THE
SERENITY
BOOK

THE SERENITY BOOK

Sensory
Awareness Training
and How it Can
Change Your Life

Marylou McKenna

Rawson Associates Publishers, Inc.
New York

Library of Congress Cataloging in Publication Data

McKenna, Marylou.
The serenity book.

Bibliography: p.
Includes index.
1. Awareness.   2. Senses and sensation.   3. Suc-
cess.   I. Title.
BF 311.M17   1977   158'.1   77-76996
ISBN 0-89256-026-6

Published simultaneously in Canada by
McClelland and Stewart, Ltd.
Manufactured in the United States of America
by Fairfield Graphics, Fairfield, Pennsylvania
Designed by Gene Siegel
First Edition

This book is dedicated to P. B., who, showing cool reserve and a military-type courage, has joined our search for serenity and true self.

CONTENTS

FOREWORD: HOW SENSORY AWARENESS PRACTICE CHANGED MY LIFE

For authors, it is said that each book is a journey. For me, this one brought curious turns in the road and an unexpected destination: I found love. I am living in a different country; and I think I am a much happier, more likable person than I was before.

To explain, let me tell you of one morning at the outset of this project, before I became deeply involved in sensory awareness training or practice. I had an editorial meeting scheduled in midtown New York City. En route from my East Eighties penthouse apartment, my taxi was delayed by traffic. Aggravated and impatient, I halted the driver, paid him off abruptly, then raced down the street to catch a Lexington Avenue subway. As a longtime resident of the town that Christopher Morley called the "thyroid gland of America," I was accustomed to coping with Manhattan traffic delays. In the subway station, I tapped my foot to keep tempo with my racing mind, or walked briskly back and forth. Others around me also were preoccupied, each of us oblivious of the other, and mostly unaware of our surroundings. Some time later, I arrived at my meeting, harried but (like other big-city residents) proud that I had survived the exasperations of getting to my destination with minimal time "wasted."

At this writing, I note the chirping of a yellow-breasted kiskadee, here at my new home in Bermuda. The saucy little fellow is perched outside my window in the poinciana tree, its profuse red-orange blossoms dripping toward the ground. As I glance around, I feel a cool breeze wafting in from the Little Sound, and I pause a moment to enjoy this sensation on my cheeks. (These days, wherever I am, I don't worry as much about being late as I used to. Usually I start out earlier to enjoy environmental "sensing" along the way.) In largest part, it was sensory awareness training that gave me the courage to trust (and to follow) my senses, leading me into a life-style that is radically different from the one I had maintained for decades.

I have now lived in Bermuda for over a year, and, in all honesty, I realize that the island of serenity that I left my crime-ridden big-city home to seek exists mostly in my mind. Even in Bermuda there are muggings, rapes, and, as the country moves toward independence, there is social and political unrest. Indeed, it is sensory awareness practice that, in complex ways, has helped me perceive that serenity must come from within a person—it is not a place. More important is the knack of being able to obtain the quiet mind, and being able to reach for this at will, under any circumstances and in any place.

That the composure this brings has made me a warmer, revitalized person is (I'm told) evident. From a personal vantage point, after being divorced for over twelve years, I am now engaged to be married to a wonderful Englishman (living in Bermuda); most likely I would not have appreciated him as much prior to sensory awareness training, for the open-mindedness that it brings teaches one to accept really different people and new experiences. But before I discuss the way I learned to love more trustingly, let's talk about health.

"Sensing" and the Art of Slowing Down

Living in a hectic metropolis for nearly twenty years, I hadn't yet acquired hypertension—I have always been blessed with low blood pressure. But in retrospect, I see I was on the way to developing a collateral illness—the "Type A Personality." This syndrome runs in my family—my father is such a person, a fine gentleman with energies flowing in various directions. His most serious heart attack was in 1969, and he has survived the ensuing years only by carefully monitoring his life and his habits.

American public health statistics agree on the deadly consequences of the "Type A Personality," sometimes known as "hurry sickness." Of the one American out of every five who still dies of stroke or heart attack before age sixty, more than *90 percent* are said to be "Type A" people. This concept was originated by two San Francisco cardiologists, Dr. Meyer Friedman and Dr. Ray H. Rosenman, who saw a consistency of traits among those patients who died prematurely. The "Type A" person, they note, is one who feels compelled to keep busy and likes to do several things at once: if he is dining alone, he feels compelled to read a book or to telephone, sometimes also trying to follow a radio or television broadcast. If he is driving a car, he is making notes about an upcoming meeting (or dictating into a tape recorder). Such a person can't sit still for long, even at the dinner table, a movie, or the theater. (To this day my dad can't simply sit and watch television, bless his heart. He "watches" it as he plays solitaire or, better, a two-man card game.)

Often it is the talented, highest-motivated person who feels the compulsion for busy hands. Americans, especially, are prone to equate making wise use of time with continuous movement and activity: quiet contemplation comes easier to those of other cultures. According to cardiologists, the "Type A" person can't relax without drumming his fingers or otherwise restlessly fidgeting. Even when this is not pathological, it is obviously energy-depleting—and it counteracts serenity and a quiet mind.

It might have been my family awareness of "Type A" that put me, as a science writer, onto what sensory awareness practice can offer urban Americans, in particular. Those who are caught up in "hurry sickness" will find sensory awareness practice fulfills a special need: when you are "sensing," you are to all intents doing *something*, yet your body and rational mind are permitted to relax, and stress buildup is relieved.

How Sensory Awareness Opens One Up for Love

Next week, my fiancé is taking me to England to meet his sisters and his brother (the youngest brigadier in the British army!). I am confident about our future, for I know I shall be welcomed. However, we Americans today are products of a full-blown, genuine culture, more crystallized than many of us realize. Whatever comes, though, I know I can ease myself through adaptation and stress; thanks to sensory awareness practice, change no longer makes me uneasy. One of the unexpected gains from "sensing" is this: a tolerance and genuine interest in persons different from oneself. Because one becomes tuned into one's own uniqueness, one acquires more respect for the "suchness" of others. I like to think of this in terms of Annie Besant's definition of tolerance, as "an eager and a glad acceptance of the way along which our brother seeks the truth."

Love, romance, and warm interpersonal contacts come easier after the sensitivity training of sensory awareness. "Sensing" eases open those defensive onion-skin layers many of us lay down, protecting ourselves from hurt or intimate, trusting relationships. And because you become a warmer, more *human* person, you are more likely to attract love from others. (My fiancé tells me he fell in love with me because I had such warmth and open-hearted kindness. By comparison, I recall an evening in Manhattan when I enjoyed playing a role as a quick-witted "sophisticate": my escort told me he thought I had a brain like a computer. And I thought of it as a compliment!)

To a large extent, we carry a form of "hurry sickness" into our emotional lives. With every weekend holiday we seek instant romance and then feel downcast that such superficial relationships do not prove deep or meaningful. Geared to speed and a fast "through-put" of acquaintances, we have become a nation of turners-on, looking for easy love-at-first-sight and undemanding, disposable lovers, attractively packaged.

Lest I mislead you, please understand that this book leans heavily on scientific knowledge and is a serious attempt to explain the practice of sensory awareness in terms of recent left-brain/right-brain research. This mind-improvement background relates to the functions of the cerebral brain and its twin hemispheres. A pioneer in this research is psychologist Robert Ornstein, who says that our Western culture's educational system overemphasizes left-brain studies and neglects the perceptive, intuitive (right-brain) truths.

The New Enlightenment

Until recently, we were a nation of church-goers; spiritual worship provided stimulation for our right-brain intuitive minds in ways I will discuss later in this book. (The Methodist congregation that sang a familiar, lilting hymn might have exercised similar brain areas as do followers of a California guru, sitting in silent meditation.) As you will see in this book, sensory awareness practice works on neglected brain areas and thus can offset the imbalance brought on by our pragmatic, detail-oriented world. It also encourages the brain "integration" that experts in the new field of left-brain/right-

brain studies acclaim. Scientists say most of us rely on one or
the other of our twin "brains" every three to four hours,
rather than shifting according to need. A less agile mentality
can get in a kind of brain rut, using just a fraction of his
mental capability in everyday life. By letting you integrate
your thinking, sensory awareness practice helps you use untapped mind power.

Our civilization is still in its adolescence in many ways.
(It is worth noting that as recently as the eighteenth century,
Dr. Johnson declined to include the word "civilization" in
his dictionary, feeling that "civility" covered this meaning.)
All across the world, what I call the New Enlightenment is
evident—a period in our civilization when larger numbers
of people (and people of all ages) are seeking studies that
would round them out as cultured, more enlightened persons.
Less interested in materialistic values than personal growth,
these people enjoy the therapeutic release from workaday
stress that this kind of enrichment brings. With apology to
the Zen and "sensing" purists, it is in this spirit that I offer
our guide to sensory awareness training, cautioning the reader
that sensory awareness is basically a *nonverbal* study. Some of
the essence of it cannot but be lost on a printed page. Therefore, I hope those who want to taste the full flavor of it, as a
growth experience, will consider formal instruction, perhaps
on a one-to-one basis from a Selver-trained sensory awareness
(SA) instructor. I'll be sharing some of my experiences in
formal SA training with you in this book and telling you
more about the remarkable Charlotte Selver, the developer
of SA in this country.

Finally, no part of our thesis would imply that Western
education's role in training the fact-seeking, rational mind
should be eliminated. This could lead to another brand of
soft-headedness. In his essay on "The New Synthesis," Robert
Ornstein calls for "an extended concept of man." This can
be achieved, he suggests, "if people make the effort to train

those aspects of themselves which are usually uncultivated in Western education."

Sensory awareness practice and this book provide guidelines for this effort.

In Conclusion

There were times when the preparation of this book was like riding a tiger. I would like to acknowledge the help and understanding of Charles V. W. Brooks, who suggested; Eleanor Rawson, who perceived; A. Durston Dodge, as well as Maude Tudor, who encouraged; Anita Lands, who aided; and my daughter, Kate Dylan McKenna, who adapted to any peaks and valleys. In Bermuda, residents and neighbors of the tiny village of Somerset (an area similar in many ways to Harper's Valley, U.S.A.) will remain in this author's memory. For extra help, I am grateful to Dr. Charles Shaw, Dr. Jerry Pikolycky, Consul-General and Mrs. Richard Rand, as well as Eileen Dodds, Helle Patterson, Jane Bainbridge, and Vicki Jensen; plus Isabel Rowse, Marlene Butterfield, Grace Rawlins, Peter F. Bromby, Alan Todd, and photographer Tony Cordeiro.

But enough of the past. D. H. Lawrence said the *present* is the most elusive, the most challenging of all time modes. It is the joy of the present that "sensing" can bring you. With its keen insight into the here-and-now, sensory awareness becomes an existential event, letting you make more out of each passing moment. With this comes a new self-esteem. This is serenity in the Oriental sense, as that composure that serves as the first step to self-actualization.

As a science writer, I am reluctant to make sweeping promises, and mental improvement is a bold thing to insure a reader just for reading a book. Even the person following our sensory exercises scrupulously may find it takes time to notice unexpected differences in himself. So a final caution:

don't expect miracles overnight. (This tendency goes with American "hurry sickness," and trying to avoid that terrible curse, being a "time waster.") Much depends on what you are today, and how deeply you are willing to invest yourself. But there is no doubt that, practiced regularly, sensory awareness will bring beauty and change into your life, even if it approaches on little cat feet. As Charlotte Selver says, almost offhandedly: "Changes will happen by themselves, once your organism is allowed to assert its needs."

MARYLOU McKENNA
"Addrianna"
Somerset, Bermuda

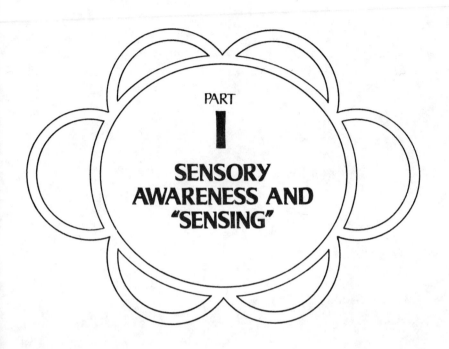

PART

I

SENSORY AWARENESS AND "SENSING"

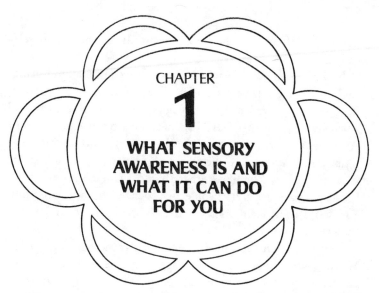

CHAPTER

1

WHAT SENSORY AWARENESS IS AND WHAT IT CAN DO FOR YOU

The primary aim of our approach is to make it possible for a person to re-experience himself as a totality, to bring him back to the degree of aliveness and receptivity of which he is capable.

CHARLOTTE SELVER

It is a Zen concept that being told what a thing is *not* will help one understand what it is. Sensory awareness is not a set of exercises, with a specific and common result. In sensory awareness practice, there is no correct and incorrect way to do things—what is most natural for an individual is what is appropriate for him or her.

Another common misconception is that sensory awareness means glancing at a pretty sunset or sniffing a bough of pine needles. Deep sensory awareness comes only when you have learned to silence your thinking—and begin to "listen" to your inner stirrings. This listening brings confidence in self and a new assertiveness. It teaches fresh self-sufficiency.

This could explain why sensory awareness training brings such sweeping changes into the lives of those who practice it. The late Dr. Fritz Perls, developer of Gestalt therapy and a student of Charlotte Selver, the woman who brought Sensory Awareness to this country (see chapter 4), puts it this way: "Many people dedicate their lives to actualizing a concept of what they *should* be like, rather than actualizing *themselves*." Sensory awareness puts people in touch with their emotions, and what they want most of life—and the kind of persons they truly are.

Perls, Erich Fromm, the eminent psychologist, and Alan Watts (who pioneered the acceptance of Zen Buddhism in America) were among the supporters of Charlotte Selver in the early days of what is termed "the work." Their esteem, and their followers, did much to make sensory awareness the highly regarded study it is today. At sensory awareness workshops you are likely to encounter educators, psychotherapists, physicians and dedicated social workers.

It should be pointed out that a major difference exists between SA training and learning Sufism or meditation studies. Like the intricacies of Zen Buddhism (which SA resembles in its focus on the here-and-now), sensory awareness is taught with a careful disinterest in quick gains and goals. Deep-reaching sensory awareness should be pursued for itself alone. (This relates to left-brain/right-brain interactions, which I will explain later.) However, from the very beginning, SA practice can open rewarding doors, and I have discovered (as an experienced "senser") that unlike some esoteric disciplines it can be put to work in tangible ways— ways I've explained in this book. As preparation, let me emphasize that, just as each person differs, wants and needs differ too: so SA might not bring the same gifts to everyone.

Yet seriously pursued, SA practice brings rewards, some quiet and intrinsic—and sometimes unexpected riches.

For the purposes of this book, it will be easier to consider that sensory awareness works on three levels:

Sensory awareness (or SA). This is taught at sensory seminars. Many of the techniques are included in this book. These are beginners' workshops and may be led by teachers who have not studied with Selver and are not conversant with deep sensory awareness. Many of the latter-day teachers rely as much on encounter techniques as on subtle, nonverbal sensory awareness.

SA-Selver. This is the deep, controlled sensory training that Charlotte Selver introduced to America. It is taught by Selver-trained teachers at such places as California's Esalen Institute, Mexico's Barra de Navidad, at Jalisco, and on Monhegan Island, Maine, where I studied sensory "work." Some of these experiments are also included in this book.

"Sensing" is the term given SA practice. After SA-Selver, this is when the noteworthy changes in a person's life begin to occur. Like meditation and other forms of Eastern study, it is sustained SA practice that brings noticeable and impressive results.

SA is a study whose time has come, it's perfect for dealing with our speeded-up, stressful age. One bonus that sensory awareness brings to almost everyone is the serenity and mental peace that come in the form of the quiet mind. (I like to think of this in the context of Robert Louis Stevenson's favorite prayer, found on his Edinburgh memorial: "Give us courage and gaiety and the quiet mind.") So often it is the bright, highly educated person who's most in need of this gentle gift.

Once one learns how to reach for the quiet mind at will, it heralds a special joy. This can light the way to self-realization in the most fulfilling, vital sense. And once one learns and practices "sensing," it is possible to block out disagreeable mental intrusions from without, and unwanted thoughts from within. In this regard, SA builds mind power. It does this in complex but scientifically valid ways that I shall explain later. For now, let me illustrate how SA works from my own experience.

How "Sensing" Helps You Overcome Fear

The incident I refer to took place the day after I had completed an advanced SA workshop, my second sensory awareness training under Charlotte Selver. I had gone to Monhegan Island, the summer home of septuagenarian Selver and her husband, Charles Brooks. Our workshop included a dozen other professionals and two nonprofessionals interested in the human potential movement, of which SA is a part. Activities consisted of nonverbal experiments such as (1) Group activities to teach us to "come to quiet"; (2) Individual "sensing" experiences to accustom us to reaching inward for sensation, rather than depending on eyes or logic— this involved working with smooth, polished stones, and lying and sitting experiments, sensing the head, sensing gravity, etc.; (3) Other activities consisted of working in twos, giving and receiving experiences, etc. We changed partners frequently, enhancing our perceptions of the way various people react to the same instructions.

The week had been filled with peace as well as growth, I recalled, standing at the airport in Rockland, Maine, the morning after our workshop concluded, waiting for my Down East Airways plane that would fly me to Boston. A cool wind was blowing about my face and the aroma of spruce trees idled in the down currents of August air there on the runway. A certain inner warmth remained with me even as I surveyed the frail-looking aircraft. While the eight-passenger light plane was probably sturdy for its size, I remembered the air turbulence that had made my arrival the previous week queasy and anxiety-filled.

Once we took off, however, I tried to bolster my assurance as our plane approached and entered a cloud bank that cut us off from landmarks below. Flying might be an old game to me (I had logged over 300,000 miles), but I was used to larger, jet-age aircraft. When I flew for thrills it was over flat terrain, with a known and dependable friend at the controls. This was different: it was blind flying over rugged foothills in a small plane with sparse equipment. My uneasiness was aggravated by my reporter's knowledge about the safety compromises allowed such small airlines and random airfields, such as Rockland, without air traffic controllers.

Within ten minutes my unease had built into sharp anxiety, as our spindly Navaho aircraft darted and dropped in the New England air gusts. The craggy landscape, no longer picturesque, now stretched perilously beneath my window. I could feel my breath coming in gasps and felt the helplessness that persons experience just before becoming airsick.

On impulse, I decided to try "sensing." Perhaps it would bring composure. It couldn't make things any worse. So, taking a deep breath, I rested my head against the metal framework of the aircraft window. I concentrated on trying to pick up vibrations from the engine, moving through the aircraft metal. Then, closing my eyes, I began to hum to myself, softly and in a monotone.

Within a few moments, the plane's vibrations seemed to become my own; the feel of the window at my head and the relentless sound of the engine became a physical reality. It reached down to penetrate my deepest core. The motions of the plane and my own surroundings seemed to merge. After still, timeless moments, it became a transforming experience. Much later (I don't know how much time actually passed) my eyes found their way open. I saw the cloud banks now as a buoyant and insulating cushion of comfort. The blue sky, once so cold and alien, came alive and bathed our presence like a friendly ocean.

Our plane began to soar, now, and further thoughts dropped away like unneeded clothes. My spirit became "unshadowed by thought," freeing itself of self-limiting logic and unnecessary explanations. Our plane continued to rise and fall, but it became exuberant. Now, gradually, I could feel my body levitate. I no longer seemed earth-bound, with a vague future or wearying memory-loads, but elated at being in this time and place. I felt a part of the steady, vibrating aircraft, part of the sky itself. I was one with the morning sun rays, now breaking through to paint a panoramic promise in the new vista below. It seemed to hail the awesome import of our human endeavor: still en route, space conquered, landing somewhere ahead. At ease, and unafraid, I felt blissfully alive and privileged to feel part of this stubbornly enduring, majestic universe.

Ways Sensory Awareness Training Benefits the Body and Emotions

For me, there was magic in the moment just described. Only later did I learn that what occurred was based on sound physiological fact. What had happened was that "sensing" had worked to tone down the mental activity in a specific part of my brain's neocortex. When I was able to focus in on the mechanical here-and-now details of the flight (engine sounds, tactile contact, vibrations, my own humming), I closed down the thinking brain, dispelling fears. I had tuned in the vivid reality of the present to tune out anxieties about things I could have no control over. I turned my attention to the here-and-now.

By helping you gain mastery over your thoughts, "sensing" lets you exercise more dominion over your life, making you less anxious about the future and putting you in easier control of present events. You'll understand this better after reading the next chapter about functions of the living brain. Right now, let me point to some early ways sensory training can enrich your life, for it has salutary effects on the emotions and the physical body.

1. *Sensory practice strengthens emotional health.* We live in a speeded-up, hectic era, with the emphasis on immediacy bringing its own adaptive stress to mind and body. Big-city living also tends to desensitize people: urban crowding, crime rates, job stress, noise, uncollected litter. If you live in the suburbs or country, you're only slightly better off, particularly when you must travel heavily trafficked highways. Automobile fumes and industrial pollutants incline us to shallow breathing and sedentary living. Even when outside, we occupy ourselves with thoughts instead of relating our minds. Seldom do we pause to notice the quiet little things. Even if we did, industrial clouds often mask the wonderland of stars at night. Our sensory input is dulled due to the pollutions that surround us. (How long has it been since you noticed the silvery moon? Days? Months?)

Yet when one becomes aware of sensory and body sensations, it serves as an emotional stabilizer, according to psychologist Fritz Perls: "Awareness, per se, by and of itself, can be curative." Other authorities agree: when humans become desensitized, emotional problems result; we become unfeeling in other regards, and apathetic. And according to Dr. Alexander Lowen, Bioenergetics therapy founder, chronic depression follows on the heels of apathy.

2. *Sensory practice helps reduce hypertension.* Much has been written about the ways meditation and raja yoga can lower hypertension when practiced daily. Indeed, it has been shown that any regular meditation practice accomplishes this. If practiced for similar time periods (twenty minutes, twice daily) so can sensory awareness, for "sensing" uses these same

perceptivity centers of the brain. Reduced hypertension, or high blood pressure, will lower the risk of stroke and cardiovascular disease; it also reduces headache and tension ailments.

But more than meditation, sensory awareness practice helps one reduce self-destructive habits like cigarette smoking. The smoking habit corrupts sensory-neural pathways, deadening feeling and sensory appreciation. Sensory practice will restore and invigorate such channels of youth and vitality.

3. *Sensory practice slows aging.* When our sensory selves are desensitized, we get old before our time. There is a biological law—what we don't use, we lose. As a rejuvenation lecturer, I like to remind lecture audiences from Ontario to California that sensory abilities deteriorate in old age— through disuse in younger decades. But when an adult revitalizes his senses, it slows aging; it perks up his mood, as well as other corners of his life. (See chapter 8: Sensory Awareness at Your Work.)

4. *Sensory practice improves the quality of life.* As a paradoxical biological law, it is *our* sensory abilities that make the earth beautiful. Alfred North Whitehead, the mathematician/philosopher, noted this: when we praise the rose for its scent, the bird for its song, the sun for its radiance, the moon for its glow, nature gets credit that rightfully belongs to man. For it is our ability to notice, perceive, and appreciate our surroundings that makes them "beautiful." He adds, "In reality, nature is soundless, scentless, colorless"— just a hurrying of otherwise meaningless atoms. Biologist Dr. Rene Dubos agrees: "It is our bodies that extract (from the jumble of sounds and external phenomena) the special colors, scents, and sounds that make up our emotional and intellectual lives. "

5. *Sensory practice brings joy.* A special joy comes with sensory work, and with steady sensory awareness practice especially. Often it is quiet and soothing, sometimes it is a flash of high exultation. In itself this enriches your life,

bringing extra beauty into it. With "sensing," your days take on a lilting, musical quality.

6. *Sensory practice can make the humdrum interesting.* You can put sensory "music" to work for you, making less wearisome what would otherwise be dull or boring. Chores you don't like can become satisfying, and even an end in themselves. Charles Brooks (husband of Charlotte Selver, and author of the definitive sensory awareness textbook) commented to me: "There are lots of things we do because we want to do them. How wonderful to find a way to help us enjoy what we *don't* want to do—and must!"

Sensory Practice Can Boost Your Mental Ability

In human brain research it's been found that it is impossible for one human mind to be equated with another— so individual and distinctive are the brains of each of us. Scientists have found that the brain is a living, growing organ—with plasticity and greater capability of growth and development (even in mature adults) than was formerly believed. The living brain evolves and shapes itself according to the needs of its owner; with training—including SA training—it can even grow larger. While brain size and weight increases will not change outward appearance, scientists believe these increases indicate heightened intelligence, particularly in terms of the size of the neocortex. (See the following chapter: "Left Brain/Right Brain.")

Much brain individuality results from the use that each of us puts our brains to, day after day. Our minds are in a constant state of unstructured flow; the brain relies on sensory impressions and messages. In this regard, sensory practice can strengthen and build your mental abilities, as follows:

1. *Sensory work accustoms you to choosing what to notice.* Psychologist George Kelly says each of us creates his own world by means of "personal constructs." This is a

sensory flow that we unconsciously select. That our minds depend on such messages for flow of thought has been shown by research in sensory deprivation. In such studies, human volunteers have been cut off from light, sound, and other environmental cues. After prolonged sensory deprivation, the mind is found to play curious hallucinatory tricks.

In one experiment, a sensory deprivation volunteer came to "see" a hippopotamus emerging from a musical instrument case. In other tests, a man envisioned purple, pink, and blue elephants. Where sensory information is lacking, an active mind can supply its own, however illogical or preposterous this might be.

But when one's sensory nature is transformed by SA practice, one's "personal constructs" change. Do sooty factories dominate your landscape, making your environment grim and polluted? Does the din of car horns or yelping dogs make you tense and short-tempered? Sensory practice can't transplant you to another city—but it does let the unpleasant loom less large. One comes to find beauty (even a kind of grandeur) in common, everyday things.

2. *Sensory work helps you avoid habituation and mental sluggishness.* Sensory impressions act on the brain constantly, often without our being aware of them. They can excite and spark mental activity or they can dull by repetition. The phenomenon of habituation can bring mental depletion to the person whose daily routine has a day-to-day sameness. Dr. Robert Ornstein, head of the Institute for the Study of Human Knowledge, illustrates this with a little exercise:

> Say the word "need" a hundred times. As you repeat it, you'll notice it becomes strange, curious. It gradually loses its original meaning and impact.

(Mere repetition, he concludes, can cause a change in consciousness.)

Psychologist Karl Pribram explains that our sensory systems react more readily to *changes* in the environment due to this phenomenon. We become accustomed to what is familiar, so our senses dull. Pribram illustrates this with what he terms the "Bowery El effect." This refers to the incidence of late-night phone complaints received by a New York City police precinct right after a certain noisy train was taken off its run. Residents of the area called to report "something strange"—shadowy figures, imaginary burglars, and so on. The people had become uneasy due to the *absence* of the noise they were used to hearing.

3. *Sensory work as cerebral exercise can increase brain size and build problem-solving abilities.* When sensory practice is incorporated into one's daily routine it serves as what scientists call "enriched experience," a factor that builds mental acuity. Worldwide research on enrichment training shows this, including work by Dr. Bruno E. Will at the Université Louis-Pasteur, Strasbourg, France, and by Drs. Mark R. Rosenzweig and Edward L. Bennett at the University of California at Berkeley. This research was undertaken to restore brain function to brain-damaged persons, but results show normal persons benefit—and adults as well as infants. In one experiment on brain-damaged laboratory animals, just two hours daily of this enriched experience (over a sixty-day period) was found to provide the same mind-building benefits as did twenty-four hours a day. Improvements included memory function and stimulating the production of additional brain hormones. This further boosted mental growth and learning abilities. There were definite physical manifestations of brain changes due to enrichment experiences when sustained over a two-month period. The size of the neocortex was built up, and brain weight increased. Some scientists associate such changes with higher mental development, and evolution to a more perfect order of being.

So notable were these brain research findings that the

U.S. Institutes for Mental Health concluded the following in their 1976 medical report:

> . . . *sensory deprivation has been found to stunt brain development. On the other hand, enrichment of the environment so that brain as well as body can be exercised, leads . . . to a larger (brain) cortex, and to an increased problem-solving ability.*

Put simply, scientists find that regularly varying one's daily activities (as with sensory practice) stimulates brain growth, and even the secretion of brain hormones. This improves learning ability and mind power.

4. *Sensory work opens perceptions, intuitive abilities.* Because it stimulates right-brain thinking, as I shall later explain, sensory awareness opens up perceptivity. This makes life easier, as well as more interesting. Let me illustrate from my own life. I've misplaced important notes. A few quiet moments "sensing" and, like a flash, I recall where they are and go straight to them. I'm riding in a car when another speeds past on a rain-swept street. With intuitive sensing, I've already braced myself for water spray, while other occupants of my car are startled and stressed. This awareness improves telephone contacts, in business as well as social communication. (I ask my literary agent about the Japanese rights on my last book: her intake of breath and pauses tell me more than her words. She feels I'm pressing—and she hasn't any news yet, anyway.)

As a science writer, I would not promise without scientific proof that SA practice will heighten intuitive powers for anybody. But fresh perceptivity results from sensory work. Will scientists find a link, eventually, between this and what has been called ESP? Dr. Charles Shaw, top British medical administrator and member of the esteemed London Psychic Research Society, says that it may be ESP consists of this—clues and signs that surround all of us continuously. But we have not yet become attuned to sensing and interpreting them.

Sensory work builds this kind of perceptivity. And, due to the brain areas acted upon during sensory awareness practice, our intuitive understanding increases, including the ability to perceive body signals and internal truths.

The Wondrous World of Body/Mind—How Sensory Work Helps You Understand Yourself

Charles Brooks says: "In sensory awareness, we are not interested in the healthy mind in a healthy body. We are interested in the total functioning person." In this regard SA is a practice with unique application to our troubled era. More medical scientists now stress the importance of the so-called holistic medium—treating the whole person in health and medicine. Don't treat the stomach disorder, treat the personality problems that brought it about, says the gastroenterologist. Don't treat the arthritic hand, natural medicine experts say: treat the person—then the body might heal itself. Even shamanism (the cult of the tribal witch doctor or faith healer) has come under scientific study—and gained new respect. These "ignorant" men treated (and sometimes cured) the whole person.

Understanding of the subtle interactions between body and mind can be aided by sensory practice. Such understanding brings insight into behavior as well as health. This is shown in the contradictory contortions of what is termed *body language,* where physical gestures reveal truths the mind won't or can't admit.

As I've said, an early booster of Selver's work was psychologist Erich Fromm. In 1955, at a joint conference at New York's New School for Social Research, the two addressed educators, psychologists, and psychotherapists. Fromm deplored the habit of referring to "body" and "mind" separately.

He called it "symptomatic of a sickness in our society." Reporting on this, social critic Theodore Roszak notes: "My body, your body; the form is grammatically correct (but) psychologically disastrous. For who is the 'I' apart from my body? How can we tell the dancer from the dance?"

As you read the following, consider your own body/ mind attitudes. Do you think of your body as merely a physical possession of your inner self—like a shell?

1. *Sensory work helps you avoid psychosomatic illness.*

Dr. Fritz Perls, originator of Gestalt therapy, liked to repeat: "Lose your mind—find your senses." It is in leaning more on our senses, he believed, that many of our ills can be avoided. This is borne out by current medical statistics, particularly the increasing incidence of stress-related illnesses. Health reports claim nearly 75 percent of sickness among affluent people today is psychosomatically linked.

As the first half of our twentieth century was heavily influenced by Sigmund Freud, the latter half is increasingly taken up with the late Wilhelm Reich and his followers. A cult-figure psychiatrist who split with Freud, the controversial Reich pioneered the concept behind many body/mind techniques. Called psychophysical methods, the current Reichan offshoots include: Bioenergetics, Rolfing, Feldenkrais technique, and others. Such therapies agree with Reich as well as Freud that emotionally disturbed minds can trigger physical illness. Latter-day concepts carry this one step further: the body that is chronically tense will muddle thinking, bring emotional depression. (Stress expert Dr. Hans Selye terms these ills "somatopsychic," or body-influencing-mind. He deplores the fact there has been only minimal research on such disorders.)

Consider the daily tensions in big cities with high crime rates. A woman walks down the same dark street every week. One night she will imagine she hears ominous sounds or see specters in shadowy doorways. Another night she breezes by, confident and carefree. The difference, claim Reich's followers, lies in whether her mind/body harmony is in balance or not. Anxiety, said Reich, begins in the body.

Sensory work brings more understanding about body tensions before they trigger emotional upset and therefore helps reduce psychosomatic illness. Consider the following list, put together by a leading psychophysical expert. There are exceptions with some cases, of course, but it holds true for most people.

Chronic tightness at the backs of legs and upper thighs (especially in the hamstring muscles) is seen in repressed persons, especially office workers with too much stress, too little exercise. It results from constantly holding yourself in check, burying true feelings. Similar tensions can be found in seemingly quiet people who, sometimes overruled, resent not having their say. Their lips are silent but their bodies speak out in protest—by tiring tensions at the rear of the thighs. Habitual resistance to control by others can also be revealed by lower back tensions.

It was Freud who first noted the way our body "puns," often in the form of dream imagery. SA helps you understand such signals, using this self-knowledge to sidestep psychosomatic illness. Tensions also reveal this. Back tensions can exemplify "digging in your heels," for example—it results from a chronic stiffening of the backbone.

2. *Sensory work lets you translate other body signals.*

Time and time again the body might try to signal one's conscious awareness to do something. When sensory work helps the person accept body messages, a new self-love results, in addition to personal growth. A Boston feminist told me her therapist commented that she seldom flexed her upper lip when talking, seldom smiled. Some time afterward, she caught herself saying, "I've always tried to keep a stiff upper lip about things . . ." Then, she added to me, "That wonderful-awful moment of self-realization: what had I been doing to myself!"

3. *Sensory work helps you in dealing with personal crisis.*

Fortunately for all of us, scientists have embarked on a research voyage to discover new insight into body/mind behavior. I would have been grateful for such professional help some years ago, during a personal crisis.

On impulse, in my late twenties, I became engaged to a popular Florida radio personality: witty, urbane, talented—and emotionally unstable. At the time I enjoyed life—I had a super job, a new car, and a busy social life for myself and my four-year-old daughter. Being divorced myself, I put aside my misgivings about my fiancé's serial marriages and the fact he had been in and out of psychoanalysis for several years. The fact that he seldom held a job longer than a year at a time might have been due to the precarious nature of the broadcasting field. His zany behavior brought a few doubts about his influence on my preschool daughter. But it seemed suitable for me to get married at that time, so we announced our forthcoming wedding.

As the date neared, I had a curious physical sensation. From time to time I could feel an unexplained opening at the back of my head, as if there were a curious gap in my skull. It was not painful—merely present. When driving alone in my car, I'd feel a wind draft seeming to enter this opening somewhere in the rear of my coiffure. Common sense could not deny I felt it, nor logic reason it away.

As most women do when they have medical problems, I talked to my gynecologist. I felt silly describing it to him and tried to make a joke of it. Perhaps I seemed over-emotional. At any rate, he "cured" it in typical medical fashion: he prescribed tranquilizers. I took them faithfully, and sedated the symptom; yet emotional confusions remained, deeply buried. Since I was then a cigarette smoker, I began to smoke as many as four packs a day. I also drank more alcohol and began to have recurrent colds.

After weeks of physical upheaval, on a pretext I broke off my engagement. Today, knowing more about this intertwining of body and mind (and ways the body puns), I think this: my body was trying to tell me that, right then, I needed marriage to that itinerant radio disc jockey like I needed "a hole in the head."

Had my physician not been so prone to dope up and sedate an overwrought patient (or had someone suggested I try to get in touch with my true feelings), much anguish and sleepless nights of turmoil might have been eased—for both parties involved.

Medical annals reveal similar tales about body puns. Our digestive system is a ready index of emotional distress. Verbal expressions like "I can't stomach it," or "He nauseates me," or "It chews me up inside" can be dramatically acted out by the body. One report suggests that frequent use of these phrases even brings on the disorder, as sickness manifests itself in that body organ so emotionally discussed. The person who chronically claims he "can't swallow" a situation can develop cardiospasm; this is a swallowing disorder in which the lower end of the esophagus tightens, interfering with the passage of food.

Faith-healing successes show that the opposite will hold true: firm belief in a medicine, treatment, or healer can speed the cure. The medical establishment presently refers to cures that are scientifically confounding as "the placebo effect." Yet, as an expert on this phenomenon notes: if the cure is genuine, what does it matter what brought it about? Scientists daily are unearthing explanations for events once considered miracles. It is said more has been learned about the body in the past four decades than in all recorded time. More of these puzzling body/mind events may be medically explained in the near future.

You'll clarify your life by getting in closer contact with your senses, suggested Perls. Sensory work puts you in touch with reality, sometimes better than intellectualized facts. "As long as you can see and hear, and realize what's going on, then you *understand*," Perls notes. "If you learn concepts, if you work for information, then you don't understand. You only *explain*." (This difference between perception and the rational mind will be further explored in the chapter that follows.)

4. *Sensory work brings appreciation of human uniqueness.*

When you get in the habit of "listening" to your inner messages, as in sensory awareness practice, a new appreciation dawns for individuality in others and the uniqueness that is you. You come to overrule ritualistic dogma as to whether a thing is "correct" or "incorrect"—and consider whether it is right for you as a person. (Are you working at that job because it was what your parents wanted for you, or is it what you want, deep down?) Sensory awareness practice teaches more respect for what it is *you* truly feel. In this way the habitual "senser" gains self-determination and control over his destiny, enjoying a heightened feeling of self-mastery.

How "Sensing" Changes People's Lives

When I started to seriously research SA-Selver, the unexpected thing was the way I found that "sensing" changed people's lives—sometimes gradually, but often in quantum jumps. Age is no real barrier to this, nor are educational limitations.

Sensory awareness training helped a sales executive in Manhattan's most competitive area (the garment industry) decide he wanted more than his present life, lucrative though it was. Mustering his emotional forces, he quit his job (although more than forty-five years old at the time) and took lesser-salaried but emotionally rewarding work at a New York settlement house. Working with deprived juveniles and ex-drug addicts whetted his interest for psychiatric counseling. Returning to night school, he completed college credits for a degree in rehabilitative psychology. The last time I saw him, he was preparing for a state examination, which would license him as an accredited social worker. These days, he looks far younger than his years.

Usually, these life changes begin with tiny things. At Monhegan Island, one early result of SA-Selver was seen in Sara, a very quiet and shy nurse. One afternoon, as we walked back together from our SA workshop, she said, "I wrote a seven-page letter to my husband last night." I absently murmured a comment. "You don't understand," she persisted. "I haven't been able to write a real letter for years. I don't even send postcards. But last night I was so absorbed in telling my husband about our sensing experiences that I kept writing and writing. And I enjoyed it!"

I suggested Sara bring this up the next time Charlotte or Charles listened to reports on our progress. When Charlotte heard this account of becoming unblocked, she merely nodded, commenting, "You had somehow lost your ability to be wonderful."

Selver's European teacher and mentor was Elsa Gindler, whose studies led the way to sensory awareness as we know it. To her students, Gindler would comment: "There is no such thing as being ungifted. You may be merely hindered, and (with sensory practice) you may shed this hindrance by and by."

There is no doubt about it: sensory awareness practice changes you. It undrapes your secret ambitions and unblocks your ability to achieve them. A quiet Manhattan editor (one not given to overstatement) confided to me: "After years of 'sensing,' I've put aside all my preconceived ideas about what I can do and what I want out of life. What I've gained through sensory awareness is already so extraordinary, I'm just leaving myself open for whatever happens."

It has been said that it is the little secret impulses, hidden in each of us, that will shape the world. Does "sensing" bring these to the surface? Charlotte Selver recalls her own experience: "(The sensory work) gave me a new desire—to explore my own capabilities more fully and to be more at home in myself. And it gave me a feeling of trust: I could sense, I could follow my feelings."

Would one learn other stories of sweeping change from former SA students? Perhaps; but as Charles Brooks says, sensory awareness is not a study—it is a practice. And major change comes gradually. Besides, what mature person will simplistically attribute new directions in his life to a single incident, when one activity generated others? Yet one thing is certain: sensory awareness opens up people. Depending on the individual, and the strength of his daydreams, the implications of this can be enormous—and unending.

Your Own Blueprint for Change—Through "Sensing"

Have you discovered the life of your own dreams? Most likely not; utter fulfillment is a rare gift of the gods, not casually dispensed. If you'd like somehow to remake your life, try these two preliminary steps:

1. *Recall your childhood ambitions.* Isn't there some early dream, deferred or forgotten, that you'd like to achieve? It might not be a profession; perhaps it is a place, or a way, you'd like to live. It might be something special you loved to live around, like flowers, or a mountain lake. Attend seriously to such yearnings, no matter how soft-headed: it has been said we are most happy when our lives grow in ever-expanding

circles from our earliest expectations. Remembering the person you wanted most to be, plan to use the sensory exercises and SA experiments in this book as a trowel; use them to dig creatively into the garden of your life. You'll relish the experience, for (as a tool for change) sensory awareness brings more joy than encounter and other methods.

2. *Believe in your body as self.* It doesn't matter if you are fat or rail-thin, balding or arthritic, sensory practice can revitalize you. Of course, this requires open-mindedness. My friend Hans Holzer (expert on ESP) says there are two persons: believers and nonbelievers. I noted that the students who benefitted early from SA-Selver were those who avoided skepticism. (It may be that "sensing" comes easier when one can switch off the doubting mind, as I shall discuss later on.)

For, whatever your age or history, you can still perfect yourself, growing into that rare and noteworthy person you always knew you could be, given half a chance. Fritz Perls used to say that most people live at only 15 percent of their ultimate potential. With "sensing" you can reach for more, and become a more confident person in the process—because you are reaching inward, relying upon yourself for reinforcement. It is still plausible for our species to evolve. Indeed, as John Steinbeck noted, *homo sapiens,* more than any other mammal "grows beyond his work, walks up the stairs of his concepts, emerges ahead of his accomplishments." Sensory awareness practice lets you compose your own kind of music and make your life a meaningful song—as well as a special one.

Celebrate Yourself Exercise No. 1: The Sensory Bath
This is a sensory experiment you'll enjoy practicing at home. You'll need: a portable phonograph or record player; a rousing, upbeat recording; and a bathtub of warm water. (What follows is based on an exercise dynamic from the new science of sports psychology.)

DO THIS: Next time you're mentally fatigued from job stress, or testy from emotional decision-making, fill up a bathtub with warm, inviting water. If you like, add spa water coloring or bubbles or bath oil. Bring your phonograph into the bathroom. Then place a cheerful record on the record player, selecting music with or without lyrics. The song should be music with a strong, lilting beat—but not one associated with your emotional past. Broadway show tunes are good. (My own favorite for this is Barry Manilow's recording of "Beautiful Music.")

THEN: Clear all thinking from your mind, and ease yourself into the tub. With the melody playing, let it fill the room and fill your mind as well. Give over your entire being to the sensory experience of warmth, wetness, and invigorating sound. Don't analyze these sensations, and don't compare; just let your body take over, as you lie back and enjoy water and rhythm. Experience the warmth on your toes, the musical mood—and your own celebration of the special feeling it is to be y-o-u, alive and vital, in this room, and at this time. Let the music move your body, flowing gently, rhythmically. After the record ends, drift relaxed in the water for several moments, breathing deeply, mind and body cleansed. Then repeat the experience. Or rinse yourself with cool, sparkling water, completing this revitalizing experiment with a towel rubdown.

With sensory practice, repetition of this tune can be put to work for you. Psychologist Dr. Richard Suinn, attached to the U.S. medical team during the 1976 Winter Olympics, used a similar method to turn anxious skiers into ready winners. He considered this a *thought-stopping technique,* using it to help them combat self-doubt (which limits success for an athlete just as it limits success on the playing fields of life). Dr. Suinn had inconsistent skiers practice to musical strains that had strong, recognizable beats. Later, during competition, if the skier noted self-doubts or negative thinking, he mentally called, "Stop!" To prevent the thought from recurring, he then recalled the music. He devoted all his attention to skiing to that remembered rhythmic beat.

In your own life, just recalling your key tune can relieve anxiety and emotional unease. It can also be used to make humdrum chores less tiring. Recalling tunes is a right-brain function, great for blocking self-doubt, illogic, and other (left-brain) activities, as I shall explain in our next chapter.

CHAPTER

2

LEFT BRAIN/RIGHT BRAIN— HOW "SENSING" BUILDS MIND POWER

When I started to work in the [Gindler group], I could not distinguish what came through visual *images, what through* thoughts, *and what through* sensing. *It usually was a mixture of all three. But I began to realize how my all-too-busy mind stood in the way of experiencing . . . [Later] what a delight! I could really feel how my head needed more easing up, how I could give to it, how efforts would begin to subside, how thoughts would gradually come to rest.*

CHARLOTTE SELVER

In "sensing," you focus in on your own inner sensations (or the external environment) as physical meditation. As sustained meditation has been proven to do, sensory awareness practice acts on the right hemisphere of the cerebral brain. As we shall see, this is the key to serenity and to building mind power.

It has been said man can *double* his present mental abilities, once he learns to harness capabilities of the right half of his cerebrum to the extent that he relies on the left.

It is the left brain that is dominant for the vast majority of us, including all right-handed people and over half of those who are left-handed. It is only man who boasts a divided cerebrum (due to the use our evolved brain has been put to). As brain researcher Maya Pines notes, this separates us from lower orders of mammals. "This asymmetry, which we all recognize when we say whether we're right- or left-handed, is the glorious mechanism through which man is able to speak."

Here's how our twin brains function. The cerebral brain grows like a double cauliflower out of less sophisticated brain areas. It is only partially divided: left and right hemispheres (or left brain and right brain, as experts call them) are joined by what is called the *corpus callosum*. (See illustration on the next page.) This thick cord is cross-wired to carry nerve impulses from one side to the other, as each twin "brain" controls the opposite side of the body. That is, the left brain controls the right leg and arm, the right brain controls the left leg, and so on. From each eye, optic nerves feed impulses into the opposite brain hemisphere.

While each of the twin brains has separate functions, we sometimes call on both brain halves for problem-solving, and even for ordinary, uncomplicated things. Consider: at a party or social gathering, were you ever asked to describe a spiral staircase? Chances are you ran out of words and (almost uncontrollably) your hand started making clumsy gestures in circles, ascending or descending. People around you might have grinned at your abashed surprise.

What you demonstrated unknowingly was the way your left and right brains interact. Your left brain is the center for verbal ability; this tried to use words to define the spiral staircase, a spatial object. If words alone proved insufficient, your right brain took over (the center for understanding spatial

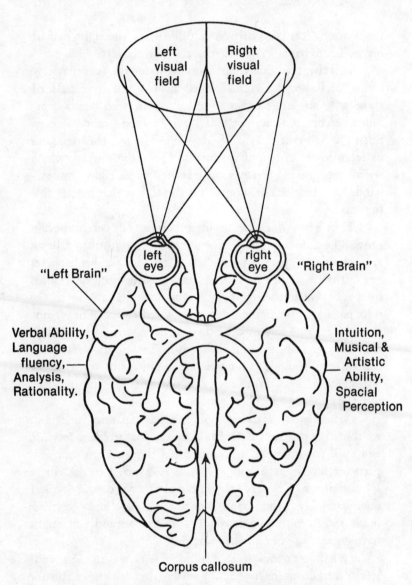

Left visual field

Right visual field

left eye

right eye

"Left Brain"

"Right Brain"

Verbal Ability,
Language
fluency,
Analysis,
Rationality.

Intuition,
Musical &
Artistic
Ability,
Spacial
Perception

Corpus callosum

THE TWIN HEMISHERES OF THE CEREBRAL BRAIN

relationships). It was your right brain that forced hand movements to convey the definition.

TRY THIS YOURSELF: Next time you're with friends, ask one to define the word "goatee" without using hands. Or try to get an explanation of what the word "zigzag" means. Chances are, your friend will use his or her hands uncontrollably, or do a lot of clumsy hemming and hawing. And if you really want to make a joke of this, wait until your "victim" has had an alcoholic beverage.

The left brain (verbal center and site of vocabulary and language learning) is the dominating side for most of us. Scientists have found this is the most active brain area during mental tasks like reading, letter writing, or mathematics. This is the brain area used by most executives and office workers in day-to-day routine. This is the brain area that can become fatigued and overstressed during a hectic business day.

It is the right brain that is our most underdeveloped body part. This is the brain area where we meditate, where *nonverbal* abilities like intuition and perceptivity, reside. Here we understand spatial relationships and designs (like the spiral staircase); here we grasp ideas and concepts and their relationship to each other. This brain region is the center for insight, for holistic knowledge, and ideas can be synthesized here. This is also the storage bank for remembered music—and remembered faces. The right brain is the creativity center for sculptors, dancers, and composers, as well as for artists.

Put simply, the left brain works in *analytic* ways; it considers facts in sequence, part by part. The right brain works perceptively and *intuitively;* it is here we obtain the overview about a problem, and the insight for solving it.

Persons who are not stroke victims or otherwise brain-damaged have active cross-connections (through the *corpus callosum*) between the twin "brains." There is cross-communication for even simple activities, such as ordering the right foot to move (a command directed from the left hemisphere, or dominant brain). Sensing pain in a specific body part can also involve this crossover, or integration. Nerve impulses travel up the spinal column, then cross over within the *corpus callosum*, entering the opposite side of the brain. (Pain from your right foot is communicated to the left brain, and so on.)

As the brain matures, however, brain dominance takes hold. Dr. Roger Sperry of Cal Tech (a pioneer in this new study) says that excellence in one brain hemisphere seems to interfere with top-level performance in the other. Brain behavior studies at San Francisco's Langley-Porter Neurological Institute agree. Notes Dr. David Galen: "In most ordinary activities, we alternate between cognitive modes [or our twin brains] rather than integrating them . . . most people are dominated by one mode or the other." Many people have certain difficulty with crafts and body movements (right-brain activities)—or they have difficulty with speaking and language learning (left-brain activities). Better brain integration could enhance such abilities, improve decision-making, and bring anybody a wider range of talents.

How Our Schools Ignore Right-Brain Development

To grasp how integration could be improved between the twin brains (and to understand the part SA practice might play in this) it will help us to look at the root of the problem. It is Western education itself that limits man's mental capabilities, suggests Dr. Robert Ornstein, of California's Institute for the Study of Human Knowledge. Schools unconsciously encourage students to believe in and rely exclusively upon left-brain reasoning—denying respect for right-brain perception and talents.

Let's consider this: from the time a youngster is out of kindergarten, teachers tout logic and emphasize the scientific approach. They say: Remain impersonal and objective, avoiding "guesswork." Don't put too much faith in your hunches if they aren't backed by scientific dogma. Stick with the known facts. An educated man (we are reminded) reasons with cause-and-effect, analysis, and other linear modes. If an idea does not prove itself out in terms of our present analytic (left-brain) rationality, it is thus dismissed as ignorant superstition or (worse yet) "female intuition."

It is only our left-brain-dominated culture that has the unarguable, patent answers, we are persuaded. Indeed, other cultures are dismissed as illiterate, regardless of their aesthetic standards. Notes Ornstein, many Westerners see those of the Far East and the Orient as self-indulgent, and performers of ridiculous "far-out" rituals—which we assume to be inferior to our own quick, "decisive" thinking.

In IQ and intelligence tests, vocabulary, language, and mathematical talents are still considered main measures of intelligence (all are left-brain abilities). Seldom are designs, spatial relationships, or other *right-brain* probings included on IQ or SAT tests—and a low IQ grade can be an embarrassing stigma that follows the creative or latently talented child from school to school. Is the student good at hunches or any other glimmer of undiscovered ESP or perceptivity? If he's ambitious, he learns to keep this to himself (and gradually loses such talents) rather than be mocked or have his "unscientific" suggestions dismissed as ignorant hogwash.

If he goes on to college, the student learns to specialize, further encouraging a single-minded asymmetric brain dominance. It is intricate, step-by-step analysis that is favored, rather than a holistic, nonlinear (right-brain) approach to problem–solving. Most schools still place emphasis on what is the correct and incorrect, or the black and white, right and wrong way of doing things. This is oversimplification and lays the groundwork for intolerance of other cultures and other intellectual modes and life-styles.

There are exceptions, and new waves of thought are now lapping at our educational institutions. But at this writing, most American and European schools accord top priority to left-brain subjects (i.e., verbal and language skills, math and science), giving lesser importance to right-brain studies, even though these would balance off mental strengths (i.e., music, art, spatial and design concepts, physicality, intuitive studies).

For the student as growing individual, body-awareness knowledge is avoided and scorned in some regions as "dirty" or leading to perverse, unspeakable behavior. Physical education classes are considered extracurricular in many schools, and are first to be curtailed if budgets must be cut. (And rare is the high school that provides adequate mirrors even in girls' bathrooms. For boys, such body awareness aids are shunned, adding to the psychological distortion many males have about their body-image, a topic I shall discuss in chapter 16.)

For Understanding the Situation: Right-Brain Synthesis

Fritz Perls urged reliance on the senses to boost understanding. Only by sensing do you *understand*, he'd say; with (left-brain) words, you would merely *explain*. Yet our educational system directs such attention to sequential (left-brain) modes, it has little time for studies that build total understanding and what advertising moguls describe as "the big picture." This is the ability to synthesize all components of a situation, obtaining the kind of overview that can turn an aspiring executive into a corporate president or managing director. This holistic approach is an earmark of the (right-brain) perceptions that SA practice will groom and exercise.

As a related factor, more training in self-regulation in our schools would encourage the graduating student to individual contributions to the outside world of business and industry. As it is, many remain cookie-cutter products of our present homogenizing educational process.

"Sensing" for Creativity and Intuitive Insight

Yet it is the right hemisphere of the human brain that might hold the secrets of creative genius. Let's explore this, looking at great people of history, and consider the circumstances under which their great achievements were sparked.

It was the classical Greeks who first gave a name to the mysterious forces that inspire man, impelling him to create his greatest works. They termed this hidden aspect of man's nature as "*entheos,*" or "a god within." Appropriately, it is from this root we derive our word "enthusiasm."

Far-seeing biologist Rene Dubos suggests the concept comes full circle; that is, bursts of enthusiasm might trigger creativity. Even scientists, as well as more emotional composers and artists, have admitted their most singular achievements seemed to spring forth almost spontaneously. Consider Descartes: no philosopher was more partial to cool, clear reason. Yet he reported that, while he was in a dreamlike state, the idea for his famous *Discours sur la Méthode* came in a flash of inspiration. Novelist Erich Segal reports one of the knotty problems in his plot for *Love Story* was resolved without effort, while he was jogging mindlessly. The French mathematician Poincaré, dismissing a perplexing problem from his mind, went for a relaxing drive in the countryside. While meditating upon the beauties of nature, the winning solution came to him as he put his foot on the brake. Chance, of course, favors the prepared mind (as another philosopher reminds us); it is seldom the untrained who are gifted with those inspired gleams that alter the course of history. Yet there appears substance to the claim that our subconscious (right-brain?) mind can work on, and resolve, a problem, while the thinking consciousness is occupied with other tasks.

Brain experts tell us that everybody boasts forgotten but useful information, buried deep in our memory banks. It remains for the right moment to nudge this data to conscious awareness. In my own experience, I've found "sensing" can aid with memory retrieval. Let me give you an example. During the final work on this book, a Bermudian friend telephoned me, asking if I knew the names of any lawyers in the Dominican Republic. I had read an article on two of them, some years previously, but had never needed the information it carried. At this request, I searched my memory for days, to no avail. Then, one chilly afternoon in my bathroom as I was "sensing" the warmth of tap water on my wrists while relaxing from work at my typewriter, the names came to me, unsought. "Sensing" works to nudge open memory banks, a theory that might be scientifically researched. (It is of interest here to note that certain memory experts urge persons who would improve their memory for names to associate the name to be remembered with vivid sensory imagery, as, for example, the name Bob Copper could be recalled by fantasizing a "bobbie" or a policeman after an accident, his blue uniform stained bright with red blood, and so on.)

In other cases, the opening of memory banks has occurred after right-brain sports exertions or sensory awareness recreations and hobbies. (One scientist of Nobel consequence, in explaining how he arrived at the solution to a puzzling equation, says it came to him as he completed his climbing of the Matterhorn, while on holiday.)

Sensory awareness practice promotes left-brain/right-brain integration, letting one do this at will and avoid the habituation that certain jobs or tasks incite. With practice, you can learn to switch from left-brain analytic reasoning to right-brain perceptivity, thus sharpening your mental agility.

In itself this can add the intuitive spark that ignites the fires of creative genius. (Toward the end of his life, Albert Einstein looked back on his greatest achievements and summed up the thought processes that lead to them. "The really valuable thing," he recalled, "was intuition.")

SA practice opens the door to what has been described as the *peak experience* (as I shall discuss in the next chapter). But what most excited me in researching this right-brain study is that SA encourages *holistic thinking*—exercising the right part of your brain that is neglected by so much of Westernized education. With holistic thinking, you can master (or at least understand) almost any personal situation—because you bring the best of both minds to it and can put any problem in perspective.

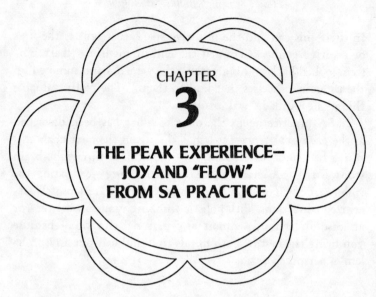

THE PEAK EXPERIENCE—
JOY AND "FLOW"
FROM SA PRACTICE

Knowing is not seeing; knowing is not thinking; knowing is feeling.

CHARLOTTE SELVER

As we've seen, SA will bring a new, more enlightened kind of joy. SA practice also heralds the possibility of a phenomenon known as the *peak experience*. This is a blissful, high-intensity moment when perception, clarity, and your own natural talents fuse together. Like the ecstasy of sexual orgasm or the heartfelt satisfactions of parenthood, a peak experience should be enjoyed for its own sake, rather than measured for (left-brain) practical usefulness. It relates to the definition psychologist Richard Suinn attaches to the New Enlightenment: "A swing away from materialistic values to new feeling states."

Yet just recalling the moment when you reached this kind of drugless high will help you create a product business clients will rave about, or let you run a longer race, or articulate a more impressive speech before your civic group. Call it inspiration or call it super power, a peak experience is an extraordinary flash that helps you bring together the best of all your possible selves.

For most persons, the joys that are experienced have a certain similarity. (It may be that some experience joy more frequently than others, a matter I shall discuss later in this chapter.) Remember, for now, the joy you felt as a child at Christmas, or opening a special birthday present. Perhaps you can recall the way you felt when your lover told you he or she loved you in return—or gave you an engagement ring.

Typical feelings of joy are self-oriented (involving tangible gain), yet they usually are dependent on other people. Even charitable acts are often considered in terms of what they bring the donor. This limits human tolerance and person-to-person communications. It also inhibits psychic growth. SA practice takes one beyond these self-prescribed limitations into a higher order of being. This enlightenment brings its own joyous *satori*, as one senses one's part in what Jung called the "collective unconscious."

Once you can quiet your (left-brain) rational mind and come to the serene aspects of SA training, you open yourself to the kind of ecstasy certain mystics have experienced in recorded history. It can be as fulfilling for you as it was for St. John of the Cross, Gautama Buddha, or Joan of Arc. And because it is not dependent on others, it also brings an inner radiance that people or circumstances cannot dim or take away.

Let me describe an incident during the Monhegan Island SA workshop that proved this to me. It helped me understand what the late Abraham Maslow, president of the American Psychological Association, was referring to when he described a peak experience.

The incident came at a time in our SA training when sessions involved such things as dividing into twosomes and exchanging a ball—an experiment in giving and receiving. This phase of the work seemed awkward at first, but came to have sweeping philosophical overtones. (As Charles Brooks instructs: "We shall wait to feel what we have in our hands and not rush to do something with it.") More than anything else, this little experiment started opening me up for deeper and more meaningful human relationships. (Later I would ask myself: Do I give love willingly? Do I receive it of others gratefully, trustingly?)

That particular morning our SA group, after our "sensing" session, was led outside by Brooks to stand quietly at one with the outdoor environment, opened up and full in the warm August sun. I was shoeless as I followed the group, who were arranging themselves like figures in a curious tapestry along the irregular landscape. As I walked outside, it was odd to feel damp grass underneath my stockinged feet. Yet there was a reassuring familiarity about the pebbles and twigs underfoot, ruling out unease or discomfiture. No one spoke; some stood on rocks, others (like myself) were balanced on both feet on solid terrain. The scent of Maine spruce trees was thick in the crisp morning air, and the sun caressed my back, as a sea breeze gently played in my hair. I reveled in how good it was to be there, right then, feeling vitally alive.

Then around a brambly bush strolled an auburn tiger cat, doubtless belonging to one of the Monhegan residents down the hill. The cat ambled lazily to a flat stone just ahead of me, stretched, then lay down on the pillar warmed by the summer sun. (Many readers have probably appreciated cats for years, adoring them as pets; I never did. I'll even admit I have actively disliked cats for vague, illogical reasons.) At that moment of deep "sensing," I became almost hypnotically fixed by that creature, just six feet ahead of me, stretching, claws out, claws now in. Artlessly yet deliberately the cat began to roll over on her back, rocking over and forward on the warm stone as she permitted the sun to bathe her underparts in a sensuous ocean of warmth. Back and forth she rolled, and, as I watched her idly (my mind peaceful and at rest), a curious transference seemed to take place. It was so subtle that I did not notice anything extraordinary about it until afterward.

For, at that moment on that rock-strewn cliff in breezy Maine—despite my lifelong dislike of cats—I became one with that cat. I did not merely appreciate how she felt; I did not just identify with the cat—I *was* the cat. As the cat lazed and rolled around, I enjoyed the summer sun on my underbelly; the sharp stone edges roughed *my* back. I felt the sensation of fur all over me and was one with her delicious warmth. I gloried in *our* sensuality. I, too, felt delight in body and a sumptuous pride of life. For a long, mind-boggling moment, the two of us (now one) also became all humanity. We were at one with all people everywhere, all animals. We became, as that beautiful Zen Buddhist prayer says, all *sentient* beings. It was a star-struck moment that had no linear duration of time as we know it. It was at once an occasion of heart-stabbing humility and of loftiness and grandeur.

Afterward, I felt an exhilaration that was greater than the joy I felt when either of my dear children were born, or on my wedding day. It was a blissful serenity I had never experienced before, not after sexual orgasm or other mundane gratifications. Indeed, the sensation was so extraordinary I was reluctant to sort out or define my feelings; like holding the world's most beautiful butterfly in my hands, I was hesitant to look closely for fear of losing it. It took some days before I wanted to share what happened with anybody.

That experience, on the crest of a hill in Maine, gave me fresh perception of the words of Zen pioneer Dr. D. T. Suzuki when he noted: "The individual becomes perfect when he loses his individuality in the All to which he belongs." It goes without saying that, since then, I've looked with an appreciative eye at cats, indeed, at all beings I previously felt an alienation toward or a vague mistrust about.

For me, this was a peak experience, and as I write this, I can still recapture the beautiful stillness of that moment. Like Transcendental Meditation and other Eastern studies, SA-Selver can bring relaxation and the quiet mind. And more than the rest of this spate of Oriental-type practices, SA will open you up for the peak experience. A single one provides a high-water mark for the rest of your life. It is a rare person who can boast a number of such occasions when he or she exulted in feeling totally alive. This is when you reach a higher order of being, and with several such zeniths, an unexpected inner power grows, helping you achieve more of your ultimate potential. (Oscar Wilde describes the best of lives as that one made up of experiences that let a person burn as with "a white-hot flame.")

The "Flow" Experience—How SA Helps

In ongoing research studying the phenomenon of joy, scientists are coming to understand more about what makes up day-to-day joy (in addition to the extraordinary peaks we just discussed). Psychologists have recently defined what is termed the "flow" experience: this is a special joy that is prolonged over a unique period. Yet one sign of true "flow" is that time, as we know it, has lost its importance. In some cases, it alters completely. Other signs of this "flow" of joy involve almost physical sensations: concentration comes automatically. There is a clarity of response that becomes its own reassuring feedback. This is merely a signal that things are progressing; the person in "flow" does not pause to evaluate such feedback. He does not have (left-brain) thoughts of self-evaluation or criticism. (Such thoughts destroy flow.) Self-consciousness is lost, even for the shy participant, and he comes to enjoy an almost godlike sensation of self-mastery and control. Whatever he is doing, there is a heightened awareness of his physical involvement in the task or game.

Indeed, top athletes have reported this phenomenon more than any other professional group. (As we shall see, being physically fit can attune and prepare one's body for the onrush of joy.) For when agile talent is combined with the sure energy that "flow" can bring, super powers can be unleashed. The self-exultation this promotes would account for a surprising agreement among certain "flow" experiencers who were surveyed by a Chicago psychologist, Dr. Mihaly Csikszentmihalyi (called Dr. C hereafter). He distributed an interview questionnaire to nearly 200 "flow" regulars: basketball players, mountain climbers, dancers, chess players. He asked them to rank suggested reasons for continuing to participate in his or her "flow" activity. Among the lowest-rated choices were "prestige, reward, and glamour." What ranked highest? An altered state of being, a curious merging of action and heightened awareness, seemed to occur when participants were enjoying their work or sport the most. It was this altered state that the majority of respondents felt was the most gratifying.

Dr. C found that professionalism, experience, and "flow" are interrelated. It starts with the ability to concentrate on the here-and-now. Describing her best performances, when "flow" occurs, a leading dancer said: "Your mind isn't wandering, you are not thinking of something else. You are totally involved in what you are doing . . . Your body is awake all over." A rock dancer told Dr. C: "[At such times] I feel I can radiate energy into the atmosphere. I can dance on walls. I can dance on floors. I become one with the atmosphere."

On the playing fields, athletes who experience "flow" claim it helps them envision actual guidelines that bring about winning the game. Ted Williams, American baseball great, said that, despite the stress and bustle of a major league game, he was able to see the seams turning on a baseball speeding toward him at eighty miles an hour. During a winning streak, other baseball players report they see and hit the ball with extra punch because it appears larger than normal as it comes up to the plate.

John Brodie, winner of the National Football League's most valuable player award, describes this feeling on the football field. "Flow" brings a new perception, even in the heat of the game; a player's coordination seems to improve dramatically. A certain clarity sets in, and the player tunes out on the noise and confusion of the crowds, as well as all extraneous thoughts and events. Time seems to slow, and everyone around him begins to move in slow motion. "The defensive line is coming at me just as fast as ever, and yet the whole thing seems like a movie or a dance in slow motion," Brodie recalls. "It's beautiful."

At California's Esalen Institute, founder Michael Murphy takes a personal interest in this sphere where sports and supernatural powers overlap. For example, Murphy likes to follow golfer Jack Nicklaus around a golf course. He observes the golfer's keen concentration at crisis moments. Such experiences led to Murphy's book on *Golf in the Kingdom*. He describes Nicklaus as a sports professional who has achieved the talent of playing in a kind of trance; oblivious to crowds, Nicklaus, his golf club, and the ball all become one. In this state, Nicklaus seems to influence the flight of the ball, even after it is hit. This kind of follow-through becomes a kind of "energy streamer." Visualized and executed in a moment of high clarity, the moving ball seems to glide into the cup, riding smoothly on an invisible streamer released by the golfer.

Can this kind of almost-mystical control be used in other walks of life? The study of what is now termed sports psychology lets us learn from the new breed of enlightened athlete. Today, sports superstars are augmenting practice with psychological techniques. In addition to efforts to "psych out" and demoralize opponents, this practice is geared to release untapped powers of body and mind. Tennis great Billie Jean King is said to meditate on a tennis ball prior to an important match. Olympic hurdle jumper Bill Toomy likes to "practice" with imagery exercises. He'll sit quietly, ritualistically imagining the feel of the way every muscle moves during a sprint. He claims this technique has improved his timing as much as hard practice. Skiing star Jean Claude Killy used an imagery method to run-through a championship course when he was recovering from an injury and couldn't practice physically. He claims the race he skiied afterward gave him his best results ever.

What these and other advocates of the new mind/body disciplines are talking about is "body thinking," a term coined by Dr. Suinn. This domain is a new frontier where, according to one psychophysical reporter, the mind is ruled by a more intuitive, almost physical (right-brain) wisdom. Once this sensation comes to be experienced habitually, it opens up a curious new perception. It helps us become more enlightened in everyday life than we could be if we attempted difficult things aided only by our conscious mind.

Essential for cultivating this secret weapon is the ability to relax one's conscious thinking, turning oneself over to physical reactions and sensations. For many, it is hard to turn off the brain's constant chatter or "noise." Yet until this is achieved, it is difficult to ease the hold of left-brain dominance. (See chapter 2.) The stubbornly practical left brain, with its endless logic and linear reasoning, can padlock the door to new perceptivity.

Sensory awareness practice overcomes this. To improve

your chances of experiencing "flow," SA aids in specific ways, as follows:

1. *SA brings the quiet mind.* This silences left-brain "noise."

2. *SA gives you more overview* on habitual routine. This lets you choose that particular aspect of your here-and-now likely to encourage "flow."

3. *SA opens you up* as an emotionally trusting person to the acceptance of joy as a self-determined experience. You learn faith in your own joy-producing capability, as opposed to being dependent on outside events or persons.

4. *SA practice helps you enjoy just being,* letting an activity become sufficient unto itself. This generates the kind of present-centeredness that sparks the "flow" of joy.

5. *SA practice attunes you to extraordinary experiences.* If "flow" is indeed a matter of coming to use more of one's untapped potential, SA practice will prepare your rational mind for such an incredibility.

How to Ready Yourself for Joy (and Get More of It)

There are specific ways you can prepare yourself for joy, until such time as SA practice works its changes in your life. First, consider your job or recreations. Dr. C notes that the "flow" comes mainly to those who passionately love their work. When one's profession is merely a job, an absorbing hobby can fill the gap. But one has to be fascinated by the task at hand for these phenomenal effects to occur.

This corresponds with the tale of the surgeon who was so rapt in his task he failed to notice part of the operating room ceiling had caved in. Chess champion Bobby Fischer is said to enter a kind of trancelike state during tournaments. If a fire were to be ignited near him, he wouldn't look at it. In certain instances, body thinking takes over naturally. One report suggests that the reason mountain-climbing, tobogganing, and skiing prove good stress release is precisely because they demand total attention. Because of the risks, the penalties for inattention are too great, so the left brain shuts down. Right-brain "flow" and a shutdown of the logical mind might explain a gambler's addiction—high-stakes players have described to me a keenness in the gambling experience that is reminiscent of this flow of joy. Some top athletes, during a winning streak, say they get to the point where they can't stop, even if they want to. On one such occasion, golfer Arnold Palmer grew so immersed in his game he played a complete round without noticing that his wife was walking alongside.

Money and financial reward don't seem to trigger "flow"; risking oneself slightly helps, however. Notes Dr. C: Those who induce the flow of joy on a regular basis say they achieve it when they try to meet a challenge at the outer limits of their capabilities. (In the Broadway theater, an acting coach puts it this way: To grow—you must stretch yourself.) At the same time, don't hazard the impossible. Once one exceeds his known limitations, self-consciousness and (left-brain) doubts arise. This might be why beginners in a profession seldom experience the joyful flow of the tried and confident.

I think a sense of humor is also important, certainly for achieving certain kinds of *peak experiences*. And here is where instruction in SA-Selver (with its Zen parallels) will lighten the somber personality. In Zen, wit and humor are as germane to living as bread or water.

The following checklist brings its own feedback, helping you prepare yourself for joy's sensual flow.

Have You Readied Yourself for Joy?
(A Reader Self-Appraisal)

QUESTIONS

Answer "yes" or "no" if you would describe yourself as follows:

1. Speed and efficiency are most important to me.
2. I spend more time planning for the future than considering the immediate.
3. I am of normal weight for my age and family build.
4. I drink (or smoke) only on occasion, if at all. If I indulge, I limit myself to a total of one or two daily.
5. While not always athletic, I try to stay physically fit.
6. I exercise daily, or keep mobile and vital in my work.
7. Even if it's only a daily walk, I encourage outdoor habits for cardiovascular health.
8. Sometimes I get so interested in my work (or hobby) I forget all about my physical self.
9. I have a good sense of humor, but find it silly or undignified to laugh readily.
10. When I'm absorbed in my work, I can lose track of time.
11. Regardless of the number of years I've spent at it, I find myself eager and even thrilled by new developments in my work (or hobby).
12. The profession at which I now work is both satisfying and provides sufficient income for my needs.
13. In my future, financial gain is of secondary importance to me.

ANSWERS

1. No. North Americans especially are victims of the mental "hurry sickness." Such compulsions pose a hazard to both emotional and physical health, hastening hypertension for those over thirty years of age. All this works against sensory pleasure in the passing moment.

2. No. If your daily work requires you to skip over the here-and-now, find a hobby that will compensate. In addition to the "flow" activities mentioned previously (skiing, chess, dancing, rock-climbing), you might tailor such things as handicrafts, sailing, or meditation to your needs. Any of these will release the job stress you're probably building up day by day. Or, best of all, take classes in SA-Selver; this will attune you to focusing in on little moments of quiet serenity—even at a hectic office.

3–7. Yes. Numbers 3–7 are key to the onrush of joy for sound medical reasons. An expert on flow and mindfulness, Daniel Goleman, claims that a relaxed body (coupled with alert attention) are needed to induce the flow of joy.

8. No. Awareness of one's physical self relates directly to the sensory manifestations of joy. Indeed, focusing attention on your physical movements can ready you for "flow" (even dull chores like scraping pots and pans can offer a here-and-now to attune you.) With practice, you can experience "flow" while changing a tire, darning socks, or doing menial tasks. In a sense, this is the best thing about sensory awareness, with or without "flow"—it brings beauty into humdrum routine.

9. No. Ask yourself searchingly whether your heritage

or social conditioning have encouraged impassivity or dour behavior. There are exceptions; but many "reserved" people develop an unsmiling attitude toward life, whereas those who are able to laugh readily do, indeed, find joy in commonplace things. And today psychophysical scientists point out that the person who seldom smiles is most likely to suffer chronic emotional depression.

10. Yes.

11. Yes.

12–13. Yes. It can spark a rewarding new life for you when you seek out honest answers to these final questions. (If your answer was a "yes," then you're en route to the flow of joy, if you haven't discovered it already.) But if money counts for much with you, ask yourself whether there isn't a job that would be fulfilling, yet lucrative. (Dr. Hans Selye, stress expert, suggests the "play-professions," or jobs where one has followed one's hobby into gainful employment, thus earning a livelihood at work one enjoys. This can bring unexpected esteem: the well-informed antique seller or health food store proprietor is most appreciated. Such a combination of public approval and work joys can prove its own revitalization treatment; it will make the doer even younger-looking than his contemporaries. As the world's "youth doctors" agree, joy is the great rejuvenator.)

Celebrate Yourself Exercise No. 2: A Sensory Awareness Meditation

Prepare for this by getting a water-filled goldfish bowl or other glass container (with or without fish). Place it in bright sunlight, positioned to reflect hues on wall or ceiling. Then select a favorite record to play on the phonograph, preferably one without lyrics or emotional association with your past.

HERE'S WHAT TO DO: Seat yourself comfortably in a straight-backed chair or on a floor cushion, legs crossed, tailor-fashion. As the music begins, breathe low and deep, from your diaphragm. Think of your lower abdomen as a bellows, pulling it inward as you *exhale*. (This expands your lung capacity to embrace large quantities of oxygen when you inhale.) As the music flows, listen with your body as well as your ears, blocking out all outside thoughts. Just let your mental "motors" idle, and see if you can note colors coming alive on your improvised prism. Try to envision the music rolling in waves of pastels, bright or muted. (If you can't shut off your left-brain "noise," try counting with each exhaled breath: one, two, one, two.) Continue for at least five to ten minutes.

CHAPTER

4

CHARLOTTE SELVER AND THE SENSORY AWARENESS MOVEMENT

A student at one of my workshops said she was surprised to find that "sensing" is such a quiet thing. She said, "From all that I had heard about sensory awareness, I expected a really big thing."

I replied, "Is not quiet a 'big' thing?"

CHARLOTTE SELVER

The wonder of Charlotte Selver's sensory awareness is not merely that it is a time-proven and medically reliable pursuit, without side effects, and a study that is curiously relevant to our times, pre-maturely-aging as they are. Equally gratifying are its un-expected origins; for there was an unlikelihood of Selver, the developer of sensory awareness as it is taught today, ever working in collaboration with her German mentor, the late Elsa Gindler.

Charlotte was a well-to-do young woman, educated and teaching the goal-oriented gymnastics of a body technique couched in music and expressive movements. She unconsciously brought to the Berlin studios of Elsa Gindler attitudes and competitive experiences that were at polar opposites from "sensing's" nonverbal, inner quiets. Yet it was the marriage of these two approaches that gave birth to the deep, meaningful practice to which Charlotte Selver gave the name "sensory awareness."

At their meeting in the late twenties in Germany, the hawk-eyed Elsa Gindler abruptly rejected Charlotte's request to study with her. Charlotte was already a successful teacher of the Rudolf Bode School of Expressive Movement, and felt taken aback to be summarily dismissed. Months passed before Charlotte approached Gindler again. When she did, she found the latter, a teacher in the stern European tradition, was one who seldom wasted words. Looking piercingly at the rosy-cheeked, physically fit Charlotte, Gindler asked how her classes in expressive movement were progressing. "Quite well," said Charlotte, pleased that she had acquired such a following for so youthful a teacher.

"Then continue with it," snapped Gindler, again rejecting her application without explanation.

Back at her own studio, Charlotte continued her bustling classes in what was termed *Ausdrucks-Gymnastik*, but her curiosity continued regarding the mysterious work she had been hearing so many reports about. She persisted now with Gindler and finally gained permission to enroll in classes to learn about what Gindler called "study of the person" rather than the body as such. That Charlotte was accepted was probably due to her dogged determination, for Gindler warned: "Be prepared—it will be a long way for you."

As I shall later explain, progress in sensory awareness can vary from person to person, sometimes for unfathomable reasons. Sometimes it is the shy, unathletic student who progresses most auspiciously. Others (conditioned to gain-seeking gymnastics or yoga's rigorous disciplines) advance at a snail's pace. Excessive weight or body frame does not impede "sensing," and age is no limitation. It is frequently the reserved, inner-directed student who gains headway from the outset. Others might have "blocks" to work through before they come to believe in their own sensory truths.

Burying her self-regard as a successful teacher, Charlotte started as a beginner with Gindler, without encouragement and with little other than faith in her own ability to learn. (As Charlotte recounts "Finally, after years of work, Elsa Gindler said to me, 'Ah, that was your first real movement: at last, we have a beginning!' ") Why should she have humbled herself, submitting her ego to a demanding stranger for a length of time that amounted to years? Charlotte explains her persistence as the result of recurring doubts about the lasting import of her work in gymnastics and rhythms. When she observed improvement in her students, the changes that were produced were temporary. Those who responded, with their bodies shedding tension, acquiring grace, soon returned to their old habits. When she spied them on the street or met them socially, she discovered that their clumsy postures and ungainly gaits had returned.

Another factor was the need for music for self-regulation in the exercises: Charlotte wondered whether a person needed music and gongs to bring about body changes. She speculated: "Couldn't such changes come out of one's inner quiet—without outside stimulation?"

The Time of Great Awakenings—When SA Began

In Germany at the end of the twenties, profound change and sweeping self-improvement were popular topics. Those last years of the Weimar Republic were unpredictable, inflationary times, when fortunes were made (and lost) overnight. Despite, or perhaps because of this, new ideas abounded, and people were eager to turn their lives around. A surprising number believed that small things might have immense personal impact—all they had to do was discover what was right for them, and make use of it. In Berlin, there were thirty-three magazines and papers specializing in astrology. In speaking of this period of pre-Hitler Germany, Carl Jung was to write of the tumultuous forces that were energizing the nation's psyche.

Bold new concepts were introduced in the field of medicine, and body studies were no longer a "for men only" world. Mme. Marie Curie, now elderly, campaigned for acceptance of her late husband's (and her own) discoveries, as women in science garnered respect and new esteem.

Just across Germany's border, Vienna's Sigmund Freud had obtained acceptance from the staid medical establishment for his unorthodox views about the links between mind and body. Actually, the human body was coming into its own, as the Continent threw off the surviving remnants of Victorian stodginess, including distaste for man's physical realities. An artist named Bess Mensendieck noted postural flaws in the (otherwise) faultless models she sketched, so she went to medical school, and the Mensendieck system of corrective exercises was born. Realign your body, it promised, and you will revitalize your future; attending to your physical being will let you change your life. In England, an Australian ex-actor named F. Matthias Alexander was teaching that body movements could bring emotional benefits. Intellectuals like Leonard Woolf and Aldous Huxley believed him and recommended his technique to others who were also open to new ideas.

Even more than today, it was an era of awesome possibilities, with people ready to believe in the unlikely and extraordinary. Enthusiasm for change was abundant and free-flowing. This enthusiasm impelled and channeled some toward leadership and originality when, in a less heady era, they might have remained unnoticed subordinates. The shy, ex-patent office clerk who, at the beginning of this era, was unexpectedly awarded the Nobel Prize was an illustration of this. His concept in physics, then simply called "the general theory," would up-end the future of our civilization. And like the Gindler-Selver work in sensory awareness, Albert Einstein's theory of relativity was not to become popularly known until later—and also in America.

Elsa Gindler and Self-Healing

What made the Gindler work on "the person" more inspiring to students than other body improvement methods, including the one in which Charlotte Selver was trained? There was little explanation from Gindler herself, for the practice was nonverbal and could not even be discussed rationally.

Perhaps it was the rumors repeated by Gindler's long-term students about the curious things that were beginning to occur within them. Whatever the reason, Gindler's students accorded a passionate devotion to the doyenne, calling her probings into self by the reverential term "the work."

For the fact that such "work" could heal and effect physical change was dramatically seen in Elsa Gindler herself. Once a physical education teacher, she had risen above her humble family origins to educate herself. But, as with many impoverished students who climb a strenuous professional path, the years of stress had taken a physical toll. Her health wavered, and a lingering illness was diagnosed as what was then a most dreaded malady—tuberculosis.

In those days, before the use of penicillin and sulfa drugs, this disease was considered fatal or, at best, disabling. So advanced was Gindler's case that her only hope for survival, said physicians, was to emigrate to the rarefied atmosphere of Switzerland. There she might live out her remaining time as a semi-invalid.

Such professional care was tempting, but it was a dream outside the day-to-day realities of this self-employed young woman from a family of meager resources. Instead, Elsa Gindler decided to probe deeply into the medical problem and into herself. She spent weeks researching, noting, then sifting what she had learned about the body from current medical literature. Elsa Gindler was to say: "If this disease came by itself, it can go by itself." She decided on a bold course, which even now sounds risky and foolhardy, if not a bit insane. Gindler became convinced she could become deeply attuned to her own inner processes, so much so that she might master and control her respiratory movements. She would become so aware of all the subtle sensations within that she could allow breathing in one lung only. For all intents, she would "collapse" the diseased lung. Semi-activity and limited respiration would rest the chest area, allowing time for self-healing.

It should be noted that this kind of self-mastery was unheard-of in Europe, and unparalleled elsewhere. It involved control of tiny, complex air passages, an extensive muscular system, and involuntary reflexes. As Charles Brooks observed, what Gindler proposed required her putting her entire sensory-neural system on the alert. Like a pebble dropped in water, any excitation at any point in the body tends to set up reactions everywhere. "In so critical a situation," says Brooks, "every disturbance in breathing was acute." Yet if the determined teacher were able to succeed (trying to sense her inner sensations on a moment-by-moment basis), functional hindrances to healing might be overcome. Tissue and lung regeneration could take place.

If this story seems incredible, so is its ending—for Elsa

Gindler indeed healed herself. There is a faded portrait of Gindler, taken nearly thirty-five years later. It shows a smooth-skinned woman, poised and aglow with health. Almost sixty, Elsa Gindler then appeared to be a woman in her mid-thirties. To say that this iron-willed patient overcame tuberculosis and confounded her physicians, who pronounced her cured at the end of a year, seems a massive understatement for magnificent self-regeneration.

This, then, was the core of the Gindler legend that attracted Charlotte Selver and others. It remained for class work, and her own discoveries and experiences about herself, to provide the reinforcement Charlotte Selver needed to urge her to continue.

Charlotte tells of one day (early in her work with Gindler) when an exasperated student complained, after an unsuccessful experiment, that he always had one particular difficulty or another and that he was probably ungifted for such work. Gindler retorted, "There is no such thing as being ungifted!"

What a wondrous possibility, Charlotte reflected. Perhaps there is no such thing as a person's being ungifted for something. The words came like a "thunderbolt," Charlotte recalls. In her previous years of training in dance and rhythm, her teachers occasionally told her that she was clumsy by nature, and perhaps the work was not right for her. Charlotte continued in it because it seemed as if she might not overcome any other problem unless she overcame such limitations.

As an advanced student with Gindler, Charlotte was to look back and recognize the differences that separated the active, competitive world of gymnastics and physical exercise and the quiet, self-oriented world of sensory awareness probings. No one at the Gindler studio showed students how to perform something, or demonstrated an exercise for the class to follow. There were no urges to "Go higher!" or "Use more power," or "Go deeper!" Charlotte recalls that one day

Gindler shrugged, "How does it help Ann when she is told 'See how high Clare jumps. Now you do that, also!' "

Rather, there was constant inner exploration, quiet "sensing," and the seeking out of one's inner impulses, learning to respect them for what they were. This was the way Gindler students made their biggest discoveries. This was the way, as Charlotte puts it, "they came to allow changes."

After a few years, Charlotte was to teach this self-exploratory practice in European schools. Then, against the advice of many, Charlotte took this singular, nonverbal work to the United States, emigrating in one of the anti-Hitler waves of 1938. It was a move that was to change the lives of thousands, including herself.

Sensory Awareness as a Cultural Pursuit

America was not the appropriate place for a subtle practice like sensory awareness to gain headway, friends warned. America was fast-moving, a nation of ambitious, goal-oriented pragmatists; people in the United States were too hearty and impatient to take time for quiet, motionless "sensing." Americans were interested in making money, not in "sensing" their own inner stirrings.

For a while, it seemed as if her would-be discouragers were correct. Setting up a studio and attracting serious students was not easy in an alien land—even for Charlotte, who had learned to trust and follow her inner instincts. But as time went on, skimpy classes filled out. SA-Selver came to attract those influential in the fields of medicine and psychology who were to engineer and channel the currents of body/mind studies for decades. Fritz Perls, his Gestalt psychotherapy still in its formative stages, came—then returned again, and again, first to talk, then to encourage and propose a mutual collaboration. (Despite tempting reinforcement, Selver decided against taking "the work" into emotional therapy, opting to maintain its integrity as Gindler taught it.) As we have seen, Perls was to base many of his central concepts in Gestalt on Selver's teachings.

Other seekers after sensory truths included Clara Thompson, president of the William A. White Association; Frances Flaherty, widow and associate of the pioneer film-maker, Robert Flaherty; John Collier, former U.S. Commissioner of Indian Affairs; Scott Nearing, pioneer organic farmer. The leading psychiatrists came to visit and learn, including Ernst Schachtel, and Elizabeth Howes and Shiela Moon, who headed the Guild of Psychological Studies.

More than anyone else, Dr. Erich Fromm offered help and encouragement, for he saw in the quiet, nonverbalisms of sensory awareness a steady path to inner truths and self-actualization. Fromm was to arrange a teaching post for Charlotte at New York's New School for Social Research, overcoming the opposition of less farsighted faculty members. In 1957, Fromm invited Charlotte to introduce sensory awareness at the influential Conference on Zen Buddhism and Psychoanalysis, held in Cuernavaca, Mexico, and jointly chaired by Fromm and D. T. Suzuki. An invitation followed to teach SA at the University of Mexico. Word spread, and sensory awareness was used to launch the beginnings of Esalen Institute at Big Sur. By this time, SA-Selver had become universally respected on professional as well as intellectual levels.

The late Alan Watts was instrumental in the spread of this work to California, and its emergence in the respectable mainstream of humanistic psychology. In a talk on SA-Selver, prior to his death in 1973, Watts observed that most of us are reared with a kind of fundamental mistrust of our physical nature. "We think of man as a sort of rider on a horse, a two-natured person who has a rational soul and an animal body. And the animal body is regarded as something vital but stupid." Reciting the story of Elsa Gindler and her intricate self-healing, Watts noted that such efforts to gain awareness of subtle body sensations and further the promptings of her own nature was an Oriental truth. "The Chinese would say this is the art of Taoism . . . [It is] called in Chinese '*wu-wei*,' or a noninterference with the Tao . . . the course of nature."

A related truth resides here, also, and rejecting it will be a barrier to true "sensing." Alan Watts recognized it early: one must ask oneself what one feels of one's *own* body and organism, rather than looking elsewhere for how, and what, to feel. Most people are not accustomed to this, Watts noted. From childhood, we are told what is correct and what to reject as incorrect. We are instructed as to what something should be, if it is not. Yet what of happenings within ourselves? "Not what one knows or thinks about, or believes somebody else expects one to feel, but what one actually perceives."

Such an easing of the questioning linear mind is difficult at first because we think we're supposed to conform to a pattern of perfection—that somewhere there is somebody who knows precisely what we ought to be and ought to feel. We persist in this stubborn notion, Watts marveled, "despite all the emphasis in the Western world on the value of individuality . . . [and] personal uniqueness."

In SA-Selver (as in psychophysical therapies like Bioenergetics and Structural Integration) this kind of breakthrough of repressed individuality might be accompanied by brief and tearful hysterical outbursts. In SA-Selver this can offer the *satori*, or enlightenment flash.

In Charlotte's case, she found that she seemed to be "holding back" from partners in the Gindler class. Unaware, she had a fear of losing control. Staying with this feeling, she worked through it.

"With the beginning of 'giving,' " she recalls, "a torrent of tears came, tears and tears—all the weeping I had held back in myself. These became tears of relief. 'I don't have to hold back any more.'" And to the degree to which her resistance vanished, her "tensions" eased. "My breathing picked up, and through me, from feet to head, a feeling of ease and life spread."

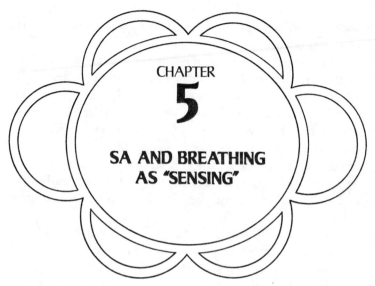

CHAPTER
5

SA AND BREATHING
AS "SENSING"

There is no "proper" breathing. Your breathing indicates very clearly what state you are in. When you are more reactive, your breathing is more reactive; when you are more habitual, your breathing is more habitual; if you are pushy, your breathing gets pushy, too, or stops. You can depend on it; as your breathing is, so you are.

CHARLOTTE SELVER

You're now ready to experience "sensing" for yourself. One of the easy ways to sample SA-Selver is to "sense" your respiration. This was the approach that started Gindler on her road to self-healing. And this underlines the way SA-Selver differs from all exercise systems.

As opposed to yoga and structured physical disciplines, sensory awareness avoids breathing exercises, as such. Let your normal breathing flow, says Selver. Trust your natural breathing—just be fully there to allow it.

In seldom recognized ways, our breathing and the respiratory process are connected with all that we do and think. We breathe slowly when we are relaxed, more slowly yet when we meditate, our respiration then centered low in the abdomen. When we are excited, or tense, our breathing is rapid and higher in the chest. Should one do exercises for relaxed breathing? One California teacher of breathing awareness warns that going around with forced abdominal breathing, as certain yoga gurus suggest, can keep you in a drowsy stupor.

In her individual way, Selver was one of the first of today's environmentalists—she considered man's role in the surrounding ecosystem. In her lectures on breathing, she emphasizes that nothing in nature is isolated, ourselves included. And it is the process of breathing that provides a vital connection between everything outside and all that happens within us.

When we allow it, we can become constantly responsive to everything about and surrounding us—and this can prove a revitalizing experience. Our whole day becomes full of sensory invitations; but we realize this only if and when we respond to them. Such everlasting invitations, she promises, "can keep us young, movable, and reactive." We will be "never repeating, always new."

This is another tenet of SA-Selver that coincides with Zen Buddhism. While a latter-day observer thinks it unlikely that Elsa Gindler ever studied Zen (which was not available in the Germany of that time), the parallels are ample. As I'll describe it in the next section, the sensory awareness approach to breathing relates closely to the Zen concept of *shamatha*, that practice with which one begins to travel the path to enlightenment, or *hinayana*. Chogyam Trungpa describes this in his writing on Zen Buddhism, as follows:

*The basic practice is to be present, right here. The
goal is also the technique. Precisely being in this
moment, neither suppressing nor wildly letting go,
but being precisely aware of what you are. Breath
. . . is a neutral process . . . We simply become
mindful of its natural functioning.*

For most of us, it is easier to gasp and pant in dramatic
breathing dynamics, rather than to simply "become mindful"
of our natural functioning. Yet it is the quiet, "listening"
way that is the way of the Tao, Zen and sensory awareness.

Sensory Breathing: An Experiment in SA-Selver

During breathing workshops, sensory awareness leaders
emphasize the spontaneous, the art of becoming fully receptive to the here-and-now. Selver thinks it is paramount to
differentiate between this "spontaneous" breathing and "habitual" breathing. Some persons, she notes, have the notion
that when they are just as they always are, this is what is
meant by being spontaneous. They say, "This is my nature;
it's the way I am." Actually, it is merely habit—and as such,
it can be a deviation away from one's true nature.

There is another caution in SA-Selver: don't let yourself
become preoccupied with your breathing to the exclusion of
everything else, even during a SA breathing experiment. Paying attention to the here-and-now includes remaining open
and mindful to outside events. "When you care only for
breathing, you are impoverishing yourself," notes Selver.

The knack one must encourage is to be totally present,
responsive, and—in other words—*all there* for whatever is
happening. Then breathing flows and can provide us with
tremendously sensitive energy supplies.

You'll understand what this means by the following

SA breathing experiment. Exploring your breathing and your respiration process helps you become more responsive to it.

1. *Try to notice when you stop breathing.* Unaware, we stop breathing many times—if we are shy or ill-at-ease, when we panic or are fearful. Selver says your breathing can stop when something is not quite right in your relationship to whatever it is you're doing. "It is very interesting psychologically to find out what makes you stop your breath at that particular moment."

2. *Stop breathing right now.* Do it gently, effort-lessly. Consider again the possibility of learning more about yourself by perceiving when your breathing slows. Perhaps at such moments, you are putting too much energy, urgency, or pressure into whatever it is you are doing. When some persons study intently or closely observe, they can stop breathing temporarily. ("When the head is too busy, breathing stops," notes Selver.)

3. *Let breathing resume naturally.* When you find you are holding your breath, wait a little. When you are not hindering it, a marvelous thing happens: your breathing resumes of itself.

4. *Have respect and patience.* Whatever you discover about your own breathing, be grateful that you feel it, and don't push yourself toward changing. If you try to force your breathing, it destroys the discovery of what really is spontaneous breathing.

5. *Allow exhalation as needed.* Being as busy as many people are today, we often don't allow sufficient time for complete exhalation. Thorough respiration is essential for internal cleansing and the removal of wastes. By holding too much exhalation within, we can rob our heads of elasticity and freedom, says Selver. Consider this, taking time to learn whether you are allowing

exhalation as needed. ("Do not *do* it, but *allow* it, until you have a feeling of satisfaction, of completion.")

6. *Let inhalation come.* Do not deliberately inhale, but let your very next breath occur naturally. Wait very quietly until this happens. When your respiration comes, allow it to distribute itself in you. Try not to manipulate your breathing—become more open for it.

Note: Due to the subtleties of SA-Selver as a non-verbal practice, you might have skimmed over the above. Read it at least twice more. Better, put it on a tape recorder, and play it once daily for a week.

In Your Own "Sensing" Practice

Consider the way you can be *all there* for other activities besides breathing. When you hear a song or a casual conversation, explore the possibility of letting it come to you with all its depth, as fully as possible. Don't reach out for it—allow what comes to you to, as Selver says, soak in thoroughly. Don't leave it "in the head, and turn it over in the brain," says Selver; receive it with your whole being. This is what happens with an extraordinary dancer or actor. "When he listens to some reading or music, it right away hits home with him. He doesn't make an effort, he's just there for it . . . It's not art, it's our natural equipment which comes into play."

And if *you* are receptive, everything within is receptive —receptive and reactive to what is happening.

PART

II

**EXERCISES
TO ACCOMPANY
SA PRACTICE**

CHAPTER

6

YOUR HARA, CENTERING AND BODY AWARENESS

We now bring one hand to the lower back and the other to the belly opposite . . . This is the hara, *or seat of vitality, of the Japanese, the "wheat fields set about with lilies" of the Bible, and the "guts" of our own vernacular.*

CHARLES V. W. BROOKS

At about the time that sensory awareness practice becomes meaningful for you, a door will swing open in your perceptive mind. You may not be aware of this right away: discovering that SA practice offers philosophical overtones is a gradual process, like growth itself. But this self-evolving is aided by understanding the *hara,* or body "center." You'll also find that "centering" makes SA training progress smoothly, for it helps you understand that SA-Selver, at its best, is a body awareness study.

In Zen Buddhism and other Oriental studies, the *hara* is the term given the vital body center, the core of self. When you are emotionally in touch with this area, it opens up reservoirs of energy and emotional stability.

To help you grasp the concept of *hara*, let me first sweep away some cobwebs of confusion that have been spun by self-termed experts. In the spate of body awareness studies, the term "centering" has been abused and overused, as beginners talk casually about who is "well-centered" and who isn't. Observers assume there is some visible locus or position on the body, and once this "center" is located and exercised, predictable changes will begin happening, preferably overnight. This illustrates the kind of goal-oriented, commercial reductionism that blurs and mutilates the sensitivities of Oriental truths. Following such a false assumption will lead you down a dead-end road; it can slow down or postpone your growth toward wisdom and the right-brain perceptivity that comes with "sensing." (Charlotte Selver and Charles Brooks seldom use the term "centering" in sensory awareness workshops, just as they do not talk casually about "energy flows." These terms have become empty and meaningless to the leadership coterie in the human potential movement.)

Nevertheless, the "center" (as Gestalt's Fritz Perls termed it) relates to a powerful body/mind concept. It is a truth born in the Orient, where perceptive truths are given as much credence as scientific fact—sometimes more so. An unclouded appraisal of the concept of "centering" will condition you for sensory awareness practice. It builds a higher regard for inner feelings and deepens body awareness perceptions. In the process, you will grow in ego strength—and come to experience more of the serenity that this book is about.

Body awareness studies have a collateral relationship to "sensing." They set great store by what is *experiential*, or what a person experiences, rather than what he is told or what he reads. (You'll note left-brain and right-brain concepts at work here.) At its best, sensory awareness is a nonverbal experience; so to make what follows in this chapter more meaningful, practice the following experiment, prior to reading further. Again, do not seek correct or incorrect results, or a preferred way of reacting: what counts is your *own* responses, and endeavoring to sense them on deeper levels.

For best results, read the following over before you follow it. Or you and a friend direct each other in the experiment, practicing alternately. Don't be self-conscious or shy about the following, and avoid (left-brain) side comments. Too much verbalizing during sensory awareness experiments will blunt the impact of the experience.

The Hara: *A Body Awareness Experiment in SA-Selver*

(This is to be practiced barefoot, dressed in comfortable, loose-fitting clothing.)

Come to standing. Relax your body and begin to breathe gently. Balance your weight evenly, moving it lightly from foot to foot.

Now bring one of your hands to your lower back, placing the other on your belly, palm inward. (*Notice how different you feel, front to back?*)

Let us consider this. In the back, your hand comes in contact with a rigid structure, distinct bone and muscle. Your hand in front is in touch with a vague, almost unknown mass. Here we have been taught that many organs rest; these parts are vital to our health and well-being. (Charles Brooks says that these organs have to do with body functions that are not always mentionable in social company. As a result, he notes, "Some of us remain faintly ashamed of them.") *Do you feel shy about the front part of your abdominal area? Does it embarrass you to touch it?* Note that this lower front part of your body is not protected by an encasing bone structure, as your chest is. *Does it feel vulnerable to you? Do you feel it should be covered up and hidden, or kept out of sight?* (Pause now, and consider these sensations before proceeding further.)

In back, under your other hand, you'll find quite different territory: firm and solid, perhaps. Certainly it is more definable. As your hand presses your lower and midback (do this now), you sense a reassuring response of bone and muscle. There is steadiness here. It is within this structure that we stand erect.

Now shift your weight gently from foot to foot, side to side. Keep both hands in place, and explore the feel of this body movement. (*Do subtle muscles come into play as you move?* Repeat the movement to sense this again.)

Sit down now, hands still in place front and back. Try to rock from side to side on your buttocks. Again, let your back hand sense the ripple of muscles, knitting and moving. You also may note a reassuring firmness beneath. (I love Charles Brooks's simile for this: he compares this contrast in body sensations to a ship's mast, rising out of the deck, while the surrounding muscles, below, respond to every rock and pitch of the "sea.")

Now remove your hands. Again, come to standing. Place one hand again in front, lightly but firmly resting on that mysterious region, just below your navel. Think for a moment about our culture's notion that courage and fortitude are expressed by "guts."

In the Orient, also, this region is considered to contain deep, powerful forces that can be called upon to manifest themselves in brave, assertive actions. As you rest your palm against your lower abdomen, let your sensations include this bold, revitalizing concept. As you inhale and exhale quietly, let your abdomen rise and collapse. Think of this as your *hara.* (*Can you sense the feeling of power within?*) Now drop your hand lightly to your side. Stand quietly, breathing gently. Do not do anything; just recognize that there is a miracle of respiration now taking place within you. (*Are you all there for it?*)

The Hara *and the Nervous System*

Even outside the Hemingway novels of guts and bravery, in the quieter, more sedentary battlefields of the business world, one hears references to "gut feelings." This term is used in New York's polished advertising profession as synonymous with deep-set conviction. Might this colloquialism have unacknowledged links with the legendary *hara*?

Consider the following. Dr. Tomio Hirai is the Japanese psychologist-physiologist who was the first to medically research the benefits of Zen practice. Dr. Hirai points to an anatomical fact about the *hara* that is of more than coincidental interest: behind the stomach, just below the navel, is a network of autonomic nerves. Such nerves direct fatigue recovery. They help one withstand hardships by energy restoration and what Dr. Hirai terms "the creation of physical and mental strength." This is the regional nervous system that exercises control over blood vessels for the kidneys, liver, and large intestines, all active in waste removal (and therefore, active in fatigue recovery). This local autonomic nervous system provides a tangible link with what our civilization symbolically terms "guts," or fortitude.

Dr. Hirai notes that numerous animal experiments show that tensing the abdomen under certain conditions can calm the body. Oriental physicians who prescribe abdominal breathing exercises for patients find this therapy can cure gastric ulcers, intercostal neuralgia, and chronic constipation. Abdominal breathing exercises have helped when medications and other therapy have failed.

Children growing up around swamps and country ponds learn early another version of this folk wisdom: tapping a frog two or three times on his abdomen, when he is lying on his back after capture, will calm his nervous flailing-about.

This phenomenon is also seen with a chicken. When it is

taken alive and laid on its back, it can be "hypnotized" by tapping its abdomen two or three times. For a short period the fowl appears to be asleep. This state of relaxed drowsiness, according to Dr. Hirai, is due to the parasympathetic nervous system. This forms a network in this part of the torso and is responsible for slowing the heartbeat, constricting the optic muscles, and related actions.

Of course, as with any body oversimplification, there are complex factors at work here that might be reckoned with in more scientific research. But for now, let's return to our body awareness and "sensing" study. I'd like you to consider occasions when this unique body/mind concept might help you understand the power of the *hara*—and use it to build inner strength.

Returning to Center: A Body Awareness Exercise

Any time you feel annoyed or overrun by outside forces, consider your *hara*. Shift the focus of your conscious attention to within yourself. If your concentration is total, even though it is momentary, such an interlude helps sharpen your feelings about complicated situations. It releases new energy and can restore your confidence.

HERE'S WHAT TO DO: Stand or sit easily, relaxing chest and abdominal muscles. Let your breath sink low, into your abdomen. Breathe gently from your diaphragm (the lower stomach region). Try to use your diaphragm as a bellows: expand it as you inhale, flatten it as you exhale. At the end of each exhaled respiration, pause briefly. This encourages a vacuum and makes you ready to welcome larger quantities of air as you inhale. Practice this in a leisurely way for two or three breaths. This exercise (which has the advantage of being imperceptible) will help you remain more your own person when in the presence of opposing forces.

Sensory Centering for New Energy—Aikido Exercises

It was the Oriental martial arts that laid the groundwork for centering and body awareness studies, particularly the work in aikido. *Tai-chi ch'uan* is another study that teaches the student to place himself in tune with universal energy as it flows and moves with the tides of life. (Most Oriental studies are couched in lyrical terms, so open up your right-brain perceptions to this kind of truth as you read further: this helps you grasp the body/mind significance of the aikido exercises that follow.)

Most of these *hara*-related studies are based on the Chinese concept of *chi*, or a body energy that flows along fourteen main body channels. Imbalance leads to sickness and disorder, including emotional disorders (one reason why acupuncture is used to treat mental problems in applications of this traditional Chinese medical therapy).

In the following exercises, note that these are body/mind arts, and they let the spiritual and mental supplement the physical. Put simply, this is a way of helping you gain access to new energies—energies that are nonphysical but no less invigorating.

The Light Bulb—A Sensory Exercise for Centering

This aikido imagery exercise builds awareness and power in those body regions once thought to be outside conscious control.

HERE'S WHAT TO DO: Sit comfortably, legs crossed tailor-fashion. Imagine there is a light bulb in your abdomen, just below the navel. This is a light that is ready to glow with radiance and warmth. Turn on this light bulb. Feel the steady warmth pulsating throughout your abdominal area. Enjoy this for several moments.

Now turn off the "light." Then turn it on again, and pretend as you switch it on that it radiates a stronger light, beaming a living warmth. Let these beams shine from your center throughout the rest of your body. Let the light beams move up through your chest and out your arms. Let each finger glow with steady light.

Let the light beams travel down your torso and into your legs. Imagine the light is so warm and bright that each body part starts to glow brightly as the light beams move through. Let such beams of light flow outside your body; extend this glowing light from your hands and feet. Beam these in any direction you choose.

Stand up. Feel this light as energy, flowing and stirring within you. Now walk forward, feeling the sensation of light beams within you as you move. Try to direct these powerful beams through your face and hands. Let your inner light touch and warm the people you will meet today. Let your light radiate power into the work you will do in the next few hours.

A Body Awareness/Centering Exercise: The Polarity Squat

The following exercise is more physical, and from the unique field of polarity therapy. This is a body art that relates to centering, and was developed by Dr. Randolph Stone. He was a California chiropractor who traveled to the Orient to study Chinese medical arts, including acupuncture. This exercise is said to boost energy, as well as aid in centering.

HERE'S WHAT TO DO: Stand relaxed, feet wide apart, knees pointed outward. Now bend your knees, and imagine there is an invisible chair beneath. Keeping your back erect, try to squat as if you were sitting on the chair. Place your hands on your knees and hunch your shoulders. Let your torso weight rest on your hands. (Don't worry if this feels clumsy: it's part of the centering sensation.) Now bend one knee as you straighten the other, thus beginning to rock back and forth. Keep your body weight on the leg that is bent. Continue this rocking for several moments. Enjoy the feeling of strength and power that is generated at your center as you rock.

Celebrate Yourself Exercise No. 3: Imagery Centering

This exercise is one of my own favorites, based on psychophysical theories proposed by Dr. Moshe Feldenkrais. It is a *body-painting experiment* that I call "the Belt." You'll be using your own mind-power and imagination rather than brush and paint. In this way you restore body awareness sensation in those regions with which you are emotionally out of touch. This can happen through day-to-day living, or through emotional "blocks" that have grown up, separating you from a more natural relationship with your center. Performing this exercise regularly does much to restore body/mind harmony. (Put this into a tape recorder for replay.)

HERE'S WHAT TO DO: Lie flat (preferably on the floor, a pillow under your upper neck and head). Relax your legs, and keep your arms lightly at your sides. Now close your eyes and breathe gently for several minutes. Then lower your breathing, centering it low in the abdomen. Again, use your center like a bellows: lift it as you inhale, flatten it as you exhale. Gently close your eyes.

Select a bright, cheerful color (such as red/orange or a shining pink). Imagine that a container of such paint rests easily on your navel area. Imagine also that you have a paintbrush, held by a mechanical arm that is suspended over your body.

As you continue breathing deeply, let the imaginary brush dip into the paint. With firm strokes, paint your waist with this colored "belt." Without moving a muscle, also imagine you are painting your back, stroke by stroke.

Return to the front, and use vertical strokes to paint your lower abdominal area, waist to pelvis. Do this thoroughly, moving inch by inch. When your brush reaches the pelvis, move it around the penis or vaginal lips, painting them directly and completely. (Women, take the brush and "paint" inside the vagina.) Continue to paint your genital area a bright, happy color.

Still with eyes closed, take the brush around your backside, painting scrupulously. Paint the area between your buttocks, all around. Pay special attention to the lower back area. Continue stroking imaginary paint around this region until your buttocks and lower back glow with bright rich paint. Then return to the front. Retracing your brush strokes, give your abdomen and center a second coat of paint.

This imagery painting should take at least five to six minutes. The longer you spend at it, the stronger body awareness you instill. As you stroke, try to vividly "sense" the feel of the paint and the brush and the warm paint as it dries on you.

If you recently have had an unsatisfactory sexual relationship—or if you are over thirty-five—you might have tensions in this region of which you are unaware. Repeat the experiment, this time doing this: attempt to "exhale" from each body site as you paint it, inch by inch.

With daily practice, this sensory body "breathing" revitalizes circulatory health and restores vitality to sexual organs. With regular practice of the above, you'll accustom yourself to radiating from your center—and *be all there* for interpersonal relationships.

Centering for Mind Power, New Composure

In addition to a lack of sensitivity training, two other studies are neglected in our present education system: how to slow down, and ways to be good to ourselves. When you learn how to reach (and respect) your center, you'll find it useful to reach for comfort and reinforcement. This curtails nervousness and a lot of tension. It also builds self-esteem, even as it gives you a meaningful way to slow down in a busy, hectic world.

The next time you're out of sorts or anxious, use the "Return to Center" exercise on page 174. Or do this: Pay particular attention to that part of your abdomen below the navel. Pause briefly, and breathe calmly. Let your breathing center in this area. Take several moments for this, wherever you are. When you return your attention to the outside world, you'll find you are steadier, more sure of yourself.

A special note: Cigarette smokers (and those who live in air-polluted cities) have a greater need for centering and might find extra difficulty in reaching their centers. This is because such environmental detriments accustom one to shallow breathing. However, when such persons sense and reach their *haras,* or centers, on a daily basis, these efforts build extra mind power. If you choose, this revitalization will whet your interest in giving up smoking.

A Sensory Centering Exercise for Mind Power— *The Mountain*

Sit cross-legged on the floor, buttocks resting comfortably on a flat pillow. Think about a mountain as a reality that is majestic and strong. Visualize such a mountain, and breathe deeply as you contemplate it. Think of the way a mountain sits solidly, dominating the environment. Imagine you are this mountain.

Consider yourself majestic and massive, like the mountain. You are rooted to earth. Feel yourself drawing nourishment from the earth. Feel calmed and strengthened from such earth-nurturing. Whatever your size or weight, imagine there is a massive feeling within, more powerful below your waist than in your head and shoulders. Like a mountain, the lower part of you is massive, and it anchors your body to the ground. Stay with these mountain feelings as you breathe deeply for several moments.

Now stand up slowly. Continue to experience these feelings, for, like a mountain, you are drawn to earth for your sustenance. Feel this vital contact with earth as you walk around slowly. Enjoy this feeling of new power, and know it brings a steadiness that you never felt before.

Remain in awareness contact with this massive feeling at your body center as you go through your day. Take whatever space you require, as you need it, wherever you are. (You are a mountain, aren't you?) Let nothing stand in your way, or deflect you from your chosen purpose.

Living from Your Center

You'll gain more than energy and mind power when you begin living from your center, or *hara*: you'll acquire an emotional stability that will make your contacts and communication with others more successful, deep, and enriching.

By now you have progressed in "sensing" and body awareness, so try a little experiment. In the privacy of your room, stand naked before a full-length mirror. Do you feel at ease? Do this regularly, until you feel comfortable gazing at your unadorned, vital self.

With body awareness and sensory practice, you'll feel good about yourself—regardless of whether you are overweight, shrunken, aging, or squat, for you grow to accept yourself as you are, rather than some phony Hollywood or fashion magazine "ideal." This builds self-esteem, and enhances your social outlook.

Psychologists tell us the way we feel about our bodies and our center can influence social attitudes, including racial prejudices, if any, and political attitudes toward minority groups. Leading American psychologist Seymour Fisher has collected extensive data on this subject. He builds a convincing case to substantiate the theory that the person who feels an uneasiness about his *own* body tends to overreact or be repulsed by any physical characteristics that radically differ from his own. In other words, the person who doesn't feel secure about his own body will feel an unfocused feeling of alarm when he sees an amputee, a hunchback, or a thalidomide victim, to name some examples. Such a confrontation, suggests Dr. Fisher, is a threatening encounter to one with latent body anxieties—it might happen to him.

On the other hand, when persons become more relaxed about their body structures (and at home in their centers), their ethnic and racial prejudices seem to lift and disappear. This was proven in research by psychologist I. M. Rubin, who measured the changes in attitude (testing ethnic prejudices against blacks) by charting reactions of a group of white persons before and after a sensitivity training or body awareness workshop. He found those persons who became more self-accepting about their bodies also became less prejudiced toward blacks. Explains another psychologist: when negative feelings about self are replaced by positive ones, there's less need for defensive (or self-whitewashing) tactics toward different minorities.

Your body can be your most dependable, stable entity. It is a bedrock fundamental to emotional security. Put simply, when you live from your center (as Fritz Perls suggested), it brings a wondrous fellow-feeling.

Celebrate Yourself Exercise No. 4: A Centering Experiment to Overcome Nighttime Anxiety and Sleeplessness

You can use centering to block unreasonable fears and left-brain "static." Middle-of-the-night emotionality (the kind that brings sleepless tossings) is aided by centering also.

Let me give you an example from my own experience. During the writing of this book, I gained great composure from the following exercise. (It is based on left-brain/right-brain concepts, as well as centering.) As you read in the Foreword, my "sensing" led me away from New York City, to live in a villa by the sea in Bermuda. Picturesque though the view, it was a rambling house; one stormy night it had its share of eerie creaks and shutters that banged ominously. This was a bleak weekend, with my daughter away, and I felt very much alone in a land not my own. I had lived for nearly twenty years in high-rise Manhattan apartments, secure and protected by twenty-four-hour doormen, so I was unused to lonely sounds at night. (And as everywhere else today, Bermuda has its share of burglars and rapists.) With the post-midnight noises, crime reports paraded through my mind, and sleep would not come—until the following exercise.

(*Note:* The directions are for right-handed persons. If you are left-handed, experiment until you hit on the hand that is most effective.)

HERE'S WHAT TO DO: Sit or lie relaxed. If performing this in bed, lie on your right side. The idea is to drum the fingers of your *left* hand on your abdomen, as you silently count to five. Then continue drumming as you repeat the first five letters of the alphabet (A-B-C-D-E). Fingers still drumming lightly, count from 6 to 10; then say the following five alphabet letters (F to J) as you continue drumming. Follow this with more counting and so forth.

Remember to breathe deeply, slowly—and from your diaphragm. It also helps if you focus body awareness attention to your fingertips: try to sense a tactile tattoo as you drum. (This here-and-now focus aids in disrupting troublesome thought spirals.) With a little practice, this exercise comes easier. It works best when your fingers alert your body center, letting the autonomic nervous system lull you and relax nervous tension. This will hasten the onset of sleep.

CHAPTER
7

ZAZEN—THE SENSORY AWARENESS MEDITATION

Zazen consists of sitting silent, motionless, and thought-less on a small cushion on a mat for extended periods . . . Thus the organism is freed of its habitual drives to act, and is left available for perception.

CHARLES V. W. BROOKS

At major sensory awareness workshops, a meditation method called "zazen" is taught and practiced. Zazen is the Zen Buddhist meditation, and it supplements sensory awareness training in several ways. As a mind/body meditation, zazen focuses in on body sensations (as opposed to use of a meditative object). This accustoms the meditator to reaching inward and helps him develop the kind of body awareness that is akin to "sensing." More than other meditation methods, zazen habituates the meditator to attend to the here-and-now, a core concept in SA practice, as we have discussed.

Studying meditation along with SA practice offers a spe-

cial reward: it accustoms one to slowing down mental processes, paving the way to the acquiring of a quiet mind. This
"coming to quiet" is all-important in SA-Selver; it helps a
"senser" attend to the whispered messages that sensory awareness brings.

There's another all-important bonus from zazen, as opposed to other meditation methods. Because it heightens body
awareness, zazen can deepen sexuality—it emphasizes the joy
of vibrant physicality.

Zazen is appropriate for sensory awareness practice, in
that it can be enjoyed in the great outdoors (zazen requires
no paraphernalia, like some meditation methods). For when
one gives oneself over to sensuous contemplation of natural
beauty, this reinforces the relaxing of internal dialogues and
left-brain "static." For example, the sun's soothing warmth
can calm a troubled spirit. So will the sound of chattering
birds, or a grassy lawn sparkling with morning dew.

So as accompaniment to SA training, let's take a close
look at zazen, the sensory awareness meditation. Zazen offers
special gains for the busy, educated mind; Western man (and
Americans especially) can gain much from slowing down
his mental processes at will. Culturally, we have come to at-
tach such priority to action that many adults find it exasperating, or unproductive, to be motionless for a period of
time. Yet this is the way to begin any exploration of one's
inner self, and understand those unidentified (and sometimes
misunderstood) forces that make each of us unique. Put another way, zazen prepares one for inner probings (including
SA practice) because it helps one find his *Tao*, or "no place"
—and a new serenity.

However, do not feel that an Oriental meditation will
endanger your belief in, or practice of, Western religion. You
can separate the body/mind benefits of Zen meditation from
its spiritual background, just as the music of Bach or Handel
can be enjoyed outside a Christian cathedral.

Zazen, as I'll explain shortly, also bolsters willpower and can release new energy. As a builder of mind power, it can broaden the attention span—a serious problem in our noisy, television-oriented era (geared more to electronic impulses than to smooth, uninterrupted activity). More than meditations that merely stress passivity, zazen builds mind power—this, in addition to the salutary gains in physical and emotional health that meditation practice can bring, all of which have been discussed in popular and medical literature.

Zazen Meditation and Mind Power

Brain studies show that meditation is a right hemisphere activity. It causes the brain to produce waves, indicating the mental "mood" of relaxed alertness, the most agreeable brain state to maintain. (Other brain waves include *beta*, marking wide-awake nervous intensity; *theta*, a trancelike brain rhythm that gurus and yogis have reached during deep meditative states; and *delta*, the deep-sleep brain rhythm). During waking hours, *alpha* waves are most associated with contentment and salutary productivity.

Regular zazen meditators attain the mental state in which alpha waves predominate *within fifty seconds* of the start of meditation. The likelihood of achieving this desirable mental state increases with the sensory applications of zazen, such as meditating in the midst of natural beauty (as in a park or garden). This makes daily meditation practice easier —you're adhering to a good habit that is also fun to perform.

Indeed, perhaps it is the pleasant stimulation of alpha that accounts for the dedication to meditation among those who've made it a habit. Once an outsider to meditation practice, I found this devotion almost incomprehensible—until I experienced it myself.

As with SA practice, daily zazen helps one come to utilize more of his untapped potential, turning even the meekest into an achiever. Practice the two together and they'll interact and cross-fertilize each other, with reciprocity that helps you grow and self-evolve in quantum gains. This means much to the busy or ambitious executive. It can mean even more to the bored housewife, or that person who'd like to make his life more interesting as well as productive. With zazen mind power, the person of average intelligence becomes equal to (or might surpass) the nonmeditating genius who has let stress or emotional problems dim his abilities. With the mind expansion possible through the sensory benefits of zazen you can use from 50 to 70 percent of your brain power and memory, according to Dr. Tomio Hirai. Most persons use less than 20 percent of what is available to them.

How Zazen Aids Body/Mind Self-Mastery

Zazen meditators, like most regular meditators, enjoy a greater sense of self-pride and feel more control over their future. (In itself, this opens the door for the wondrous changes that sensory awareness brings into a person's life.)

Harvard University research shows that meditators enjoy lower anxiety levels and suffer less from psychosomatic problems, including headaches, colds, and insomnia. Dr. Gary Swartz, noted stress researcher, devised an experiment that shows the way meditation improves one's ability to deal with stress. Because this teaches the practical dividends of a quiet mind (a side effect of SA practice), I'm going to report the research here.

Dr. Swartz decided to measure the biochemical reactions of two groups of volunteers: nonmeditators and meditators of at least two years' experience. The nonmeditators were persons interested in the idea of meditation, but inexperienced in its practice. Each participant, on entering the test area, was asked to relax quietly (or to meditate) for a twenty-minute preparation period. After this calming interval, each was shown a short film that depicted a series of stress situations. (This film shows bloody accidents in a woodworking shop, and is professionally accepted by psychiatrists as a way to induce stress for surveillance testing.) During the viewing of the film, a special apparatus measured the endocrinal reactions of all participants, noting changes in other vital signs as well.

The Harvard medical team found all volunteers had stress reactions that were consistent, person to person: whenever an accident was about to happen in the film, their heart rates increased; so did their respiration rates. (These changes are normal manifestations of what is termed the "fight or flight" response, recognized as the way a healthy body mobilizes for stress.) But the meditators recovered more quickly, once the accident sequences were over; their body signals returned to normal more promptly than did those of the nonmeditators. Later, after the screening of the test film, the meditators showed greater ease and appeared more relaxed than the nonmeditators. The latter remained tense, keyed-up, and ill-at-ease. Concluded the supervising psychologist: regular meditators acquired the kind of mind that lets them recover rapidly from stress situations.

As I shall explain shortly, meditators have an extra hand up the emotional control ladder, providing the kind of emotional stability that is all-important today. One of the Harvard psychologists went on to note that anxious people subject their bodies to continual endocrinal upheaval. I know big-city residents who turn themselves into taut bundles of nervous tension just from receiving busy signals on a telephone call. With mounting exasperation, they'll re-dial the call every few seconds, rather than just trying the call later on. They create an emotional crisis from everyday trivia, so that misplaced house keys or a lost change purse becomes a nerve-wracking catastrophe. By comparison, a zazen meditator—particularly one with sensory awareness perceptivity—might have been able to "sense" where his keys or change purse had been placed.

Lest we forget, the right-brain intuitive side of the cerebrum has its practical values, also.

The meditator also eases up after an arousal situation, thus breaking the threat-arousal-threat cycle. On the other hand, a nervous or anxious person (and a nonmeditator) acquires a low-threat threshold, setting him up to overreact to the next unpleasantness. By avoiding this, meditation (in this regard alone) can slow the aging process. Zazen meditation does this with an extra flourish: because it heightens body awareness, it probably stimulates vital capillaries, the tiny cardiovascular connections that, without stimulation, become rigid and account for premature old age.

More than other meditation methods, zazen sharpens perceptivity, particularly when it is pursued as an adjunct to "sensing." It offers as much as other meditations in terms of physical and emotional health. Dr. Herbert Benson of Harvard says that all medically accepted meditations have similar effects. It is regular meditation practice that makes the difference, not chants or mumbo-jumbo. Dr. Robert Ornstein agrees: "It is the attitude and attention of the meditator that is important, rather than the specific form of his practice."

And here is where zazen offers a big plus: unlike certain yoga meditations, it can be practiced anywhere—on a train, waiting in the dentist's office. So faithful daily practice comes easier for zazen meditators—they don't have to rely on a method they must rush home to enjoy.

Therefore, why not learn to practice a meditation that lets you rely on *yourself* for reinforcement? You'll find it is easy to learn, simple to practice—and lots of fun. Expensive lessons are not necessary; nor is it essential for the beginner to obtain a special mantra (a custom-tailored phrase or sound that is handed down in solemn ceremony from one's guru). Fact is, many Orientalists take a dim view of the Westernized meditation cults and elitist ashrams. Let me tell you a little Sufi story.

One day, a well-known dignitary was gazing across the lake. He heard chanting coming from a tiny island. It was a beggar, beginning his daily meditation. The dervish dignitary, being highly esteemed and considering himself lofty and benevolent, felt it was his duty to correct the beggar, who was using improper sounds to hasten the meditative state. So the dignitary had his servants row him out to the tiny island.

Interrupting the meditator, he corrected his chanting, then gave him a brief lecture on proper procedure and improving his style. "Thank you," said the humble beggar. "I had been using that phrase for many years and didn't know how wrong it was." The dignitary turned, pleased with his efforts, and had his rowers convey him back to shore. Almost there, he heard a voice calling after him. It was the beggar, and as he called he was walking on the water. The astonished dignitary heard him say, "Excuse me, sir. Would you repeat the correct phrase for me? I have forgotten it!"

The ABC's of Zazen Meditation

For any meditation method, the real gains come with meditation practice, week after week, month after month. With zazen, the beautiful simplicity of the rules—coupled with the possibility of outdoor practice—makes it easier to adopt into your life-style. To understand what I mean, consider the fact that there are only three rules you need follow to begin zazen. I call them the ABC's of zazen, and they are: Awareness of posture; Breath regulation; Control of mind.

1. *Awareness of posture.* In zazen you sit comfortably; it isn't necessary to sit in a lotus position on a hard floor; use a chair if you like. (Later, you might enjoy physical contact

with floor or earth to benefit from "grounding," the emotional gains from which are discussed elsewhere in these pages.) At the outset, just sit casually erect, with firm but easily held shoulders. Charles Brooks adds: "The eyes are partly open, but lowered, and though wide awake, and of course seeing, they do not look." As opposed to yoga meditation, the eyes are not rigidly controlled. "Only the impulse to wander is controlled."

Posture, in zazen, can serve as a body awareness reminder —use it to return your wandering mind to attention and focus. Don't worry about slight discomfort: it is a meditation phenomenon that ignoring slight discomfort (or working through it) will make it disappear. This relates to ancient Buddhist concepts, as a historic text suggests:

> *During meditation, one concentrates on the hands. When one's mind sinks, it becomes necessary to concentrate on the top of the head, or on the space between the eyebrows. When the thoughts ramble, one must concentrate on the abdomen; and when the mind seems to float unattached, you must concentrate on the feet.*

I've found it also helps to practice zazen barefoot, and outdoors when convenient. Sensing the twiggy grass, rough cement, or cool breezes also can serve as the kind of body awareness reminder to return straying thoughts. This is awareness attention to the kind of here-and-now that has great meaning in both Zen and sensory awareness (and it really works to induce a right-brain meditative state).

In zazen, there is also a special way of holding your hands.

HERE'S WHAT YOU DO: Sit comfortably, hands clasped, palms cupped and turned inward to create a tiny compartment. In zazen tradition, the meditator's hands are cupped enough to contain an imaginary bird, gently to avoid harming it, yet closed enough to postpone its flying away.

2. *Breath regulation.* Zazen procedure differs slightly from SA-Selver in one regard: to induce the meditative state, gentle efforts are made to regulate breathing, directing attention to slow, more rhythmic breathing. Experienced meditators do this without thinking, but for the zazen beginner it can build self-mastery. Oriental medical studies on zazen meditators show that rhythmic breathing coincides with entering the deeper meditative states. Tokyo's Dr. Tomio Hirai says this underlines the secret of the longevity of many Oriental zazen meditators: slow, deep breathing eases the strain on the heart and vital organs. Such respiration also expedites the removal of wastes.

There are emotional benefits, too. The person who makes an occasional effort to regulate his breathing has been found to remain composed during unpleasant events and emotional upset, even during nonmeditative hours. Zazen experts consider this rhythmic breathing technique as important to successful meditation as it is on athletic playing fields. Swimmers, football and soccer players rely on the same principle to build stamina; many find it easier to win when they can use rhythmic breathing during stressful play periods. This makes medical sense—our vital organs function more smoothly when body/mind harmonies are integrated: easy, rhythmic breathing patterns can accomplish this.

Notes one zazen expert: when the posture of the body is correct, and when the breathing has been regulated, the mind will enter that calm state in which profound meditation is possible. When a Buddhist priest is meditating, and finds his mind wandering he has only to regain control of his breathing in order to re-enter a deep meditative state.

There are two basic aspects to breath regulation: (1) deep breathing, and (2) reducing breath frequency. The habitual zazen meditator breathes only four or five times a minute, compared with the eighteen breaths a minute taken by people under ordinary conditions (and this speeds up under excitement or stress). Breath is slowed by exhaling slowly. Do this breath slowing gradually at first; four to five breaths a minute only comes with advanced practice. As a zazen text says, do this "so gently that the flow of air would not disturb a feather attached to the tip of the nose."

Rhythmic breathing practice helps. Select a poem or short text you memorized in childhood. Practice repeating it over and over in a fixed pattern. Do this aloud at first; later your respiration will adapt itself as you smoothly recall the words. Notes Dr. Hirai: as you repeat aloud the words of the (brief) text you have chosen, your breath will gradually conform—most important is to concentrate on the rhythm of the poem.

TO BEGIN ZAZEN, HERE'S WHAT YOU DO: Seat yourself comfortably. Begin deep breathing, trying to prolong the length of your exhaled breaths. Slowly count your breaths to yourself: one, two; one, two. As you continue this, let your center of breathing drop to your abdomen, maintaining a regular rhythm. Let your diaphragm work like a bellows: flatten it as you slowly exhale, expand it as you inhale.

If your mind wanders, attend to your breathing—or body sensations, as I have discussed.

3. *Control of mind.* In zazen, an undisciplined mind can be returned to meditation through breath regulation and body awareness. (Attention control thus deepens sensory awareness practice, for it is your own inner signs you attend.) This strikes at the core of the Zen concept of mindful-

ness, to pay attention whatever happens. Because zazen rules act as a mindfulness exercise, it also broadens your attention span, and makes you easily attentive during the nonmeditating hours of life. In *The Heart of Buddhist Meditation*, Nyaponika Thera explains: Body mindfulness exercises will increase the awareness of one's behavior when going, standing, sitting, or reclining. With most persons, what happens is that they become preoccupied about the aim and desire of going—they are looking to the future rather than living in (and enjoying) the present. This blots out present consciousness.

Attention and careful focus on the here-and-now (or "bare attention" in Zen) offers what I shall call the "Art of Slowing Down." A Zen teaching illustrates:

> *A disciple asks the Zen master, "What is the way?"*
>
> *"Your everyday mind," replies the master. "When I am hungry, I eat; when tired, I sleep."*
>
> *Puzzled, the disciple asks whether that isn't what everybody else does also.*
>
> *"No," replies the master. "Most people are never wholly in what they are doing when they are doing it. When eating, they may be absent-mindedly preoccupied. When 'sleeping,' they are not open for sleep to come. The supreme mark of the thoroughly integrated man is to be without a divided mind."*

As you begin SA practice, try to set aside twenty minutes daily for zazen meditation. This will allow deeper gains from "sensing."

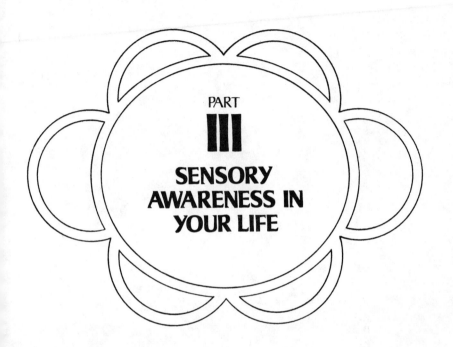

PART

III

SENSORY
AWARENESS IN
YOUR LIFE

CHAPTER

8

SA AT YOUR WORK

Attention to "sensing" quiets what is compulsive in our thought, so that the mind becomes free and available.

CHARLES V. W. BROOKS

By the time you read this, you will have come to recognize that SA is a deeply personal body experience—rather than just sensory appreciation. I hope you have used our sensory exercises and SA experiments to discover the beauty that can exist in nonverbal (right-brain) experiences. If so, you are coming to understand a Zen maxim: *Let the mind abide nowhere.* And you are recognizing this in terms of the vital serenity it can bestow.

However, nowhere in this book would I limit or rob the carefully educated Western mind of its zealousness for practical self-improvement. This section of our book, therefore, will offer guidelines to let you incorporate into your everyday life the golden excitement of sensory awareness. For it is "sensing" that will help you perceive the enrichment of another Zen promise: the path of enlightenment opens when one learns to harness and ride the stallions of thought, and cease being dragged around the ring of life by them.

This chapter will show you ways to use "sensing" to build mind power for your work, whatever it is. You will discover that when you include sensory awareness in your business day, it makes the humdrum assignment less boring and labor less tiring. You'll also offset the bane of desk-bound office workers—executive stress. When you periodically make use of your senses as well as your workaday (left-brain) rationality, it lets you focus in on a greater percentage of your talents and mental ability.

Consider your contacts with others during the business day: company meetings, telephoning, employee conversations. Under job pressures, people don't always take the time (or have the poise) to communicate persuasively and fully. And as Hegel, the eighteenth-century German philosopher, reminded his followers: *richtigkeit*, or "correctness," is not always the same as *wahrheit*, or "truth." Getting in touch with hidden but nonetheless true feelings is not easy for some, even about impersonal business matters. Sensory awareness helps.

With SA practice, you'll discover that your ability to understand situations and grasp "the big picture" is quickened—and so is your intuitive perception. Pioneer psychologist Carl Jung opened the way to this uncharted territory of what I call business-ESP when he said: "There is no such thing as a coincidence."

As I've discussed throughout this book, exercising the brain's right hemisphere deepens your perceptive thinking and can let your light shine like a superstar. No matter how successful, or problem-prone, you have been, left-brain/right-brain balance can let you unveil more of your ultimate potential. Did you know that when success comes too early it can stunt brain development? That's the belief of right-brain/

left-brain medical researcher, Dr. Roger Sperry. He warns that excellence in one hemisphere tends to interfere with top-level performance in the other.

You'll understand more about this as you read this section. For now, think of SA as a way to brighten your business hours. Your job bores you? Attending to the here-and-now will let you discover beauty you never dreamed was around. Wordsworth might have been remarking about man's obliviousness to the present when he wrote: "Look for the stars; you'll say that there are none/ Look up a second time; and, one by one/ You mark them twinkling out with silvery light/ And wonder how they could elude the sight."

For, more than TM or other forms of enrichment training, SA (and SA-Selver especially) offers ways to make daily chores imaginative—and even self-renewing.

Lengthening Your Attention Span

Do you sometimes have difficulty concentrating? More workers and executives today complain of shortened attention spans, particularly those in big cities. This could be a result of urban tensions and our electronic age: much of life unfolds in spurts and spasms, as thought processes are interrupted by transistor radios, sudden noises, and general cacophony. When such confusions are truncated and outside our control, a unique space-age stress results; this can short-circuit our brain's neural cross-firings. Even flashing lights have been shown scientifically to subject our human nervous system to extraordinary stress. Such thought-interruptions make one impatient and tense—and inattention becomes a habit.

In seeking self-taught ways to build up mind power, the most intelligent persons can mistakenly diffuse and shorten their attention spans. On two occasions, two Manhattan professional men bragged to me that they had learned to perform several mental tasks simultaneously. One advertising agency vice-president said he learned to read while "watching" favorite family TV programs. Another professional, a brilliant plastic surgeon, congratulated himself that, after enormous effort, he had learned to "double-think"—entertaining two rational thought processes at the same time.

Unaware, both gentlemen were aging themselves prematurely (a fact to be seen in forehead/eye crinkles and early graying of the hair). Equally tragic, they were hastening the deteriorating effects on their mental resources. For the mind that is habitually divided weakens its own ability to provide undivided attention.

Executive habits like this would horrify most Japanese industrialists. (In the Orient, concentration is described as becoming so enrapt in a problem at hand that a wastebasket could catch fire next to you and you'd hardly notice.) Oriental executives utilize Zen concepts (and sensory exercises) as self-improvement in the way Americans and Englishmen take Dale Carnegie courses and memory improvement seminars. Orientalists feel that building single-focus attention pays other dividends—the serenity it brings can build wisdom in later years.

How can Zen and sensory practice help? Japanese industrialists consider the Zen concept of *samadhi* as self-help psychology (called *sammai* by many contemporary Japanese). In *samadhi*, one devotes all of one's attention to a single thing or task, varying the attention object according to need. Dr. Tomio Hirai explains that there is a *samadhi* for each business activity. "In an office, only a very skillful and experienced man can answer the telephone, and do one or two other tasks at the same time." (And whether he performs at his best under such distracting circumstances is debatable.) Answering the phone is a job that merits total attention.

Consider your own interest in undivided attention when it is urgently required. (Remember how grouchy you became when you were threading your way through heavy traffic while a companion persisted in conversing about trivia or hectoring you with questions?)

Dr. Hirai adds that each kind of work demands the concentration of the people engaged in it. "In other words, each job has its *samadhi,* or whole concentration. There is a *samadhi* for the technician, a *samadhi* for the office worker, and a *samadhi* for the housewife."

In a moment, I'll show you how sensory awareness can help you enjoy your own *samadhi.* First, consider the way one can put this SA/Zen concept to work unknowingly. During the writing of this book, my teenage daughter returned from her high school elated. She said she was making new progress in her typing class, a study for which she had little dexterity or interest. But coming from a household where there is much talk about using the here-and-now as a new reality, she tried a little experiment. During speed typing tests, she directed her full attention to accuracy, instead of rushing to type as fast as possible (with resultant errors). And by honing her attention to focus on one particular aspect of the assignment, it relaxed her anxiety and nervousness; it freed her real ability. "My fingers fairly fly over the keys," she remarks, "and now I make better time—with fewer errors."

For yourself, you can build new mind power with attention to the here-and-now. Age is no limitation: it is as easy to build good habits as it was to acquire bad ones—it just takes time and practice. Try the following sensory experiment: it will boost your powers of attention.

HERE'S WHAT TO DO: Next time you answer the telephone, devote total attention to the call itself. Don't doodle, finger cords, or fiddle with pencils or cigarettes. These are nervous tics and you can avoid them (and broaden your attention span); rather, during lax moments, pay sensory awareness attention to your palm and fingertips.

Note the cool feel of the plastic instrument in your hand. Try to listen for the breath intake of your caller. (This "reading" of cues will advance you along the road to business-ESP, as we discuss elsewhere in this chapter.) Still talking, close your eyes, and concentrate on your own voice, its tone and diction. Really open your ears to each response from your caller. Let his words and pauses limn in a sensual drawing of whoever is on the other end of the phone. Keep your mind's eye unclouded by mental criticisms or (left-brain) comparisons; let your mental motors idle while your perceptions take control.

However fatigued or stressed you might have been at the beginning of the above experiment, chances are you'll return to work composed and more relaxed. You can continue this sensory mind power in other tasks: next time you pick up a newspaper or magazine, try to block out all environmental distractions and sounds. Avoid the popular habit of playing a radio during demanding close work or study. Don't interrupt yourself by impulsive telephoning, or lighting up a cigarette—it breaks mental focus. With practice, you'll find it easier to concentrate for longer periods (and employ a larger store of mind power) because you're using your senses to make the most of the here-and-now.

Sense What the Other Fellow Thinks (Business ESP)

SA practice helps build perceptivity, and in the business world this can be money in the bank. Consider the past month at your place of employment. Wouldn't it have proved a special advantage to have a "sixth sense" about situations and problems? There is nobody who wouldn't benefit from a ready grasp about the true state of affairs, and the ability to cut through what customers or clients say, and get down to perceiving what they feel.

Making more regular use of your sensory perceptions lets you develop this kind of business-ESP. Dr. Rene Dubos explains it this way: ESP, or extrasensory perception, could be considered as using "crypto-sensory responses." These are channels of communication that are so elusive that they once were dismissed as nonexistent or impossible; with practice they would enable us to acquire valuable information.

You'll understand this more readily in terms of the psychology of cybernetics, born of the computer age. This is the business world self-help that finds comparisons between the human brain/nervous system and electronic computers. Information retrieval is important in any job. Consider your own work. Right now you probably get through the business day by relying on your own memory bank and impulsive guesswork.

Most people call on simple memory tapes and stored information. As need arises, you reach into past experiences, education, and other input at the time of making decisions: sifting, sorting, rejecting, selecting. But if you employed more elaborate sensory "tapes," you would have a sophisticated set of tools at your disposal. These would be perceptive tools, enabling you to perform confidently and with a higher degree of success. Like English philosopher Sir Humphrey Davy, you'd realize you can learn as much from your failures as from your successes.

With SA practice, you can sometimes call on your brain's perceptive right hemisphere. Working in holistic ways, this lets you grasp the overall gist of a situation, and lets you easily lace the bits and pieces of a complex matter into recognizable patterns. If you have latent creative talents, they can rise to the fore. Executives will uncover the knack of projecting past and recent trends into future predictions. Top management encourages promotion when it is seen that a worker is able to lift his head above day-to-day assignments and is not confounded by advance planning but comes to relish it.

SA practice helps you build the kind of business world ESP that reinforces executive talent: any of the SA exercises and experiments in this book will exercise and develop your right-brain perceptivity. For bonus benefit: try one of our Celebrate Yourself exercises at noontime, to add spice to your business day.

Overcome Nervousness During Job Confrontations

Did you ever get nervous or anxious when your boss suddenly called you into his office? Are you at your best at business conferences? If (like most of us) you'd welcome a method for keeping your composure during tension-filled meetings, why not learn from Oriental warriors. In *kiai-jitsu* or *tai-chi ch'uan*, combatants believe in emotional composure for body and mind alertness. This, they feel, frees super powers.

In meditation (particularly those methods involving the use of mantram or meaningless phrases to bring sensory quiet to left-brain dialogues) your talent can rise to the surface. Anxiety and other forms of negative thinking will be stilled.

Here's what you can do. Silently recite to yourself any poem learned in school—and recite it line by line during the business meeting or argument. If you prefer, use a few verses of a speech like Lincoln's Gettysburg Address; just select a verse or speech with a familiar beat or cadence, and one with minimal emotional interest. This lets you focus your (right-brain) mind's eye on the intrinsic cadence when you feel under business pressure. Social critic and writer Adam Smith calls this sensory Zen technique "mantram as a block." Here's how it works:

> YOUR BOSS: *Mr. Johnson will explain to the rest of us why his report is overdue, when everybody else got theirs in on time.*
>
> YOU: ('Twas the night before Christmas and all through the house) *I don't want to claim that we were really short of help during the final report period, but* . . . (Not a creature was stirring, not even a mouse.) *Fortunately we picked up some new business for the company that was most gratifying. Of course, this demanded priority attention* . . .

Try this yourself, next time you're uptight with business tensions. This SA right-brain meditation will also bestow new poise, helping you keep cool during arguments with your spouse, exasperating discussions with your children, or testy exchanges of any kind.

SA and Gamesmanship for Left-Brain/Right-Brain Balance

Long before scientists began studying left-brain/right-brain specialization, the eminent Swiss psychiatrist Dr. Leopold Szondi came up with a related way to relieve executive stress. Szondi noted there are at least two distinct types of minds in professional use. For the sake of discussion, I'll term them the A and the B. The "A" mind is strong on (left-brain) detail: statisticians, librarians, editors, bookkeepers. The other type of mental personality, the "B," is more of a (right-brain) dreamer, and (in addition to jobs requiring dexterity) can be found in creative or service pursuits: artists, musicians, inventors, dancers.

Most people are a combination of "A" and "B" traits. In terms of self-help psychology, it was Szondi's brilliant theory that a person can compensate for becoming excessively "A" or "B" by performing a task requiring the opposite mental abilities. For example, the "B" can get fuzzy from excessive (right-brain) imaginings and brain-storming for ideas. He can anchor his mind to solid foundations with down-to-earth detail, such as setting up a telephone index or revamping a file. (The person who works at home might organize a recipe file or clear out dresser drawers.)

An "A" individual can become overstressed with his own love of detail; he can compensate for this by devoting extra time to artistic (right-brain) endeavors. This could include meditation (use an aquarium or scenic picture if you have never studied formal meditation or try one of the meditations from this book). Or listen to mood music, your mind idling. Or daydream about nonsense as you study the shapes of clouds overhead. (The childhood game of making out animal shapes in cloud formations is a dandy right-brain exercise.) Or enjoy "sensing" the furry leaf of a desk-top plant, focusing awareness on your tactile sensations only. Or, if you haven't access to greenery or open sky, take a pencil and idly sketch a tranquil scene—your imagination can help you meander on an instant vacation from workaday desensitizings.

Such sensory gamesmanship, practiced regularly, can sharpen and enhance your decision-making abilities—it enlivens and enriches left-brain/right-brain integration and builds mental acuity.

SA To Counteract Job Boredom

It is also sensory gamesmanship to focus in on a detail of the here-and-now to offset job boredom. One medical report says psychiatrists claim that the two most common complaints they hear are boredom and depression. They usually interrelate. As a psychiatrist warns, we need stimulation so much we sometimes choose emotional pain rather than remain caught in familiar ruts.

Job boredom can get you into a vicious cycle. It's a self-destructive attribute that decreases your chances of getting rid of it because it renders you fatigued. When this is chronic, training in SA-Selver will help. Formal instruction and quiet moments of "sensing" will help you realize what your next step should be.

Or try a sensory mind power game, with Zen here-and-now focus. You'll see ways to put this to work in your own life with an example from the classic novel, *Anthony Adverse*. In the book, an aging financier used this kind of sensory gamesmanship to fight boredom—and maintain sanity. Ouvard, the financier, was confined in solitary prison for several months at the whim of Napoleon. Day after day, inside bleak prison walls, Ouvard began to feel the deadening effect of boredom. For want of other stimulation, he bribed the jailer's wife for a box of tiny dress pins. Each morning, he'd scatter them on the cell floor; then, after elaborate preparation, he'd pick them up, one by one, counting carefully to make sure none was lost.

On hearing of this experience, later, his friend Anthony noted that Ouvard described it always in the present tense. "It is the hunt for the always missing pin that keeps me sane," Ouvard said, half closing his eyes. "There are a thousand and one of them, and one has been missing for a week. I find it at last in a crack in the stones of the floor. There is not, I am sure, a happier man in France now than I. I am successful once more."

You can use this Zen/sensory game to perk up your mental spirits—or use it to make vexing routine less annoying.

HERE'S WHAT TO DO: Next time you drop a box of paperclips (or break something requiring a cleanup), put your full sensory attention into the assignment. As you pick up the pieces, feel the smoothness of the glass or metal. Or notice the impression the broom makes on your hands. Or try "sensing" the smooth coolness of the tile floor. Or, if nothing else offers itself, hum one of your favorite upbeat tunes. The idea is to distract your exasperated (left-brain) rationality with your sensory self. Then what must be done will be quickly completed, with less wear-and-tear.

Celebrate Yourself Exercise No. 5: An SA Meditation to Build Self-Esteem

Whether you're ahead of (or just beginning) the game of business, confidence and ego strength count for much. The following sensory chant is performed as a meditation; the more you practice it, the more self-esteem you nurture.

The idea is to select whatever form of your name you feel most comfortable with: Charlie Ryan, perhaps, rather than Charles P. Ryan, Jr. (or the reverse, it's up to you). Nicknames can be used, if you prefer: "Midge" Williams, rather than Elizabeth Mary Williams. Complete this by adding a final "omm" syllable. (This resonance is believed to relax tensions; the most potent mantram meditative phrases have endings rhyming with the "omm" sound.) This becomes, therefore, "Char-lee Ry-an-omm."

HERE'S HOW TO USE IT: Sit comfortably, alone in a darkened room, or anywhere with your eyes closed.

Breathe deeply, exhaling slowly from the lower abdomen. After several moments, begin to gently say your special name-mantram as you exhale. Gradually this will establish a simple rhythm. If your name is long, repeat your unique name-mantram each second or third breath. Concentrate on making your name resonant, on your breathing, and on the warm, dark velvet of your closed eyelids.

Clearing all thoughts, practice this for five to ten minutes, at least four days a week. As your name grows as a power phrase, you will find it strengthening and making resonant your inner rhythms.

SA—and the Office

Mark Twain defined work as "what a body is obliged to do; play consists of whatever a body is *not* obliged to do." Since Twain's day, there has been an emporium of changes in office work, especially observable in office furniture. Not all such designs are a civilized step forward, according to SA experts.

Take the executive chair. In health terms this is a postural distortion that is foisted on unsuspecting executives. With an outward sloping back, the cushioned seat can be extended past the kneecaps, further deforming posture, and throwing the body's weight on weak sections of the lower back. When you sit for hours in such a chair, it encourages sluggish blood circulation, a hazard for that executive who needs to maintain alertness for the parade of business world papers and events. When such a chair is constructed on a swivel base, it ages and fattens the occupant—for ungainly stomach muscles are habitually used to twist and turn the chair, encouraging the unsightly "executive paunch."

Charles Brooks says most of the seating designs of the last fifty years seem directed to enveloping the body rather than providing support for it. He suggests that Detroit-designed big-car seating perpetuates this, only permitting body movement in head and foot areas. With the bulk of the body forced to remain sedentary, unpleasant side effects result: (1) Breathing is restricted; (2) Limited limb mobility discourages alertness (and the homeward-bound executive or worker is deprived of the ready response required for motoring safety); (3) Backward sloping seats encourage that chronic malady of stress-prone commuters, the "bad back"; (4) The spinal curve is distorted by heavily upholstered head rests; (5) However sleek auto (and executive) seating appears, such over-cushioned ease does little for self-sufficient body awareness or a sense of self.

F. Matthias Alexander, body-awareness pioneer, was outspoken in his dislike of chairs in general, calling them inappropriate to man's natural construction. An Alexander follower, biologist H. S. Cogswell, agreed. He noted that ignorant natives in backwater villages maintain better health when they squat on their haunches, sometimes for hours, conversing. Is there another way? At SA-Selver workshops, stools are used, in addition to floor-sitting.

Making Use of a Chair—an Experiment in SA-Selver

The following experiment will revitalize your thinking during a hectic business day. All you need is a firm-backed chair and a few minutes' privacy. (You'll find the nonverbal impact of the following directions will be increased if they are dictated into a tape recorder—or read to you by a friend.)

HERE'S WHAT TO DO: Stand beside the chair, barefoot if convenient. Sit down slowly, paying awareness attention to the way you deposit your weight on the seat. *Have you given any weight to the back of the chair?*

(*Or does it feel more like lumpy pressure?*) Now stand up, trying to relax your body as you rise.

Come again to sitting. This time, leave nothing behind your buttocks but air. Pause, then return to leaning backward. Remain alert and sensitive to the feel of the chair's wood, or the upholstered fabric.

Are your legs awake for the floor? Sense and consider this. Relax your legs more, raising and lowering your torso in order to experience the feel of your body coming down to the floor. Experiment with moving your knees back and forth; become aware of the flexibility of those intricate muscles that connect your legs with your torso.

Come to standing. Then prepare to sit again, this time trying to sense the way you give up vertical support. Learn to rely on the chair without pressing on it. *Are your feet in confident contact with the floor?* Experiment with this thought by raising and lowering your heels. Then spread your toes, fanlike, relaxing foot muscles afterward. Can you sense the feeling in your second toes? Can you sense your tiniest toes? Try this first on the right foot, then the left, then both together.

If you are an office worker, or another who sits for long periods, try to achieve more awareness in your buttocks area, the body part in contact with chairs. Do this by rising a little from your seat. Pause and close your eyes. Find your way back to sitting without using your hands or your eyes. As you come into contact with the chair, stay alert to the way your buttocks yield to the firmness of the seat.

Now explore this part of your body directly; place a hand underneath your buttocks. Sit on this hand. *Notice the firmness of your body?* Even through soft layers of flesh there appears to be strength and a kind of majesty.

Now remove your hand, and place your other hand underneath your other buttock. Notice the similarity of feeling. (*Do you notice any differences?*) Now raise your other buttock, and sit on both hands. Balance your body weight back and forth, if you like, to avoid crushing either hand. Then remove both hands. *Can you use your sitting bones to "walk" back and forth on the seat?* Do this now, gingerly, and close your eyes for greater "sensing." Pause, then open your eyes and repeat the "walk."

For Executive Planning: An SA Checklist

Whatever your work, sensory awareness can make you a more flexible instrument of talent and ability. And in their own way, SA influences make work hours more enjoyable, without interfering with competence. Consider the following guidelines, and apply them to your own work environment. Use them to spark your own SA ideas.

A meditation room. At the United Nations, in New York City, delegates and dignitaries agree they benefit from the tranquilly lighted meditation room. So would business-world thinkers in company-owned buildings. Time might be restricted for use, but the presence of such a facility would prompt that winning attribute of top management: the quiet mind.

Sounds of nature. Birdsong and pounding ocean surf add unexpected value to music recordings for offices. Even the sharp sound of thunderstorms would aid in helping recall the wandering minds of tired office workers to the here-and-now of the business world. Shocks serve a valuable purpose, said Gurdjieff, the Middle Eastern guru: they can keep one present-tense and emotionally independent.

Music in bathrooms. Elevator music has long been a soothing office building innovation. Employee lounges, washrooms, and other relaxation areas would benefit from this kind of sensory relief from pent-up work tensions.

Noontime exercise sessions. There are body awareness (as well as serenity) benefits from supervised exercise sessions during office hours: they offer right-brain relief from routine and job stress. In Japan, industrial giants like Mitsubishi find they boost efficiency, increase output, and improve employee morale.

Water walls. One of the more salutary trends in the construction of office buildings has been installation of "walls" of water (or vertical fountains) in employee recreation areas. These miniparks offer sylvan serenity, as well as recharging the ion content of the air. Factory and executive recreation space with this sensory touch would be less tiring to work around.

Indoor office aquariums. The more stressful a business day, the more workers benefit from the physical meditation made possible with a tank of colorful goldfish or other tropical fish. One author confessed to me that his most creative ideas came after spending moments idly studying a deskside aquarium.

Chanting to bolster endurance, minimize stress. African bushmen carry loads longer distances when they follow a tribal chant or syncopated drumbeat. Japanese fishermen chant "Ya-taga-yu-u" when hauling in heavy nets. In the U.S. and British infantry, soldiers march cheerfully with cadence count and chanted rhymes led by a drill sergeant. It may prove that assembly-line workers would benefit from sea chantey songs or chants. When work is less monotonous, absenteeism is reduced.

Scented air in washrooms. Sensory decor would do much to overcome the impersonal, cold atmosphere of factories and many offices.

Flowers in all offices. Waiting in bleak offices can deplete morale, make a company look austere and unmindful. When perishable flowers are impractical, the sculptured look of cactus or other exotic plants brings aesthetic soothing.

Cool water on wrists. For decades, athletes have appreciated the restorative values in a hot/cold shower. For anyone, cool water at the wrists or a bracing whiff of cologne or aftershave lotion will lift the spirits. Remember your skin (and your nasal passages) are reliable sensory organs—give them agreeable surprises and you'll revitalize your business day.

Leaf awareness for psychological reinforcement. In similar ways, you can ease executive anxieties by focusing attention on a veiny leaf or petal: stroking, smoothing, inhaling, noticing the furry underside or ice-slick surface. Practiced prior to a business discussion at which you want to be at your mental peak, it encourages left-brain/right-brain balance—and builds self-assurance.

Use wind as sensory meditation. During workday stress, you can obtain quick release in a few moments, outdoors or on a windy terrace. Even opening a window lets the harried executive discover that nature's breezes (playing on facial skin cells) are bracing, tranquilizing.

For yourself alone: "the teapot" chant. This sensory exercise was developed by speech consultant Dorothy Sarnoff. Nervous executives (or anybody else) can use it prior to any meeting that makes you feel uneasy. It firms up your voice, as it grooms and readies your best personality. Here's what to do: sit comfortably, feet flat on floor. Lips parted slightly, pretend you're a steaming teapot, hissing soundlessly. Count from 1 to 5 to yourself as you unobtrusively let "steam" escape.

SA practice as you reach for the phone. A similar sounding improves vocal clarity: practice saying z-z-z-z to yourself whenever you reach for a ringing telephone. Man or woman, your tones will sound more youthful and competent when your telephone voice boasts resonance.

Flower Meditation

Fresh flowers exemplify the right-brain existential truths of sensory awareness: their function (if any) is ephemeral; their beauty is a vivid statement of the here-and-now, and it can permeate and enrich your day as a momentary event. Aesthetic beauty plays a key role in what I like to term the art of slowing down. This can be salutary to the overactive executive mind—and any other person who tends to spin his mental wheels needlessly. For the mentally fatigued during a hectic workday, the flower meditation that follows can revitalize business thinking. (With practice, this right-brain meditation will enhance cerebral function.) Try this for just ten minutes, during your lunch or coffee break: you'll return to work refreshed and looking composed, serene, and confident—executive attributes that mark the employee management likes to promote.

One preparatory note, so you'll understand how this simple flower meditation (practiced regularly) can build mind power. It is a Zen concept that natural beauty makes it easier for one to advance toward a rewarding Zen state known as *mokusho*. This is that deep meditative stage wherein the meditator and the meditation object seem to merge, a oneness that can unify the troubled spirit. Medical studies on Zen meditators by Dr. Tomio Hirai show this to be not a state of mental sluggishness but one of heightened awareness. The meditator enjoys extraordinary sensory powers. *Mokusho* (which only comes with practice) is said to be reached when the mind is as calm as a "shining body of undisturbed water" or "a mirror wiped clean of all dust."

HERE'S WHAT TO ARRANGE: Seat yourself comfortably within arm's reach of a vase of flowers (or a potted plant). Or a single flower suffices (I prefer just one rose or carnation). Sunlight coming through a window promotes the proper mood. Ample fresh air enhances this sensory exchange between flower and meditator. Privacy helps—but if you haven't your own office, you can enjoy this flower meditation in an employee lounge. (I've worn sunglasses, even indoors, when I've wanted to meditate in secret.) Remember: power-building aspects are advanced when you meditate at the same hour daily.

HERE'S WHAT TO DO: Breathe deeply, lowering respiration to your abdomen. Count your breaths: one, two; one, two. Then focus all your mental attention on a single point of the flower (or plant). Select the center of a velvety petal or the prickly edge of a leaf. Mentally transfer and submerge your total being into the lush softness of this flower (or icy slickness of the plant greenery). Let the color surround and overwhelm. Feel the tactile sensuality becoming your own. (Heighten this by reaching out and touching the plant, if you like.) For five or ten minutes your sensory goal is not merely to look at the flower but to *become* the flower.

This flower meditation builds mind power—with practice. At the outset, don't feel annoyed if your mind strays. Let persistent thoughts unreel, but make sure you don't choose or single out the contents. Later you will be able to fix rapt attention for longer periods. For now, the following shortcuts can rein in the straying mind:

Return to slowly counting your exhaled breaths (one, two; one, two).

OR

Tense and relax your buttocks a few times. Try to sense added sensation in this body part (particularly if your job keeps you desk-bound). Then return to your meditative object.

OR

Hum the phrase "omm" to yourself, trying to center its resonance in your chest.

OR

Close your eyes and concentrate for four exhaled breaths on the forehead area between your eyebrows. Then open your eyes and return to flower awareness.

OR

Note the coolness of inhaled air at your nostrils.

OR

Take a few seconds to bob your head gently.

OR

Silently say this seed-thought: *At the center of all peace I sit, and naught can harm me here.* Repeat this gently to yourself until your respiration seems to move in cadence with the words. Then return to the flower—in harmony with it and at one with yourself.

CHAPTER

9

SA AT HOME
AND FOR THE
HOMEMAKER

We would all be connoisseurs ourselves if we only re-spected our natural gifts. No art-lover sensing out a painting, no lover of music savoring a fine quartet, in-deed, no ordinary person pausing at the song of a bird or relishing a sunset, is differently engaged from a baby tasting his juice when he is just allowed to do so. One cannot be taught to taste, for it comes naturally; one can only be distracted from it.

CHARLES V. W. BROOKS

In your own home, more than anywhere else, sensory awareness practice will have a lasting impact on your life. If you work outside the home, sensing helps you grow as a person because you have turned your place of residence into a haven from workaday stress, sensori-ally fulfilling yet soothing. If you're a full-time homemaker, sensory awareness practice rewards you with three bonus gifts: (1) It helps you build mind power; this is beneficial for those many homemakers who feel their humdrum life is penalizing them more than those who enjoy the ostensibly more challenging give-and-take of professional life. (2) It helps enliven the long, lonely hours of the sometimes isolated homemaker. (3) It can ease boredom and other stresses peculiar to the problems of full-time homemaking.

Sensory Awareness and Homemaker Stressors

1. *SA and the feeling of isolation.* Surrounded by four walls and endless trivia, many homemakers feel cut off from the excitement and meaningful events of the world "outside." In some cases, hostility and alienation grow; if one's spouse is living a very active life outside the home, jealousy can manifest itself—jealousy of scarcely known business associates, of your spouse's interests and of his time away from the house, which you may feel has become a sort of prison. Sensory awareness, however, is a practice that builds a steady pride-in-self. It is a practice that gives the homemaker the joy of being at one with the rest of humanity—not isolated from it. As discussed elsewhere in these pages, it also builds mind power, offsetting the mental sluggishness that life-at-home can bring.

2. *SA and boredom.* The day-after-day sameness of stay-at-home living and working is an extra stressor for the homemaker. Life seems a grim round of repetitious meniality. Stress expert Dr. Hans Selye agrees that boredom is a deadly serious stresser, and for homemakers it can give birth to physical and emotional breakdowns: housewife's ulcer; the so-called trapped housewife's syndrome; and the "trauma of eventlessness." The latter two emotional disorders are psychological illnesses that trigger unexplained fatigue, chronic depression, and psychosomatic illnesses. They are known to afflict the college-educated homemaker, whose scholastic background prepared her more for the executive conference room than

the home laundry room. (When depression and mental illness
come, few sympathize with the homemaker's plight. Her husband and relatives shrug: "Why isn't she happy? She has
everything she needs!")

Sensory awareness practice can dispel such boredom and
the seeds of discontent. The person who once felt victimized
by her surroundings and feelings of isolation comes to enjoy
them. Even familiar routine takes on a new radiance. The
difference is that the homemaker now can find events and
sustenance in the here-and-now; she or he no longer pines
for faraway impossibilities, for what is near reveals its own
enchantment. Sensory awareness brings with it a new feeling
of wondrous fascination with seldom-noticed detail: the
sparkle of a spider's web in the sunlight or the uniqueness of
a taste of cool water.

With sensing comes a new creativity that further casts
out boredom. Fresh ideas for decorative excitements abound:
tucking flowers or potted plants into unexpected places
(under the stairwell, to brighten a dreary garage window);
using a leaf arrangement as dinner table centerpiece; recorded
music (and the selection and location of it) becomes a heady
experience.

The family also benefits. A new human warmth seems
to emanate from the person who regularly practices sensory
awareness. He is more considerate, understanding. Loved
ones are caressed and touched, quietly but meaningfully. This
warmth and ability to show affection where it is warranted
is an assurance-builder for younger members of the household.
Child psychologists report the toddler or young person who
is bereft of physical family contacts (hugging, holding) can
become withdrawn and vulnerable to schizophrenia, among
other emotional afflictions.

3. *SA relieves noise stress.* Slam, yelp, whimper—the
life of a homemaker can become a constant cacophony, particularly if there are small children and animals underfoot.

Noise, proclaimed Schopenhauer, becomes the most annoying and impertinent of stressers: "It is not only an interruption, but a disruption of thought." And the more a homemaker is interrupted, the more difficult it is for her to concentrate mentally when she chooses. In busy households, the noise factor alone brings some homemakers to a state of chronic tension and frayed emotions.

Some people are more sensitive to noise than others. For such persons, "sensing" offers special rewards. If you can't root out the source of the noise that bothers, you can block it out with sensory soundings.

For example, suppose your next-door neighbor is a carpentry enthusiast. You like the family well enough, but every time your neighbor starts up his woodworking machinery, the jacksaw and electric drill bring a b-u-r-r that seems to bring hackled edges up your spine; your neck tenses and you get an awful headache.

HERE'S WHAT TO DO: As the electric saw begins, start quietly sounding z-z-z-z-z to yourself. When and if the noise level heightens, soothingly raise the intensity of your z-z-z. Keep this up indefinitely, if you like. (Most people can habituate themselves to harsh noise irritants in just a few minutes.)

What this sensory exercise does is to temporarily block out the brain's ready acceptance of exterior sound waves. It can be used on other home noise irritants: low-flying airplanes, persistently crying infants, "souped-up" cars and cycles, construction work next door. Whenever your home noise level becomes irksome, your own sensory soundings can block it out.

Lest the skeptical reader think this is an oversimplified way to offset nightmarish discord, I'll tell you a personal experience. During the final weeks of work on this book, editorial changes required meticulous attention and a clear head. Just then, our family dog developed the habit of shrieking with a gut-piercing tremolo whenever she scratched—and she scratched often. With several treatments, a veterinarian rid her of pests. Before (and during) her convalescent stages, the z-z-z-z sounding exercise, mentioned above, let me keep my own composure and do what I had to do.

Housekeeping Chores and "Sensing"

SA and "sensing" won't turn what is gritty and most disagreeable about housework into a joyous delight. But sensory practice can prove a powerful distractor while you are in the midst of hard jobs. The unpleasant task then gets completed faster (and usually better)—with less wear-and-tear on your nerves—and with good humor.

The exercises in this section will give you a workable idea of ways that "sensing" can brighten the homemaking day. (Again, our practical approach does not minimize the greatest charm of sensory awareness—enrichment for itself alone.)

Celebrate Yourself Exercise No. 6: A Psychorhythm Experiment that Lets You Dance Your Way Through Housework

Woman or man, few housepersons like the gritty, grim details of housecleaning. Dancing as you work helps in many ways: stretching to a musical beat releases tension; the wit and frivolity of such unexpected conduct will lighten your mood. With practice, this becomes a sensory experience that blocks your mind to housekeeping rigors.

To primitive man, dancing was a creative expression of self. He danced when happy, when forlorn, when about to go into combat, when victorious. Let your own unstructured dance movements help you dispatch disagreeable chores with style and grace—if not with wholehearted joy.

Before beginning this psychorhythm sensory experiment, decide what background music you'll use. It should be instrumental (to avoid lyrics that might recall memories or start your mind working). Your chosen music should maintain a steady beat. I recommend Caribbean reggae or New Orleans jazz. Or if it's easier, just tune your radio to a music station that will furnish lots of music, little chatter.

Next step is to set up a housework plan, possibly in terms of rooms. *First:* bedmaking (perhaps); *second:* breakfast dishes; *third:* living room floor-sweeping, rug cleaning; etc. (A hint: schedule an easy task first as warm-up. Then let your activities flow, room to room. And keep at it: the fewer interruptions you have, the sooner you'll put the disagreeable behind you. How to dress? Consider what is described in show business as "rehearsal clothes": loose shorts and shirt, or try a dance leotard just for the fun of it.)

HERE'S WHAT YOU DO: As a prelude, do a little body-shaking when the music starts. This helps you loosen tensions and begin to enjoy your body for the simple sake of being vital and alive. To music, shake your right leg, then your left leg. Shake your right arm, then your left, then both together. Shake your hand from the wrist and lower arm, gradually working up to the shoulder. Then shake your shoulders. Follow by undulating your torso (and really move your hips sensually—it helps you "center"). Now shake your body, side to side. You probably have rhythms buried deep inside you (old loves, half-forgotten joys). Celebrate the person you are today by letting it all loose.

As you progress along your chore list, continue a modern ballet movement around the house, kicking here, bowing your body there. Keep movements as sinewy or as wide and exhilarating as you feel. Just try to let your body move in direct expression to the music: let your body take the lead and suspend all thinking.

If you pass a staircase, go ahead and dance back and forth for a few steps—I do, and I'm no Shirley Temple moppet. But it is fun to feel like one, and there's sometimes lots to be said for unrestrained impulses, sensuously speaking.

Celebrate Yourself Exercise No. 7: A "Sensing" Experiment During Laundry Chores

Try this sensory meditation next time you're using a laundromat or clothes dryer. It adds color and motion to work, easing (left-brain) emotional tensions. It also can build perceptivity. Even just practiced once in a while, it turns a humdrum chore into a restful sensory experience.

It can be used with any laundry appliance: the only requirement is a glass window or door for viewing.

HERE'S WHAT YOU DO: Place clothing within; include one garment of bright yellow, red, or orange. Then set the mechanism—and seat yourself a few feet in front of the windowed door. Breathe deeply, from the abdomen, as you idly watch the colors and designs pass and tumble before your eyes. Let your mind reel and consider the whirling clothes as a colorful kaleidoscope. Let your senses spin as the bright colors move: tumbling, pausing, reversing. (Uninterrupted background music here adds to sensory and hypnotic effects.)

With practice, your breathing naturally comes slower, easily centers itself from your lower abdomen. Continue this for at least ten or fifteen minutes. It is great for building esteem or restoring serenity when the stay-at-home "blues" get you down.

Sensory Awareness—and Cooking

If you've occasionally grouched about cooking and culinary entertaining, it might surprise you to learn the number of film stars and the social elite who celebrate cooking as a sensory feast. Most do it unaware; they just find it relieves stress.

Whatever your social interests, you can enjoy cooking as a sensory feast. When your social calendar isn't too busy, make dinner at home a sensory awareness occasion. For family fun, plan a sensory feast at least once a week. You'll give your children memories they'll always cherish—and enhance your own esteem in their eyes (as well as your joy-in-living).

The following initial guidelines will help you make cooking as fulfilling to the senses as it is to the appetite. Then let your own experience show you ways to form specific sensory plans, tailored to your kitchen, social needs—and the cuisine you prefer.

HERE'S HOW YOU BEGIN: Concentrate on a limited menu (the idea is to make the sensory most out of this endeavor, not turn it into a homemaker hassle). Clear the kitchen. (The world's great chefs agree: clutter depletes culinary fun and sensory appreciation). Clear the air. *Caution:* If you're influenced by TV advertising, you might be making habitual use of chemical air sprays rather than fresh air, Mother Nature's own room deodorant. This robs you of sensory enrichment by a kind of housekeeper's Gresham's Law: unpleasant odors drive out agreeable ones. In other words, the smell of good cooking is a savory treat, a sensory memory that might come to symbolize home to your loved ones. Dress appropriately: a cheerful apron helps you concentrate on the here-and-now, just as a chef's cap adds significance to his cuisine as well as his looks.

HERE'S HOW YOU ENJOY: Experience the sumptuous feel of cooking ingredients, their individual aromas: moist lettuce leaves, sticky sauces, grainy herbs, salts, the perfection of an eggshell. The longer you savor such excitements, the closer you are to sensory awareness. Give extra time, also, to those plastic-bagged premixes that offer a spongy, sensual appeal. Suspend all thinking and let your sensations take over to stimulate, relax.

Asks Charlotte Selver: "Can you smell the aromas as you sample foods? Does each aroma come to you when you allow it, or must you sniff it out? As you bite and chew, sensuously speaking, try to go inside yourself. What happens to the food as you chew it? How long can you taste it? As you continue chewing and sensing, is there a natural moment when the food seems to dissolve? Does it progress into your being? Have you considered this mystery of life as a kind of meditation, this changing from one form to another—life into life?"

HERE'S HOW YOU SERVE: Don't let your culinary talents go under-appreciated. Only half-humorously, Lord Bulwer-Lytton wrote: "We may live without poetry, music and art/ We may live without conscience and live without heart;/ We may live without friends; We may live without books;/ But civilized man cannot live without cooks."

Plan table decor for this festive occasion: candles, crystal, a color scheme with flowers, linens. Before serving, change to formal garb, perhaps, with soothing background music on the radio or phonograph. Whether you are dining alone or with guests, celebrate yourself. Display your foods with precision, flair, and a sense of color (the cherry tomato garnish, parsley sprigs). There can be, for all of us, a theatrical exhilaration in serving one's friends or family. (Is it just the joyful sense of offering a gift—the work of your own hands—and of setting the gift before the recipient? Can there be another element, the joy of movement—as Selver says—"a choice of addressing oneself intuitively and unhesitatingly to the situation.") Next time you serve food, take time to sense your breathing as you move. Feel the weight and shape of the objects as you handle them.

When you dispense food, stay physically aware of each gesture; serve it up with style and dignity. A self-pride grows in seeing a sensory feast through from the planning to its successful enjoyment.

HERE'S HOW TO CONCLUDE: All-important for (left-brain) relaxing—remain silently relishing, enjoy just being alive, physical, appreciative. Restrain yourself from asking guests, if any, to comment on each dish, analyzing this food over that one, this dinner over another. (A Zen master said pointedly: "When hungry I eat, when tired I sleep.")

Like great sex or other peak experiences, a sensory feast is best enjoyed and relished without appraisal—for itself alone. Adds Zen expert Christmas Humphreys, "If the sunset is glorious, why not enjoy it instead of spoiling enjoyment with thoughts about it or attempts to describe it." Intuitive awareness (like sensory appreciation) should be its own authority. "Though thought may follow it, it will do so at the expense of the original experience."

Sensory Awareness and the Home as Environment

As we have seen, home is where the senses are—at their fullest, at their most serene and relaxed. Many of us forget that our homes are more than a place of refuge from stress; they are also our strongest environmental influence. Whether you spend twelve to sixteen hours a day, or longer, in the cocoon you have spun to live in, it will be enriched by sensory details. And the more sensory taste you use to embellish your home, the more you will evolve in personal growth. In subtle, subliminal ways, our homes are environments that can make, shake, or reinforce us as achievers in the outside world. And for its own sake, the home that breathes with serene composure makes your life a more articulate (and interesting) statement.

How can one furnish his environment to enrich his senses? For starters, consider (if you are an American) the way other cultures make sensory statements, even in crowded parts of the world and despite small living quarters. When touring Danish villages, on the islands of Fyn and Zealand, I seldom saw a window without cheery flowers in freshly greened windowboxes. Afternoon tea, seated amid the colorful abundance of an English country garden, is a sensory and highly civilized experience. In Japan, visitors invited to participate in the *chanoyu,* or traditional tea ceremony, perceive (but cannot explain) the nonverbal serenity it leaves afterward. The *chanoyu* has a structured formality, as does any ceremony; but each person performing this kind of cultural music expresses his own self—and the more solemnity the player brings to the sensory event, the more beautiful (and memorable) the result.

Each one of us has a sentient self within, perhaps imprisoned, perhaps in steady, communicative control. In order for "sensing" to turn your life around (as it has mine) you should accustom yourself to respecting your inner impulses. And once you habitually come to "listen" to the person you really are, the person you most wish to become can emerge more distinctly.

As one reads this book, almost unaware, the perceptive reader who notices the way others bring sensory enrichment into their lives will creatively sensitize his own. In time, this awareness of sensory significance will give your home an individual style—a kind of *genius loci*.

This was the quality the ancient Romans believed endowed important towns and villas—an unseen "spirit of place." This invisible spirit, omnipresent and ready to protect, was what explained the fact that certain places had their own mood or feeling, notable to visitors, making them different from other places.

The sensory *genius loci* of a home makes it a memorable place to visit. Those who are fortunate enough to reside there develop an unspoken homing instinct: wherever they roam, they turn home with anticipation and happy memories.

More than expensive furnishings, sensory details will help you help your family make the most of themselves. Over the years, sensory awareness decor and artifacts become your own style and éclat. (As the Comte de Buffon explained to the French Academy, *"Le style est l'homme même"* or, "The style is the man himself.")

You'll understand this better with a brief look at the lives of the celebrity elite. Those who wander the world widely usually have one home or retreat to which they enjoy returning, again and again. These are the places that bring serene relaxation in ways the analytic (left-brain) mind can only guess, but the tired body can perceive and know.

Sometimes the architecture of such a home tends to make the pictorial most of the surrounding terrain: windows offer a soothing vista for instant meditation. An appreciator of woodland beauty is country singer Johnny Cash. With his wife, singer June Carter, he lives outside Nashville, Tennessee, the home of country and Western music; they enjoy their own sensory life-style. Their multilevel home opens its windows on giant spreading trees, glassy lakes. No liquor is permitted in the Cash home, but music serves as a sensory substitute when guests are present. At some point during a party, a guitar is passed around. Each person is expected to sing, play, or recite a selection of his choosing. Whether the guest is a professional or amateur, this is a house rule. The Cash family considers impromptu music a sensory refreshment.

Music as sensory appreciation takes many forms; some of the world's business achievers take special joy in birds' song, particularly as a sound to begin their days. Whether birds are free-nesting or caged, the unexpectedness of birdsong builds a sensory ambiance within a house that makes it *home*, not just another place. One industrialist told me his happiest recollection from his children's early years was the look of his youngest toddler, listening with wide, wondering eyes to the chirping of a nearby canary.

As I mentioned earlier in this chapter, dancing at home can prove a fulfilling kind of sensory expression. Longtime film stars like Mitzi Gaynor and ageless Ann Miller rejuvenate their outlook by practicing dancing for its joys, as well as for exercise.

Others, for whom music represents their world of professional stress, find sensory serenity in nature. Rock singer Linda Ronstadt (the recording star whose first four albums sold so well she was termed "the most successful singer in U.S. recording history") likes to spend long hours just sitting by the seashore, watching the ocean roll before her $325,000 Malibu Beach home. Up the California coast, 50's film star Kim Novak keeps a woody retreat near Big Sur, one of the most scenic areas along the craggy coast. She enjoys a sensory release by painting and is said to have become proficient at it. She also finds great pleasure in her pet dogs; intimates claim she grooms and strokes them as a soothing relief from any occasional problem.

It may be that, unaware, pet owners enjoy animals as sensory meditation objects. Claude Lévi-Strauss says that certain animals have been singled out as symbolic or totemic creatures, not because they are "good to eat" or "good to prohibit" but because they are *bonnes à penser,* or "good to think." Any perceptive beholder will find that the antics of a puppy or the feline grace of a stretching cat can offer a meditative pleasure. Suspending all thinking as you view such playful postures will bring stress release and ease mental tensions. (During the final hectic months of writing this book, my black English cocker spaniel, Koko, eased work stress by nestling warmly against my feet, regularly permitting herself to be stroked despite the clacking typewriter overhead.)

With homes in various countries, as well as northern Virginia, film star Elizabeth Taylor travels with a household menagerie that usually includes five dogs and a cat. Friends say Elizabeth has another method for sensory meditation: all alone, she likes to try on jewels from her multimillion-dollar jewelry collection. These gems bring the luminous-eyed star as much personal joy as they did Faust's Margarite; the "jewel song" of cool precious stone on warm sensuous flesh brings its own (right-brain) sensory experience.

Another home sensory experience was savored by the late cosmetics tycoon, the indomitable Helena Rubinstein. Her favorite home was a magnificent triplex apartment, high above Manhattan's Park Avenue. Visiting it on occasion, I was struck by the generous abundance of modern paintings, lavishly lining the long walls; they were three-deep in the living room. It was a more private room that held Madame Rubinstein's sensory secret—a room given over to displaying gigantic Salvador Dali paintings, some from floor to ceiling. Mme. Rubinstein had lounge chairs designed for what she termed the Dali Room, but everything was dominated by the eerie landscapes and mystical imagery for which Dali is famous. The chairs themselves were grotesque, like sculpted hands of a silver-green metal that reached around to grasp and hold the occupant. But it mattered little to multimillionairess Mme. Rubinstein whether visitors liked her chairs—she enjoyed them and they were appropriate to the setting. Reports are she would enjoy long hours in serene meditation, seated before her enigmatic Dali canvases.

To illustrate the way a painting can offer deep sensory excitement, I'll tell you of an experience I had on my first visit to New York's Metropolitan Museum. Brought up in Florida, I was twenty and in Manhattan for a holiday. Earlier, I had studied the life of Vincent van Gogh, and although I was familiar with prints, I had never seen an original van Gogh painting. At the Metropolitan, one view of his version of a cypress tree became a vivid and powerful experience, one that was almost orgasmic. Hot-faced and alone (oblivious to the milling strangers), I stood gazing, and could hear my heart speed up, feel my cheeks flush. I could not move from the museum floor, part of me was one with that tree: I was the bark, I was the oddly tinted leaves. I felt a fleeting anxiety that others around me would notice my crimson face, hear my heavy breathing, and think me ill or crazy—or both. Afterward, looking into a mirror, I was amazed to find I looked the same as before, when so much had happened to me. Now that I know the term for it, I can identify what transpired as a peak experience (see chapter 3). Then, I knew only that it was one of the most important moments in my life; the word "thrilling" seems a mild way to describe that momentous sensing experience.

Besides art in the home, many overstressed achievers enjoy sensory pleasures and artifacts of a more physical nature. During his presidential days, the late Lyndon B. Johnson put the White House steam room and pool to daily use, after an afternoon's work was done. He'd follow with a light supper and, often as not, feel so refreshed he'd return to the Oval Office for two more hours of executive work. (This was not endorsed by his assistants, most of whom were not as skilled as the Texas rancher at using sensory exertions to provide stress relief.)

Another who retains his own style and taste is film star Burt Reynolds. He selects sensory decor featuring macho trimmings in his California home: hides, fur rugs, steer horns, saddles. Burt shrugs aside any debate about whether such taste is original or modish; he says this is the decor that makes him feel relaxed and comfortable. (This bedrock honesty is a sensory awareness truth: rather than attempt to furnish your home by other people's standards, what counts is how *you* feel.) Across the American continent, at Long Island's Sagamore Hill, explorer-politician Teddy Roosevelt's retreat featured the trappings of macho masculinity: tigers' heads, mounted swordfish, hide rugs were everywhere. It is said the proud father encouraged his children to romp on the fur rugs, enjoying their squeals of sensory delight.

Ecstasy, like meditation, comes in many guises. The great religions succeed in combining these on occasion, although the religious might not offer sensory appeal for everybody. (It should not be surprising that it is the devout who have the most moving religious experiences: more than anything else, you get out of a religion what you put into it.) In the home, religious objects can play a sensory role in achieving a meditative or tranquil state. Ethel Kennedy, widow of the late U.S. Senator Robert Kennedy, has had major rooms of her McLean, Virginia, home fitted with holy-water fonts. Such sacramental minutiae permit easy devotionals, crossing oneself before entering major rooms, on leaving in the early morning, etc. For the spiritually indoctrinated, there is no question that such gestures provide a sensory satisfaction as well as a religious one.

In itself, the at-home celebration of a religious feast or holiday can prove fulfilling in sensory awareness (right-brain) ways, in addition to the spiritual. Repetition and use of rosary beads and other ritualistic prayer tools bring a deep meditative tattoo. With practice, this in itself could calm anguished mental "static" and left-brain dialogues. For Mohammedans, the at-home hearing or repeating of the muezzin's cry of *"La ilaha illa'llah*" ("There is no god but God") brings serenity that is right brain in origin. In terms of home sensory awareness, Jews also have a hand up the perceptivity ladder because so many rituals are celebrated in the home from childhood on: Passover, Yom Kippur, Purim. Such home sensory celebrations make up the most vivid recollections of Jewish adults.

For secular persons, such as collectors and hobbyists, touch-me displays of collections accumulated over the years will offer meditative and sensory awareness appeal. One major American politician quickly "unwinds" when relaxing over his china elephant collection. The late newspaper tycoon J. David Stern prominently displayed his collection of chessmen in all his homes: Palm Beach, New York's Fifth Avenue, Bellport, Long Island. Whatever their home design preferences, it is such sensory awareness details that hand-stamp a dwelling place as a home, a sanctuary from the stressors of the outside world. In the ultimate sense of the word, as Pandects noted in the sixth century, home thus becomes one's "safest refuge."

Home as Environment: A Sensory Checklist

For your own sake, are there initial ways to make your home a sensory and restful experience? Thanks to mass production, sensory and free-form furniture designs are increasingly available and need not be custom-ordered: water beds, bean bag chairs (great for children's rooms), free-form chairs, lighted displays of water beads, moving endlessly, hypnotically. Posters with graphic art designs can and are being used as meditation objects, a concept from Mandala yoga. Art in the form of print reproductions is within the budget of everyone, permitting at least one wall of the home for visual meditation. Art can be as much of a sensory event in today's homes as it was in the palaces of the Medicis.

Other shortcuts help you make the sensory "most" out of your home: quiet nooks (where one can enjoy just sitting and being); throw pillows (to permit sprawling, unregimented body awareness—on the floor as well as couches); upholstery and draperies chosen as much for sheen and texture as for match and practicality.

Rethink the present use to which you put each room of your home. More sensory excitement as well as here-and-now appeal will result from rearranging your furniture. Architectural genius Frank Lloyd Wright liked to say that truly great homes offered several places for dining, some formal, some impromptu. Dining flexibility is an easy way to broaden sensory enrichment: indoor/outdoor picnics on the stoop, at redwood tables, or by an oversized fireplace; weekend outdoor brunches; afternoon tea by the swimming pool, rose garden, or even by windowboxes; outdoor cookouts (is any aroma as appealing to the senses as that of a barbecue in the great outdoors?). For indoor dining, frequent use of candlelight adds the sense of an event. (Sensual enrichment grows when candles are placed to reflect in mirrors or silver tableware.)

In any room of the home, dashes of color, goldfish, music, greenery—all add sensory statements that will both enrich and soothe. (Bathrooms are especially hospitable to green plants because of the continual humidity in the air.)

To help you generate your own sensory ideas, attuned to your present life-style (and the person you most want to become), consider the following checklist.

Wherever you reside, do you make creative use of available sunlight for interior decor (antique bottles in windows; wrought-iron room dividers or shutters for chiaroscuro effects, etc.)?
Does your decoration include nature's signature symbols: shells, cool stones, driftwood, Japanese ming trees?

(All are useful for "sensing" and physical meditation.)

Have you ever used pebbles or colorful weeds as table
centerpieces? (When children are present, this is sensory education, calling attention to commonplace
beauty that is often overlooked or underrated.)

Does your decor include at least one object that responds
to passing wind currents and breezes (Chinese chimes/
feathers or pussywillows in floor-standing pots/ hanging, wispy plant trails, etc.)?

When alone, do you regularly spend time just quietly
listening to outside, or domestic, sounds (without the
distraction of TV, phonograph, or radio)?

In balmy weather, do you have an outdoor (or window-
side) seat for enjoying the sunshine—*being,* in the
fullest sense?

Do you regularly call your family's attention to unusual
outside sounds, exotic, unexpected noises? (Do you
enjoy this with youthful zest or is it done with whin-
ing complaint?)

Do several rooms in your home make decorative use of
mirrors? (This increases body awareness, as well as re-
flects light.)

Do you use unexpected containers for flowers? (Wine
bottles, pitchers, boxes. At elegant parties, soup cans
have been used successfully for "pop art"—and to
provide sensory effects.)

At least once daily, do you take time to notice a still-life
glimpsed through your windows, whatever they face?
Do you contemplate this in terms of overall artistry?
When you catch a random glimpse of sudden beauty,
do you spend a few moments in serene meditation?

As your family's sensory environment, do you deco-
rate your home for at least three festivals a
year (Christmas/Passover/birthdays/St. Valentine's/

Thanksgiving/patriotic holidays/New Year's, and
so on)?

Do your window curtains or blinds permit maximum
penetration of sunlight?

Do you have living plants or flowers in at least three
rooms of your home? (Why not throughout?)

During seasonal changes, do you open windows to allow
sensing of different wind temperatures on your skin?

Do you take pleasure in the sound of insects, particularly
crickets, bees, or cicadas? (If not, make time; the low
tone of insects like the cicada is one of the first sounds
to be lost when advancing years decrease hearing
ability.)

Wherever you reside, do you make the decorative most of
your surroundings, bringing indoors what is the best
in the outdoors and taking open-windowed sustenance
from whatever is scenic in your environment?

For yourself or your family, the final item on our checklist can make your home a sensory powerhouse of emotional
reinforcement. When the best of your outside environment is
allowed to gain entrance into your home for decorative emphasis (from conch shells to wheat sheaves or more urban artifacts), a fountainhead of self-confidence can be created for
future achievers to draw upon. Such a unanimity of indoor-
outdoor deepens one's *sense of place* and builds bedrock assurance and ego strength.

Dr. Rene Dubos has noted the impact sensory details in
one's childhood environment have on the adult. In a psychological study made by Dr. A. R. Luria, one instance drama-
tizes this link between sensory awareness and memory. One of
the Luria patients, Dr. Dubos reports, had a memory that was
phenomenal in its ability to retain detail. Dr. Luria found this
was chiefly due to the man's habit of associating remembered
words with sensory impressions. This man could make his

pulse race by vividly recalling his walking the cobblestone streets of childhood, sensing the village railroad station—its sounds, smells, and the overall *feel* of it. We must not underestimate the conditioning we receive, early or late, from our sensory environment, says Dr. Dubos. It is those sensual images, derived from the world around us, that help most of us to reason and think.

Celebrate Yourself Exercise No. 8: A Sensory At-Home Experiment to Build Mind Power

Whatever your job, age, or ambition, you'll be better at it with more assurance and self-esteem. The recent spate of dream research points to ways we can build confidence—by controlling our dreams.

This dream research is based on studies of the Senoi Indians in Malaysia by anthropologists. The Indians are a peace-loving tribe that make the telling of nightly dream-incidents part of at-home discussion and future tribal planning. During their dreams, Senoi children are encouraged to stand up and face any nightmare figures, rather than "running" from them. The Senois believe this builds courage during daylight hours. Control your dreams, they say, and you grow in self-esteem.

The following dream-power experiment might take weeks or months to achieve, but it's worth it. I find the effort alone pays daily dividends: ego strength grows with each serious attempt. And once you succeed in asserting some control over your dream state, you'll awaken the next morning with a *satori*-type exultation, feeling that "Nothing can stop me now." For days afterward, you'll sweep through testy detail with grace and new capability.

HERE'S WHAT YOU DO: Sleep studies show that everybody dreams several times nightly, whether we recall it or not. Next time you're "in" a dream, make a deliberate effort to raise your (dream) hand, still in your dream state. You won't wake up, so don't worry; if you do, you'll drop right off to sleep again. But persist in this nightly effort, endeavoring to raise your dream hand up in front of your face. If and when you achieve this, turn your hand over (still in your dream) and try to study it carefully.

(This is a power-endowing experiment. It is espoused by the legendary Don Juan, wizard-teacher of Carlos Casteneda, the American chronicler of non-ordinary reality.) This phenomenon works in mysterious ways, but it really works. Once you've exercised control over your sensory dream state, you are awash with a feeling of confident power over events in your waking life.

CHAPTER

10

SA IN YOUR TRAVELS

*Young people, gathering about a guitar, unhesitatingly
prefer the floor to the use of chairs . . . Western adults
soon lose this faculty . . . The trouble is, when we lose
our elasticity for sitting, we lose it for everything else
also.*

CHARLES V. W. BROOKS

By letting you focus in on the
vivid here-and-now of the travel experience, sensory awareness practice makes any trip more meaningful and less aggra-
vating.

Much of today's travel means sitting, hour after hour—
in cars, on planes, in trains, waiting at terminals. Body sensitivities get dulled, and the details of travel can test one's
patience. Body awareness stimulation is needed, particularly
for the traveler who is past thirty. Without on-the-road distraction and sensory excitement, a chronically tense, under-

exercised body pushes emotional reactions out of hand. If un-expected delays occur, the desensitized traveler becomes irate and can stew for hours about travel trivia: schedule changes, abrupt clerks, delayed or mishandled baggage.

Confucius said, "Everything has beauty, but not every-one sees it." More than any other enrichment training, sensory awareness lets you make the most of new vistas, diversified people—whatever your reason for traveling.

Sensory Awareness and Business Travel
SA—to Relieve Stress

When you've got work on your mind, travel can be dou-bly fatiguing—you've more stressors than the person who is just up and away on a holiday. The following sensory aware-ness exercises will be of special help on your next business trip:

"Sensing" engine vibrations. If this trip is a hassle, seat yourself beside wall, window, or post (on plane, train, ferry, or motor vehicle—it doesn't matter). The idea is to position yourself to "sense" vibrations when you get tired—or if your (left-brain) mental *radio* won't shut down. In itself, this can bring on travel anxieties, particularly when your body is ex-hausted or under-exercised.

HERE'S WHAT YOU DO: Begin tuning up your senses, turning down your mind with these three steps: (1) Breathe deeper in your abdomen (use gentle motions rather than abrupt, forceful respiration); (2) Lean your head or shoulder against the vibrating cabin wall or window; (3) Give yourself over to this sensation: let your body take the lead, your mind follow. Now let the engine vibrations enter your body, run down your arms and spine, enter each foot. Suspend all thinking—just enjoy yourself in this time and in this place. (This should block out troublesome thoughts. If emotional thinking persists, pick up the engine vibrations in your throat, and begin gently humming to yourself.)

Tactile game-playing, "sensing." When waiting in line, or other travel aggravations, get you down—let your sensors take over. The tactile sensory nerves in your hands will put you in distracting contact with the here-and-now; this calms turbulent thoughts.

HERE'S WHAT YOU DO: Seated or standing, use your inner hand as "eyes"; try to sense your suitcase or handbag, instead of merely holding it. Focus full awareness on the feel of it, the weight of it. How does your arm relate to it? Note how your fingers curve around the handle. (Experience taught me to carry a suede shoulder bag with a cool metal zipper. I use this for "sensing" to build composure, pass time, awaiting plane departures, waiting in lines, etc.).

"Grounding" as sensory gamesmanship. When air travel was for the elite, airline travelers were given tiny footlets, allowing them to walk about shoeless and carefree. Do it yourself for sensory awareness gains. Pack shoe-socks in your cabin luggage. When your body is tense and your feet tired (and sometimes swollen from displaced circulation), try "grounding" yourself. This brings emotional serenity, as well as easing business travel fatigues.

HERE'S WHAT YOU DO: Sit in stockinged feet with your feet flat on the floor. Lift your toes, then return them to the floor; now lift your heels. Roll your feet outward to the side, then return. (Do they rest lighter on the floor?) Move and expand your toes, feet flat on the floor, really stretching them. (Can you sense each toe separately?) If necessary, touch your toes with your hands—do whatever you need to sense each toe. Now spend several minutes just riding with your feet flat, shoeless; try to pick up any engine vibrations coming through the floor. Let them flow throughout your body, beginning at your feet.

SA—to Offset Travel Boredom

For distraction, play color games. Early on, children discover it's fun to watch for colored cars, red trucks; excitement can break up the sameness of traveling along a road, mile after mile. It is a here-and-now stimulation to, say, count red trucks as you pass them. On a train, look for varying shades of yellow in passing landscapes or city streets. Airline travelers will enjoy their own sensory color game, as follows:

HERE'S WHAT YOU DO: Close your eyes (this helps shut down brain "static"). Then start to listen, unthinking, to the rolling waves of the aircraft engine. After a few moments, let the sound convert into moving waves of color or design, moving across your darkened eyelids. Do not direct them, let them pass as they will; avoid forcing them and do not single out or mentally examine them. Breathe low in your abdomen and give your mind over to your imaginative colors and designs. Let your jaw drop and relax completely. Continue this way for several minutes. When you are ready, you can open your eyes, "returning" to the external environment, refreshed and no longer mentally sluggish or bored.

SA—for Revitalizing

Sensorially exercise your buttocks. Lengthy travel (particularly under business travel stressors) can deaden body muscles. When this happens, your limbs feel cramped, and body/mind anxieties worsen. Use the following sensory awareness experiment to restore circulation and return serenity and confidence.

HERE'S WHAT YOU DO: Relax your legs and torso, and sit motionless; then tense and relax your seat muscles. Activate the muscles in the right buttock seven times, then the left. Repeat both together, tensing and relaxing seven times. Now place one hand inconspicuously under one buttock. (How does your lower buttock feel now? Any difference from before? How does your hand feel underneath?) Let your hand remain underneath until your body weight begins to press and tire; then remove your hand. (Do you now sit lighter in your seat?) Practice this procedure with the other buttock.

Now remove and place both hands under the buttocks. Hold for several moments, then remove. (Can you still sense your hands underneath?) Enjoy sensing this for several moments. Then, when you are ready, get up and move about. Return to your seat, and lower your body into it, gingerly now. Let it rest lightly on the seat rather than plumping it down, heavy and formless.

Try centering to reinforce, revitalize. When travel seems at its most demanding, reach into your inner spaces for serenity and renewal.

HERE'S WHAT YOU DO: Let your breathing slowly find its way to your lower abdomen. Continue breathing, gently, slowly. Now imagine your entire lower torso area is cuddled in a downy, warm loincloth. It wraps and blankets you around the navel, encircling your body comfortably. Feel this glowing warmth; let it spread from your gravity "center," enjoying this power as it radiates throughout your body. Stay with this feeling for several minutes. (If tiredness persists, practice switching your mental attention, back and forth, "sensing" the warmth of your lower abdomen, then notice the cool feeling of air to your nostrils as you inhale.)

SA Practice—for the Daily Commuter

Mile after familiar mile (or train junctions—day after day), habitual commuting can be enlivened for the business traveler by sensory awareness techniques. One idea is to play sensory games and prove that "getting there is half the fun." Counting yellow buses, "Welcome to . . ." signs, or red trucks is more of a mind-occupying absorption when *color* is included as sensory gamesmanship. Another (right-brain) sensory technique—remembered tunes; let one title lead into a related one and try to "hear" the songs in your head (humming along secretly if you like).

When driving, if you get bored, let movement excite your senses: the rush of wind on cheek or hand; moody or spirited sounds brought by air currents; the way your body shifts to adapt to road turns and twists. Make an extra effort to keep your perceptivities open and you'll find more sensory exultation in travel, even short-range. You will feel at one with Robert Louis Stevenson's comment: "I travel not to go anywhere, but to *go*. I travel for travel's sake. The great affair —is to move."

There is another way to enliven what might be considered the monotonous aspects of commuting—make your mind's eye a camera lens. Each familiar town and way-station has an ever-changing scene quality. Catch a sun-shadowed landscape here, a cluster of rustic townsfolk there. Above ground or on a subway, even grim, depressing scenes take on their here-and-now pictorial impact: American artist William Hopper built his success around renderings of eerie, deserted bus depots, dark beaches, mysterious shacks. As one art critic applauded, they look as if a crime is about to occur (or has just happened).

Whether a daily commuter or a long distance business traveler, one thing is key: try to differentiate between over-active (left-brain) *thinking* and sensory or physical *per-ceptivity*. When you let your intuitive perceptions roam unfettered, travel is less stressful. But too much critical com-paring (this trip with the last) and rational (left-brain) prac-ticality will lead your mind back to the world of workaday stressors you wanted to leave in the first place.

Sensory Awareness—and Pleasure Travel

Holiday travel lets sensory awareness come into its own as an enrichment experience, helping you get the most out of your travel dollar.

As a way of recuperating from jet lag on your first few days in a foreign nation, let "sensing" speed adaption. Lying on a beach in warming sunshine (or in sensuous bathwater) works through complex neural pathways, and eases your adaptation to the strange and unfamiliar. Just let your mind float out to sea; when you rouse yourself later, your outlook will be clearer and your mind and body ready for sightseeing fun. If spirits tire, make here-and-now sensual contact with your hotel room: "sense" the feel of satin coverlets, window drapery textures, woven rugs. Take time to notice warm ra-diators, feel balmy breezes.

Sensory awareness deepens your gastronomic apprecia-tion of food (in itself thus stretching your travel funds). A common side effect of holiday travel today is weight gain. Travelers overeat due to fatigue or boredom, downing food frequently and rapidly. Offset this with sensory awareness, making each meal a festive occasion.

When dining, devote full attention to the food experience. Sense the different taste in each morsel, savor food appearance, textures, colors. Let the aroma of new foods become a sensory appreciation in itself.

There are enrichment values in the unfamiliar that "sensing" brings to consciousness. When the pleasure traveler remains sensorially open for this, travel is less stressful, more rewarding. The strange feel of foreign currency, for example, can become a here-and-now sensory awareness experience.

> HERE'S WHAT YOU DO: Hold the foreign money (coins or bills, it doesn't matter) within your closed palm. Suspend all thinking and close your eyes. Focus attention only on the touch and texture. Slowly rub your fingers across the surface. Sense the sides, the weight. (Does it have an aroma? Does its age betray the richness of centuries? Or a minted penny-bright newness?) Again, breathe deeply from your abdomen, slowly—try to feel and be, rather than think.

For the pleasure traveler, SA perceptions can also relieve fatigue. Consider the following:

Cool metal revives: On ferry, train, or waiting room, armchair metal can perk your spirits, ease stress.

> HERE'S WHAT YOU DO: Prepare your central palm for "sensing" by rubbing the fingers of the opposite hand over it, back and forth. Then place your hand on the cool metal surface. Give yourself completely over to the sensation of sleek, cool metal against your warm, compliant flesh.

OR

When all else fails, try "sounding." Human resonance is uncharted sensory territory: for reasons not yet understood, it can ease anxiety, calm stress, restore good spirits. When travel gets you down, in airplane, motor vehicle, or train, imitate gently the z-z-z-z of the engine. This relaxes turbulent (left-brain) thinking, lets travel become truly restorative.

THEN

Watch the children. When a child is emotionally healthy and unrestricted, he "senses" unawares. On a European bus at rush hour, I saw the way a little French boy, about nine years old, kept his calm in the midst of the swarming passengers. Somewhere he had picked up a feather, and he stood, gamely holding onto a seat, idly stroking the feather back and forth across his cheek, smiling with pleasure at participating in the overall, unique experience.

SA Bridges Cultural Gaps

When the traveler comes jam up against different cultures and people whose opinions are 360 degrees away from his own, sensory awareness promotes universal tolerance. This might be the most significant SA value for travelers, lovers, or anyone else in the midst of an emotional or geographical flow. Because "sensing" teaches you to respect your own inner impulses and feelings, you are more willing to accord another the right to his own uniqueness, whatever it is.

Celebrate Yourself Exercise No. 9: A Sensory/Imagery Exercise for Travelers

This is a body-painting sensory experiment, similar to body awareness centering (chapter 7). It brings new self-knowledge also, and was proposed by Israeli scientist Moshe Feldenkrais. What you are going to do is to close your eyes and imagine a paintbrush dipped in bright orange or purplish paint. With it, you are going to gently and thoroughly paint your entire body. Practicing this en route (silently, eyes closed) can perform small miracles for the bone-weary traveler.

HERE'S WHAT YOU DO: Sit comfortably, feet on the floor, shoeless if possible. Breathing deeply, eyes closed, take a mental paintbrush and begin "painting" your body, starting with your head. Enter your hair, moving your brush between hairs, pausing here, moving briskly there, covering your scalp. Then paint around the outside of your hairline, around and into your ears. Linger inside your ears (one at a time), then move your brush around the back of your head. Paint the back of your neck briskly and completely (this relieves neck tensions, considered central to body tensions elsewhere).

Paint your face carefully, gently, dipping "paint" into each tiny crevice and plane until your complexion tingles. Paint your eyelids, each lash, your eyebrows, then minutely inside your nose.

Continue around the back, going slowly down your spinal cord, moving your brush in sure, steady strokes. Pay special attention to the middle and lower back. Then move the brush around your buttocks, between them, around to the front. On your chest, now, paint underarms and each breast with tiny, sure strokes. Then paint your navel, going inside it, then down to the abdomen. Now drop to the penis or between your legs to the vaginal opening; take the imaginary brush and go inside and around the vagina.

Pay extra attention to the upper leg area. Give the back of your legs an extra paint coating, going over each one separately. (This region might have become desensitized with travel fatigue.) Now go down each leg separately, thoroughly. Spend time behind the knees, around the back of the calves, around the ankles. Paint each foot separately, painting around and between each toe. (Try to sense some feeling in each toe as your imaginary brush "touches" it.) Then paint the bottoms of your feet.

Now step aside, mentally, and "inspect" your handiwork. Is there a place where you sensed little feeling, or that was difficult to reach? This might be a place you feel "out of touch" with. One body awareness expert says any area such as this is a potential "trouble spot"—a locale prone to chronic infection or breakdown. (Some city dwellers find the throat area feels strange, alien. This might be why chronic sore throats trouble many urban residents, even those who do not live in polluted cities.)

In all, this sensory experiment should take at least five or six minutes, preferably longer. When completed, just sit back, eyes still closed, and savor the sensory feeling of letting your freshly painted body "dry." When your eyes find their way open, you will feel serene—and curiously refreshed.

(*Warning:* This is a powerful invigorator and should not be attempted for forty-five minutes after mealtime.)

CHAPTER
11

SA IN HEALTH
AND BEAUTY

If you are receptive, everything will be receptive—receptive and reactive to what is happening . . . you would be like a healthy child or animal when it is interested—simply there for it. In the moment a person is really interested, it shoots into the very bones.

. . .[Otherwise] you are closing off from experience very important areas in yourself. Often this brings about great physical difficulty.

CHARLOTTE SELVER

There's no doubt there are self-healing aspects to sensory awareness—Elsa Gindler proved it. And at advanced sensory workshops (particularly those where Selver and Brooks are in attendance), you'll hear legendary tales about longtime "sensers" who used sensing to restore inner organismic harmony, which allowed the body to heal itself.

Using sensory aromatics to heal will be the "new" wave

of the future, according to Dr. Ivan Popov, rejuvenator and essence-expert. Ancient Egyptian medicine was made up largely of aromatics and inhalation therapy (documented by the medically influential sixty-five-foot Papyrus of Thebes, circa 1550 B.C.). Our own medical establishment is finding that inhaled essences can be given in smaller dosages, with fewer side effects than occur with swallowed pharmaceuticals. Popov prescribes using sensory awareness techniques for health benefits, such as aromatic bath salts which bring sleep without drugs or pills. He also recommends aromatics to relieve frigidity or sexual impotence, *all* of which can be inhaled in the privacy of one's room. He recommends sensory aromatics for energy, others for a glowing complexion.

But it is the less esoteric use of sensory awareness aids for health and grooming that will open tangible and easily defined new doors in your life. And this kind of enrichment is fun for everyone. As you'll see in the following sections, it is remarkable how much meaning (and luxury) this kind of sensory enrichment will bring to your daily life—at little or no extra cost.

SA to Revitalize

In addition to its aesthetic beauties in your private world, a sensory awareness approach to living opens up new ways to boost energy and mood. Here's what you can do:

1. *Water temperature "sensing."* When you splash alternate currents of cool water on a tired face you'll revitalize your skin cells and perk up your outlook. One international beauty expert touts water therapy so much that he recommends thirty-five cool-water rinses after each use of his costly soap. When it is inconvenient to splash your face, expose your inside wrists to alternate hot and cold running tap water. (As I've said I use this technique when I am trying to remember

important facts and data. In still uncharted ways, "sensing" opens up memory banks.)

2. *Sensory sounding as a "grounding" exercise.* For relief from tension, here's what you do: stand upright, legs relaxed. Stretch your arms upward briefly, then drop your arms and torso so that your body droops like a daisy. Bend your knees and touch your fingers to the floor. Head tucked under, continue breathing deeply. Hold for several moments, mouth open. Now quietly hum and begin to sway your body gently, back and forth and around. Keep your fingertips on the floor, "grounding" you to Mother Earth. Hold for one long minute. Then return upright. You'll have a glowing complexion—and a lighter, more confident mood.

3. *Fresh air hourly.* Most city people work indoors in closed-air environments—these can become stale, particularly with large numbers of people over extended periods of time. Opening your lungs to fresh air once an hour (at windows, on noontime reliefs) helps a lot. As an SA approach to offset work stress, try this occasionally: "sense" the cool quality of fresh air on your face, particularly on the cheeks and chin.

4. *Towel rubbing.* At home, one of the least expensive (and most invigorating) beauty rituals is an after-bath toweling, using the towel as a sensory stimulant. Rub briskly, paying close attention to the back of the neck, the buttocks, the upper arms and thighs. Better, gift your lover with Hers and His turkish towels. After showering together, enjoy the togetherness fun of a sensory towel massage.

5. *Slapping as sensory stimulant.* Related to the above is a favorite experiment from SA-Selver. At a moment alone, use your hands to slap your neck, behind, around. Then quickly slap your arms, your thighs, up and down your legs, together, separately. This is a SA-Selver method for restoring the feeling of life and vitality. With a few moments of privacy, you can practice it anywhere.

6. *Carry wet packs.* One of the most civilized additions to sensory health and beauty is the lemon-scented damp napkin. Good for dining away from home or traveling, these napkins bring sensory stimulation prior to meals or after the main course.

7. *Carry a cologned handkerchief or purse flacon.* Seventeenth-century dandies had it over us: they knew how to restore aplomb with scents (even snuff or smelling salts). When you're fatigued or under stress, a sudden shock of aromatic scent revitalizes your sensory and neural passages, clears your thinking.

8. *Change your scent semiannually.* As a final note on aromatic "sensing," remember that scents habituate. After regular use, you'll no longer notice you're wearing any. Don't minimize your own importance—changing your scent regularly lets you stimulate yourself, as well as your public.

SA for Calming

The last three methods mentioned above can soothe as well as stimulate. In addition, the following SA practices will bring instant calm when you are tense or upset.

1. *Serenity colors.* Color may have tangible physical effects on us that scientists have yet to measure. While these vary from person to person, you know those colors or designs that make you feel peaceful (light blues, aqua, pinks, delicate floral prints, etc.). Make decorative—and permanent—use of these individual serenity colors in the rest and grooming areas of your home. Pastel powder puffs, tissues, and decorative accessories (in your serenity colors or prints) can unruffle a furrowed brow as you cosmetically smooth it. (Forget about whether or not what you choose is decorative chic—trust your own tastes and your "sensing" impulses. Besides, if it doesn't work out, you can gradually replace articles as they are used.) Another sensual touch that soothes the

troubled spirit: fluffy cotton balls to remove cosmetics and to provide decorative fun when displayed in glass apothecary jars.

2. *Strategically placed mirrors.* Throughout this book, I emphasize the use of mirrors in the home: a big builder of body awareness and ego strength. No matter how physically attractive you are, you grow in assurance when you come to honest terms with your appearance. Consider placing a mirror on the exit door of your home grooming area. This lets you double-check your grooming as you leave to greet the world (and be welcomed by it).

3. *Make home beauty care a sensory experience.* Grooming on-the-run is fun, but don't make rush and hurry your constant companions. Take time out to voluptuously enjoy beauty and grooming in your own at-home spa or home beauty area. Make it a relaxing leisure experience. Play background music as you shampoo or manicure; enjoy furry rugs underfoot when your hair is drying, flattering lights and colors as you lounge. This pays dividends: grooming is more effective when your face and body are untensed and made serene. And when you enjoy a sense of harmony and beauty, deep inside you, it shows on your face.

SA for Beauty Rejuvenation

What follows is a sensory beauty meditation. It is taught at a handful of select beauty salons in England and California. The idea is to single out one area of your face or body that would benefit most from smoother, younger-looking skin. (Most persons select the upper eyelids, forehead, or under-eye area.) Then you are going to visualize that skin region as dewy-fresh, smooth, and youthful. For this imagery meditation, you will use a beauty fantasy: imaginary pink air—foaming deep into those skin pores.

(The following exercises takes just five to eight minutes,

but with daily practice over at least a month, it pays astounding beauty dividends—particularly for persons over thirty.)

HERE'S WHAT YOU DO:

1. Sit comfortably in a quiet, relaxing area. Breathe deeply for several moments. Try to activate your diaphragm as you breathe, using your lower abdomen as a bellows: suck it in flat as you exhale, push it out as you take in air. As you exhale, attempt to remove as much air as possible from your body.

2. Close your eyes. Now, as you inhale, imagine a lovely froth of pink air coming gently toward you; it enters your body through your nostrils. It is warm, pink, beautiful—route it smoothly to your problem skin area. As it reaches this region, hold your breath momentarily. Envision this skin area as becoming youthfully pink, glowing with new beauty, unlined and alabaster-smooth.

3. Hold your beauty breath for a slow count of 5; then gently exhale. Continue this intensive color breathing for eight long breaths for each problem area. (Saturate left and right eyelids separately, and so forth.) Then relax for normal breathing for several moments. If you are treating only limited areas, repeat another sequence of color breathing until your exercise period is over.

If deep wrinkles or aging problems exist, practice this sensory meditation twice daily, at least five minutes a session. As with convalescence from plastic surgery, patience is paramount here. Healthy skin cells require at least nineteen days for replacement. The most noteworthy improvements after color breathing take at least three months.

This exercise might at first seem frivolous, but there is scientific proof for such mind/body changes. Yogis have learned to partially control and direct their blood flow. At New York's Rockefeller University, scientists have taught mice to "blush" in one ear at a time.

How does color breathing work? With faithful practice, you'll come to open fresh capillaries in aging, dried-out skin. Enthusiasts claim color breathing brings skin rejuvenation that is more lasting than cosmetic skin peelings, or dermabrasion. Whatever your age, self-regeneration is within your capability. And with this five-to-eight minute sensory pause (twice daily if possible), you'll also find more serenity along the way.

CHAPTER

12

SA AND YOUR CHILD

*A glance at the actual training of your children . . .
reveals the problem. The parent invades every aspect of
the child's development. The child is taught when and
how much it is good for him to eat, when and how long
he ought to sleep, what parts of him are bad or dirty,
what is good social behavior (smiling), etc. When he
falls and cries, he is taught not to allow the pain and
shock to go their way but to seek instant distraction from
them . . . A little later he will be taught that exposure
to cold or getting wet in the rain is unpleasant and
dangerous, as it will actually become after the lesson has
been thoroughly learned.*

CHARLOTTE SELVER

$\mathbf{D}$o you try and speed up your
child's development? If so, do you coax and urge him or her
to sit, walk, and talk early and correctly (or, rather, as you
would have him do)? Or do you allow your youngster to

open and develop unhindered, like a flower revealing its petals, learning to relish the joyousness of progressing at his own speed and with his own interests.

The butterfly that is "aided" to emerge from its chrysalis becomes crippled or loses out on the spectacular colors that might have been his, had nature's way been allowed. So, unaware, you might be separating your child prematurely from the innate sensitivity and wondrous body symphony that is his or hers by birthright.

Charlotte Selver likes to tell of an afternoon when she was to visit a household where a young girl's sensory growth was being stunted just when she was on the threshold of discovering life's beckoning wonders and enjoying body as self. Called from her play abruptly, the little girl was made to come into the living room and was expected to sit quietly while adults talked at length. When the child fidgeted, she was corrected. When she put her tiny leg up on the window-seat (her toes could not touch the floor), she was reprimanded. When she did not sit up straight in her seat, she was told, in increasingly annoyed parental tones, to sit "correctly." Self-alienation begins this way, says Selver, when one is a child—and not encouraged to let one's body express itself.

Wordsworth's belief that "the child is father of the man" was a philosophy that was tinged with sadness. For much is lost when childhood's magic splendors fade and the shades of doubt and skepticism begin to close upon the growing youth. A young child is eager for new experiences, regarding all around with wide-eyed appreciation and alert interest. Recall the delight with which a baby studies his hands, looks with fascination at his toes. Each moment is intently explored. When a baby starts to sit, he does so in a natural posture that nobody had to teach him. And when he plays, he gives himself over in rapt concentration. The young toddler and his environment seem to become one, interacting harmoniously. As a result, the youngster confidently dominates his "space"—he has little need for so-called assertiveness training.

Loss of Childhood Spontaneity

Growing up brings a dimming of childhood's radiance. A baby is able to communicate what he does and does not want; and he can do this effectively before learning to use words. But after the age of two years or so, the patina of parental supervision often depletes a child's spontaneous self-assurance. The child's wishes and cravings come to be overruled, if they are listened to at all. This brings a dawning recognition that Mother, Dad, or nurse knows more about his body than he does: when he should be hungry; how much to eat; when to get sleepy; what foods are "good" and which are "bad."

Consider the exaggerated behavior and grimaces of young parents, influencing the young baby's ways of perceiving the world: sniffing at flowers, smacking lips at "yum-yum" tastes; speaking artificial baby-talk. All of this behavior implies that communication cannot be easy, simple, and peaceful. From the very beginning, Selver observes, "the young gain an impression that something *extra* is necessary." A child is constantly told there is a right way and a wrong way—and he must do things Mommy's way.

The toddler soon comes to suspect his inner urges, or to deny their existence. ("I don't seem to know; Mother knows!") As Selver warns, the genuine expressiveness of the child is transformed into a holding back, or into lifelessness. "It is not difficult to see the effect of the constant admonition of parents, teachers, and important adults to: 'Speak thus and so! Sit straight! Put your shoulders back! Chest up, buttocks tucked under.' Advice like this, if followed (and who has not at least tried?), blocks spontaneous motion and stifles natural behavior."

She adds: "And what about directives such as 'Pay attention!' or 'Make an effort!' or 'Think hard!' " Have you considered what conflict and confusions this can create within the formative spirit? "The sad thing," Selver adds, "is that most children give in. With this they drift away from the true language of the organism."

Nobody is herein suggesting that disorderly bedlam is salutary; permissive parenting carries its own pitfalls. But children unfold with greater self-assurance when their growth stages are permitted in God's time, rather than by pre-set parental rules. As Hungarian pediatrician Dr. Emmy Pickler urged: Let the child "live in peace and develop according to his own pace and needs."

To be in contact with ourselves physically and emotionally can appear to some people to be a waste of time. Ours is a civilization that has been described as "the Take Society," where social approval revolves around "gaining," "going," and "succeeding." In some areas, much social distinction is made, even to children, between winners and—that death knell criticism—"losers." Competing, as we generally force our children to do from prenursery school, leaves little room or time in their awareness for *existing,* in its purest, most fulfilling sense.

Nowhere are the sensory needs and development of a child more conspicuously ignored than in the way parents will interrupt a child at play, setting little import to what he is attempting. Rather, the preoccupied parent sets great store by the child who promptly leaves whatever he or she is doing to impulsively "come when Mother calls." It comes as no surprise that such conditioning breeds an inability to concentrate, inattention, and fosters the nervous habit of beginning another task before completing the first one.

Through continual interruption, Selver warns, the child "comes to feel that there is no natural rhythm in things, and that it is right for activities to be cut off in mid-air, and for

others to be begun, as though magically, without preparation."
Television's truncated stop-and-start interruptions further
encourage this living of life by nervous twitches. "Presenta-
tions are violently interrupted by the ones that follow," she
notes, "and the only preparations are shouts or blares."

When the child has been interrupted often enough, his
innate sense of rhythm and what has been called *zeitgedächtnis*
(German for "time sense") suffers. Selver notes that a child's
confidence in the social value of his own experience also becomes confused.

Current Western educational standards, as noted in
chapter 1, endorse the pragmatic, fact-loving, linear (left-
brained) approach to mental development. Vocabulary learning is stressed (and, surprising for this enlightened time, a
child's so-called IQ is often decided by the vocabulary words
he recognizes). Logic, reasoning, and pragmatic mathematics
are emphasized, often to the neglect of perceptive abilities
and (a word still used in the pejorative or patronizing sense)
intuition. Children are taught to believe, from kindergarten
on, that their eyes are the major source of information. Their
other senses are neglected. Facts are only acceptable to the
intelligent mind when they can be proven by other facts.
Truth must be scientific or it cannot exist at all.

When in ready contact with perceptions and sensory
truths, a child of any age gains new assurance and even tranquility. For example, the sensorially uncorrupted child feels
an instinctual relationship with the earth or floor; he enjoys
it as a base of support. He rests on it, he feels at home on it.
He grows strong by using what Selver calls a floor's "good
hardness," often in preference to the seductive softness of
couch or chair. Like the adult when sensory training prompts
his anxieties and alienations to drop away like old clothes on
the seashore, the natural child feels free to move around and
enjoys the feeling of being supported. Civilized constraints
rob childhood of such joys—but they can be restored with

sensory awareness training. We return to an awareness that, earth or floor, there is something under us inviting us, comforting, "always there to support us in everything we do." Adds Selver, "That something is the earth. We have returned to our home."

It might be that regular and reassuring contact with earth (or the indoor substitute, the floor) is essential for emotional health. In his clinical work as founder of the Bioenergetics method of psychotherapy, New York's Dr. Alexander Lowen has found that neurotics and persons with emotional disorders have a distrust of, and unfocused resistance to, earth as a support. Most emotionally disturbed people are strangely afraid to let themselves fall. (Dr. Lowen adds, "The act of falling evokes the feeling of aloneness, which the individual is loath to reexperience.")

It is a sensory irony that patients in psychotherapy are now urged to sit on their haunches; other exercises are given involving touching the floor for emotional "grounding." Yet children are reprimanded by their parents for floor sitting when chairs (mostly sized for adults) are available.

Sensory Awareness for Children: Educators Approve

Educators are beginning to recognize the meaningfulness of self in today's hectic classrooms. Alert to the learning values of sensory experiences, children's museums are installing "Please Touch" exhibits. A few schools are teaching sensory awareness at kindergarten levels and in high school psychology classes. Experts agree that this is the new wave of education—reeducating a child to appreciate self and body —for by respecting himself, he comes to respect others, and their rights.

A social behavior study among fourth-grade students found another benefit of sensory awareness training: mutual trust. Three educators collaborated: Wanda K. Franz of West

Virginia University, Lawrence W. Berning of U.S. International University at San Diego, and Eileen M. Reilly, on the faculty of dependents' schools at the Ramstein Air Force Base, Ramstein, West Germany. They selected four classes of students of similar age, taking two out of school to a nearby hostel. There, one class of students was taught sensory awareness "games." The other studied regular work. Back at the school, one of the two remaining classes was given classroom training in sensory awareness, the other used as control to measure results.

Training stressed group activities: students were encouraged to move about the room, eyes closed, touching one another if they liked. Or they were divided into pairs, then instructed to touch and "sense" one another's faces. Pairs of students also went on "blind walks," one blindfolded, the other acting as leader. One of the most telling experiments involved a "falling" game: one student, acting as "It" stood in the middle of a circle formed by classmates. Closing his eyes, he would fall backward, as another student caught him. The classmate playing It was then passed around the circle, "falling" and being gently caught.

Participants were rated on the Horace Mann-Lincoln Social Distance Scale, and checked before and after instruction. This scale is accepted by educators as indicating the extent to which individuals accept associates and are, in turn, accepted.

Results were consistent. Students given sensory awareness orientation showed a lowering of alienation and distrust. Those trained away from the classroom showed the biggest gains in the closeness they felt for each other. In reporting this landmark research, an editorial in a psychology journal said that many adults recall that first week in school, when the only way to get to know other students was to start a fight or stick a pigtail into an inkwell. "Perhaps these tactics could be avoided," the psychologist commented, "if teachers were to use sensory awareness training" to bring youngsters together more compatibly and comfortably.

Games for Sensory Awareness: Family Fun (and Learning)

Think back to your own childhood. Single out one or two memorable moments or experiences. Chances are your most vivid recollections are those that somehow were linked with sensory experience: taffy-pulling, licking the spoon for Mom after she made chocolate icing; swimming or fishing with the morning sun on your relaxed body; eating salty popcorn during Saturday movie matinees. It is not a coincidence that your brightest memories have sensory recollections. One body awareness expert claims it is sensory experience that opens up deeper memory banks, particularly touching or being touched.

To help along your own remembrances, I'll recall an incident from my childhood, during the Depression years. Fortunately for me, we lived in the tropical beauty of south Florida, and my mother sometimes let me "make" the butter. In our small kitchen this consisted of a squashy bag filled with white margarine (the manufacturer was not legally permitted to pre-color his product, making it less competitive with butter). So this cheaper but good and nutritious product had a red spot of dye attached to the bag. My chore (which I relished) was to puncture the dye, then knead the soft mass inside the margarine bag until the color was mixed throughout. What emerged was the golden color of real butter, and I helped create it! Molding that bag for several minutes was a sensual experience I can feel in my mind's eye, even now. I thrilled to the touch of doing this—and felt a special pride when I was, all alone, responsible for getting just the right color for our dinner table.

The following sensory games will give your own child

memories of fun, and sharing them will increase your joy of parenting. Played in a relaxed, encouraging manner, they will help along your youngsters' sensory development and reinforce their growing pride-in-self.

For some, this can have immeasurable results, for a child's confidence in his or her self (and intuitive perceptions) comes early.

These games cost only the time it takes to play them— and will return love and the joy of shared experiences. Materials are items already available in the kitchen or playroom —or are free for the picking from nature's ample bower.

"The Tone/Tune Game"
(For toddlers and early school years)

Teaching relaxed use of a musical instrument is one of the great sensory encouragements a parent can give his child. If this carries over into a desire for formal musical training, it returns countless satisfactions, including an evolved development of perceptive, nonverbal abilities. And you are probably aware that playing a musical instrument provides salutary release from stress, for children as well as adults.

HERE'S HOW YOU PLAY: Give each youngster a simple musical toy (a miniature lute, xylophone, or piano). First ask "players" to let you play at guessing: Each participant plays a musical note. Then they play other notes, asking you to guess which is higher or lower. Then you take the instrument, sounding notes as they listen, and attempt to place them higher or lower on the "scale."

For children over four years: Ask them to work out a simple tune in private, selecting one that is familiar to all. Let them make up clues to identify it for you (you probably won't recognize it from their playing!) Each player setting up a recognizable tune gets a prize.

All get congratulations. (It is a right-brain perceptive function to remember tunes, worth encouraging in all youngsters anytime.)

"Primal Play"
(Sensory fun for any age, from two to sixty-five years)

This experience in sounding offers something for everyone. It teaches nonverbal communicating to youngsters. It brings a unique relaxation to adults. For both, it offers a special sharing.

HERE'S HOW YOU PLAY: Place throw pillows on the floor and clear the room of breakable objects. Players spend advance moments romping shoeless among the pillows. Then ask the players to select a favorite animal. They will "imitate" this being for the first part of the game: searching for food, feeding, at rest. (Give each youngster a chance to sensually consider how he would behave as a bear, tiger, elephant, etc. Then allow at least four minutes for play.)

The second half of the game begins with a new rule. The plan now is to conduct an animated conversation, using sounds from your chosen animal rather than words as we know them. Players can switch to an easier animal offering greater nonverbal range, such as a cat or dog. It's their decision. The group leader begins as his chosen animal by moving around on the floor, player to player, "asking" and "discussing." Players in a group are divided into pairs. Arguments and (nonverbal) disagreements are permitted as long as they continue in good spirits.

"The Patterns Game"
(From late toddler to preschool age)

This is a version of a Piaget perceptivity game. It provides early confidence with geometric shapes and sets the stage for later training in mathematics.

HERE'S HOW YOU PLAY: Take heavy colored paper in four easy colors (i.e., red, blue, green, and yellow). With scissors cut hand-sized designs in three shapes: circles, squares, and triangles (one design for each color). The following directions are for two players, adult and child.

Keep for yourself all red and blue designs, giving others to the child with whom you are playing. Now arrange your shapes on the table. Point to your red circle. Ask, "What shape is this?" (Give the term, if they don't know.) Ask, "Do you have a card like this?" Say, "What color circles do you have?" Then, "You can use a yellow circle to top my red one." Take this offering, placing it on top of your own.

Repeat this procedure with other circles, then with squares and with triangles. Discuss what is different about the shapes with the child. Recall similar examples from life: wheels, square rugs, and so on. Most important: help the child to understand that his shapes in yellows and greens relate to your reds and blues.

(This concept is known as "mapping." The child learns that each object of a single set can be associated with a corresponding though not identical object in another set. This is similar to the way a dot on a map represents a certain town. The mental ability to perceive this is the key to basic education in mathematics, among other pursuits.)

"The Leaf Game"
(For ages two and a half through nine years)
This game relates to the above, but can be played with

older children also, encouraging them to select and gather their own materials.

HERE'S HOW YOU PLAY: Ask the players to gather five or six leaves of various sizes. Suggest they arrange them on a table or other flat surface, planning the arrangement in order of size, perhaps small to large, and left to right. If appropriate to the season, they can then rearrange them in colors, moving from light to dark, left to right. With several players, color comparisons are found.

Comments and approval follow each display. Time can be spent touching the veiny surfaces or furry backs, and listening to details about where each specimen was located.

"Blind Walking Game"
(Good for any age; particularly good when players
are of varying ages)

This version of the beloved blind man's bluff helps a child have confidence in his instincts and self-awareness.

HERE'S HOW YOU PLAY: Instruct youngsters that the idea is to boost "secret powers." When played with a group, urge teamwork as you divide players into pairs. Encourage them to aid and cheer rather than ridicule or poke fun at one another. When played in teams of two, this can be a get-acquainted game that fosters interpersonal trust and friendships.

The person who is "It" is gently blindfolded, then led around to familiar corners. His teammate gives clues to help him guess familiar objects, rooms. When the answer is given to each "leader's" prompting, the twosome moves on. The first twosome to complete a prescribed route around the house or yard "wins" the game. (*Note:* This game is a great "get-acquainted" activity at children's parties.)

"The Taste-It Game"
(All ages will love this one, including adults)

This experiment teaches any number of "players" to more sensually relish their ability to taste. If you like, you can follow this with a little lesson, as I shall discuss, making this a memorable learning experience.

HERE'S HOW YOU PLAY: Distribute spoons to each player, having previously selected foods and spices for comparison tasting. Begin by explaining that there are only four basic tastes: sweet, salt, bitter, sour. Give samples for comparison tasting (such as sugar, salt, lemon, pickles). Point out to youngsters that all their favorite foods are combinations of these basic tastes. Discuss the way one's sense of smell affects taste and food judgment. Enjoy "testing" foods with pinched noses. You can conclude this game with potato chips, salted pretzels, or other examples of tastes that combine two or more basic groups.

In simple terms, explain to youngsters that they will relish their foods more when they keep food in their mouths longer, chewing thoroughly. This lets their bodies distribute juices to begin the digestive process in the mouth. Sometimes this changes the taste of foods right in the mouth. Encourage youngsters to savor the individual taste of each food they eat, consuming food slowly; this avoids overeating or hurry-up snacking. (Both habits contribute to childhood obesity, a serious health problem in the United States and Canada, especially.)

"The Touching/Feeling Game"
(From three to twelve years: for older children, select
more complex objects for guessing)

This game alerts children to the magic of their tactile
senses; all ages enjoy perceiving surfaces with closed eyes.

HERE'S HOW YOU PLAY: Round up any number of
surfaces or objects that would be familiar to the players.
Depending on the ages, this collection could include ice,
warm cereal, dry toast, polished tiles, aluminum foil,
tissue, satin, velvet, and so on. Blindfold the child; then
take the first two fingers on either hand and glide them
across the surface of the objects one by one. Ask the
child to describe how each "thing" feels, using any words
that occur to him. (This is important: it helps the child
learn to reach inside himself for personal impressions.)
Originality counts here, along with perceptivity—and
the pleasure that comes with "sensing."

"Sensitive Spools"
(A game that delights any small child, from toddler to
preschool age)

This quiet game is perfect for occupying an only child.
If you like, a few minutes' play also can lead into an opportunity for a meaningful health discussion about our most
underrated sensory organ: the human skin.

HERE'S HOW YOU PLAY: Obtain one or two empty
spools of sewing thread. Place a thin pencil or ice cream
stick inside, making a horizontal roller. Small children
love repetition, so let them gently roll the spools up or
down their bare arms. Older tots might be encouraged
to hum as they roll, to discover the curious resonance of
"sounding."

After several minutes of quiet play, seat the child comfortably. Explain in simple terms how our skin performs other "magic" besides the sensations of feeling: it "breathes"; it acts like a blanket, protecting us against cold winds. When weather is warm, our skin perspires away moisture to cool us. While our skin appears soft, it is really thick. Deep layers protect us against germs and bacteria all around in the open air.

When the skin breaks, this protection is lost. Then we must kill germs until our skin has time to heal itself by growing back together. (This learning experience is doubly effective, educators say, because it backs up instruction with a game that demonstrates function.) Our "game" can conclude with a brief discussion of the importance of soap and water for cleaning our "feeling" friend, and perhaps actual props to show how to keep this sensory arm clean, hygienic, and "happy."

"Sunlight and Shadow"
(This little game is a big hit with toddlers, who like both the repetition and the grown-up attention)

HERE'S HOW YOU PLAY: Seat the toddler comfortably outdoors or before an open window. Position the child so a single arm's gesture places the palm of the hand in either sunshine or shade. Gently taking the child's elbow, now place his hand so as to let him experience the warmth of the sun, perhaps saying, "Sunlight!" Then move the hand into the shade. You can blow on the child's palm to nonverbally demonstrate the sensation of cool. (Older tots can be asked to close their eyes during this, if they are good at following directions.) Then say, "Shadow!" Continue thus, alternating hand movements for several minutes. Then let the toddler identify whether the hand is in sunlight or in shadow.

When the game is played with an older toddler, the child is asked after several minutes to guess whether the hand is in sun or shade. (This sensory play helps to advance a child's perceptive awareness.)

"The Rain Game"
(A good natural sport for all ages)

One of the joys of childhood is the wonder of raindrops. Physicians now agree that, appropriately dressed, healthy children are not harmed by exposure to gentle rain. Actually, this can reinforce the sensory joy of youth more than many other carefree childhood experiences.

HERE'S HOW YOU PLAY: Garb all "players" in galoshes and rain hats or umbrellas: impulsive splashing is part of the sensory fun. Ask participants to rain-stroll for ten minutes, enjoying environmental experiences; they are to observe what has been changed or altered by wet weather.

The game is to feel and identify these as factors that would be unlikely or impossible on a sunny day (i.e., feeling raindrops on cheeks, walking through puddles, the sound of rain on slicker or umbrella, etc.). Urge players to particularly notice the way plants and wildlife react to rain: how flowers protect themselves. Where the birds have gone.

At the end of the rain walk, the group returns for hot chocolate, cookies, and—for those willing to share it—a recitation of their discoveries in nature's dew-swept fairyland.

"Secret Instincts"
(A perceptive learning experience for all ages)

Top psychophysical scientists say we evolve faster when

we rely on our instincts as well as our intellect. This game teaches a child to respect his intuitive know-how—and thus grow in self-esteem. For this game you'll need a family pet, preferably a cat or dog; with school-age youngsters, an illustrated book about the Old West helps with the second part of our game.

HERE'S HOW YOU PLAY: Let players spend several minutes in quiet play with their pet, smoothing and stroking its fur. Then encourage their discussing those instincts that help the pet lead a better life: stretching after naps, wagging tail or meowing to signal pleasure. Ask for examples that illustrate ways the pet used its instincts in recent weeks.

Then talk about instincts your youngsters can number in their own selves: hunger, sleepiness, pulling hand away from fire, toilet signals, tiredness. Discuss these (the way pain is a signal that something is wrong; the way we get satiety signals to stop eating; the way policemen and hunters learn to "sense" when something is threatening them). Discuss the way learning to "listen" for body alerts can develop more perceptive body sense.

Help develop the perceptivity IQ of older youngsters with a few illustrations of the Old West, particularly Indians and trail scouts. Discuss the way expert trackers used their powers of observation to track dangerous animals or runaway criminals.

Older youngsters might welcome an opportunity to divide into Indian scouting parties. If there are woodsy areas nearby, so much the better—one team can blaze a trail for others to track. If your terrain is not appropriate, let players use their imagination from here on out: a creative child benefits as much from illusion as from reality, often more so.

"Sand in Your Toes"

(A body awareness experiment good from toddler to early school age)

Remember how you used to enjoy "this little piggy goes to market"? It brought a natural delight in your own special body parts. Return to this innocent pleasure with the following version of this old favorite. If sand is hard to come by (or the game is played in winter), soap bubbles can be used instead of sand grains.

HERE'S HOW YOU PLAY: Cover both of the child's feet with sand (or bubbles). Ask the child, eyes closed, to wiggle the toes on the right foot. (Make sure sand is between all toes.) Then ask the child to try to wiggle toes one at a time—then each foot separately. Have him or her practice this with eyes open, then eyes closed. Now, eyes still closed, ask the child to guess which toe you are touching, as you pull each "piggy."

After guessing all the toes, take a washcloth to clean sand from between the toes. The idea is to encourage the child to "sense" feeling between each toe as it is cleaned. Suggest to your youngster that he will enjoy his body more if he practices "stretching and wiggling" toes at random times during the day. You might mention it is only in this part of the world where tasks are confined exclusively to the hands. On tropical isles, children use their toes to pick berries, to help climb trees. In Mexico, shoe workers use their feet to thread thongs of leather for sewing. In England, there is a woman who, graciously and without fuss, serves afternoon tea with her feet (she is armless). Another young man, a paraplegic, learned to paint beautiful pictures, holding a brush between his teeth. (Scientists say the multipurpose use of extremities can etch new pathways in the sensory nervous system and build brain power.)

"The Sound Game"
(From three to twelve years; schoolchildren can play with
pad and pencil)
This sensory experience alerts children to a perceptive
ability often overlooked in big cities: the ability to identify
sounds.

HERE'S HOW YOU PLAY: Ask players to lie back on
pillows on the floor (or outdoors, if convenient). Keep
eyes closed and take some moments to come to quiet.
Then ask each player to devote attention to listening
to special sounds: identify all that are familiar. (Ask
older children to list these after three full minutes pass.)
Sounds can include indoor murmurs: refrigerator hum,
faucet dripping, clock ticking. The idea is to build
awareness—and listening sensitivity. (If you like, the
game now can have a "winner"—the player who lists
the most sounds during the three-minute period.)

Creatively advanced children will benefit from part
two: furnish crayons or paints, prior to another three-
minute listening period. Ask players to select a single
sound, then illustrate how it "looks" to them in colors
and shapes. The most imaginative description "wins."
All should be individually commended on their keen
hearing and ability to "listen" quietly and detect.

"Scents and Nonsense"
(A sensory game for youngsters from four to twelve)
Children love guessing games where jokes and surprises
are included. This game helps develop that most neglected
(or misused) sense in urban environments: the ability to appreciate aromas.

HERE'S HOW YOU PLAY: Set up plates with six or
more different herbs and aromatic objects. Include "sur-

prises," such as odorless flowers, low-scent lettuce, empty plates. Then blindfold players and ask each to identify the items by scent alone. Selections might include: wheat or rye bread, Mother's cologne, coffee, chocolate candy, spaghetti sauce, Father's cigars or pipe tobacco, blades of grass or hay, pizza, onions, etc.

If you wish to give a prize, players can get points for each aroma or food correctly guessed. The person with the most points can get a bag of aromatic candy (peppermints) or flavorful fruit (dried apricots, raisins, etc.).

"How Do You See It?"
(A quiet game for youngsters under ten,
alone or in a group)
Children relate instinctively to color and drawing. But too often we insist they reproduce according to life, rather than encouraging their untarnished perceptions. This game respects a youngster's imagination and gets him used to calling on inner resources.

HERE'S HOW YOU PLAY: Give players paper and a wide range of colored crayons or pencils. Display a plant or flower. The idea is to draw the object as each player sees it, not like a photograph. Allow five to ten minutes. Legibility does not count, but wide use of color can. Each player wins and should be individually congratulated: he has learned to reach into himself and project his own views.

"How Do You See Mommy/Daddy?"
(A quiet game, as above, but best for use
within the family)
This game is good for preschoolers. Lead off with a discussion of how Daddy or Mommy spends the day, particularly when away from home.

HERE'S HOW YOU PLAY: Rules are like those of the previous game, only the child draws exclusively on his imagination. Allow as much time as needed, and display "portraits" for appreciation when the absent parent returns.

"How Do You See Me?"
(A quiet game, similar to the preceding one)

HERE'S HOW YOU PLAY: This gives you an opportunity for telling the child about any upcoming changes in daily schedule (a new sitter, Mommy going to work, going shopping tomorrow, etc.). Then, as before, the child is permitted to do a creative rendering of how he or she sees the supervising adult. (*Caution*: Don't overreact if your portrait is less than flattering—and never poke fun at it. Preschool children, especially, are deadly serious about their artistry—and the early shoots of creativity are easily stifled.)

"Centering"
(Ages four to upper school years)

As discussed elsewhere in these pages, learning to relate to one's *hara*, or body center of gravity, helps develop body awareness. Let your children sense the joy of their bodies with the following.

HERE'S HOW YOU PLAY: Plastic hoops known as hoolahoops provide exercise for the body center—and kids love them. Try to keep the activity joyous rather than competitive: let them "twirl" to music. For extra fun, get your own hoop and join in. Your youngsters will be proud of their gleeful friend. (And this torso exercise slims the hips!)

"Round-Robin Story-Telling"
(From four years to about fourteen years)

In our electronic age, many parents have neglected to encourage the development of childhood imagination. Dr. Robert Ornstein (pioneer in left-brain/right-brain research) says that story-telling develops the perceptive side of the brain's cerebrum. The following will also be a stress-release for you, after a hectic business day. Most important, such a sharing of ideas fosters warmth and more loving parent-to-child, and mind-to-mind contacts.

HERE'S HOW YOU PLAY: Encourage all participants to sit on the floor or ground, in a circle if there are enough players. The leader begins a story, improvised on the spot. The idea is to reach a suspenseful, thrilling point, then "pass" the story abruptly to a youngster. This "player" then moves the narrative along, before passing it to another. There are two rules: each player must spin the story for a required period (three to five minutes, depending on the age of the participants). And each player should try to "pick up" the story with a surprise twist. Play until children tire of the novelty of this. Then do not "finish"—just adjourn until next time.

"The Light Bulb"
(From preschool to about twelve years)

This aikido centering game is as useful for alert youngsters as it is for adults. Older children (girls as well as boys) will love this introduction to the often publicized Oriental martial arts.

HERE'S HOW YOU PLAY: Read the aikido section in chapter 7: "Centering Exercises." Then describe the "light bulb" exercise in words your "players" will understand. (*A hint*: Use as many sensory verbs and adjectives

as possible—"warm," "burning," "glowing," etc.).
Then ask them to envision such inner strength the next
time they are on the "alert": reading a paper before
class, taking a note to the principal, paying a cashier at
the local candy store, etc.

"A Family Favorite—All Your Own"

By now you've developed a flair for adapting these sensory ideas to bring more enrichment into your child's life:
put your own creativity to work and plan special games of
your own devising.

HERE'S WHAT YOU CAN DO: Get children to help with
baking; even household chores like sweeping or dish-
washing can be fun if set to music; or devise a chantey-
type song for singing as they help wash or hang up
clothes.

Certain toys and play-aids will help: building with
blocks (or creating sand castles) stretches the imagination—
so will fantasy games with old-fashioned paper dolls. Useful
for developing right-brain spatial cognizance is the Spirograph, a kit that teaches nonlinear relationships and graphic
artistry. Jigsaw puzzles also provide right-brain stimulation.

Most important in all play: keep interruptions at a minimum, and commend your youngster's originality, regardless
of the direction it takes. And try not to discourage a creative
imagination, even when it leads to telling an occasional "whop-
per." With your own perceptive example, that bundle of
"noisy impertinence" could evolve into one of the Mark
Twains and Jules Vernes of tomorrow.

CHAPTER

13

SA IN RECREATION AND SPORTS

The concern with breathing . . . is not for the purpose of improving it, but simply that one may become more and more conscious in connection with it.

CHARLES V. W. BROOKS

Recreation and sports pastimes become more relaxing (and lots more fun) when SA values are considered. In many cases, using SA to attune yourself to the here-and-now will sharpen your sports proficiency and make recreation a more rewarding stress-release.

Consider bird-watching, a recreation that exemplifies the sensory awareness/Zen approach. To enjoy stalking or lurking in wait for one of our feathered friends, one must become at-one with their natural habitat. The overactive mind should be stilled. For the avid bird-watcher, breezes and sounds are observed, the slightest rustle of color is heeded, bird calls are "sensed." For the experienced bird-watcher, the paraphernalia (binoculars, notebook, pencils, hiking boots) impels his attention to the here-and-now. When the yellow-breasted warbler or cardinal is finally sighted, all focus is concentrated on the bird and his movements. Sounds and his presence force the exclusion of past thoughts or future expectations. It may be that, in itself, such a combination of present centeredness and sensory soundings is what makes bird-watching satisfying as a stress-release.

One reason why bird-watching (like risky sports such as rock-climbing or skin-diving) is so relaxing for overtaxed executives is because the urgent need for instinctual (right-brain) perception automatically shuts down (left-brain) mental turmoil. You just can't twitch around in nervous agitation when near a chirping kiskadee—he'll up and away.

Another recreation that shows sensory awareness at its best is dancing—and much can be expressed in the dance. As Havelock Ellis noted: "Dancing is the loftiest, the most beautiful, the most moving of the arts, because . . . it is life itself." You can ease tensions by dancing, you can relieve the sense of loss—in addition to expressing joy and imaginative yearning. The next time you go dancing, you'll get more out of the experience if you endeavor to close down your thinking mind and let your body (and the music) take over. If it is difficult to silence your thoughts, try "sensing." Note the texture of your partner's suit or dress, his or her cologne. If you're a woman, run your hand over the rough stubble of hair at the back of your partner's neck (he'll love your touch). All the while, let the music move into your body, not merely stay in your ears. Let your body speak with it. Feel the music moving down your arms and out your fingers, in addition to the vitality it brings your legs and hips.

Handicrafts as SA Here-and-Now

If working with your hands is your favorite recreation (knitting, carpentry, etc.), you'll get more out of your hobby when you attend to the sensory aspects. For example:

When knitting: Sense the rough warmth of the yarn, letting it nestle around your fingers; unwrap it from time to time to renew the tactile feeling. Take additional time to note the colors of the yarn, the singular scent of it; "sense" the cool metal of your needles. If your mind dances back to disturbing thoughts (during stressful or overworked days), use the sharp point of the needle to return your awareness.

When woodworking: Let your fingers do your thinking. Glide your palms (as well as your fingers) occasionally over unvarnished surfaces, polished wood, beveled edges. Take time to occasionally "sense" the vitality of tools, enjoy the weight of them in your hands, the relationship they have with your fingers. Feel their icy power, their unique construction. Learn to move with your tools, developing a oneness, rather than considering them as dispensible, inanimate trivia. If you have electric equipment, accustom yourself to the soundings—they can serve as (right-brain) meditative tattoos when you are troubled, restoring you when you are depressed.

Sports as a Re-Creating

Left-brain/right-brain research has shown that physical exertion (where the total body is involved) is mainly a right-brain activity. Most sports, therefore, provide hemispheric integration—in addition to the benefits of fitness as such. SA concepts can be used to bring added enrichment from your favorite sport, boost your left-brain/right-brain integration for playing it—and even enhance your ability for it.

Here's what I mean: consider your sports activity as a re-creating (using Webster's definition of "creating," or "investing with a new form"). That is, when you tense up during a game (and anybody can), just direct your attention to the gear you use for play. If you are a golfer, and are driving a long shot, try to "sense" the weight of the golf ball in your hand as you place it on the tee; enjoy the texture, the size. Feel the rough warmth of the club against the palm of your driving arm. "Sense" your golf glove; use your foot to particularize the feel of your golf shoe as you move your feet into place, readying for the drive. Invest each piece of your playing accouterments with a sensory life and new vitality.

The idea is to suspend those (left-brain) mental dialogues that would hold you back and keep you anxious and tense. You're playing outdoors, so briefly "sense" the terrain, the rolling greenway. Attend to the breeze playing across the branches of trees bordering the greenway, shrubs decorating it. Feel the cool breezes on your cheeks, against your cap or your hair. Sense the sun on you, any dew on the grass. As your caddy hands you a club, let sensory awareness heighten your receiving it (although no word will be spoken, and he will never know where your mind rests).

And in golf or any other sport, quiet all thoughts about instructions once you are playing. Let your body take the lead and your mind follow. You can trust your body—and once you relax and do this, you'll play a better game.

This "sensing" approach works for team sports also. In softball or soccer, avoid making (left-brain) critical comparisons between one play and another, one player and another. When the ball is in play, focus total attention on it. Study the seams on it as it moves. Watch the patterns it makes. If you start to tense up during a game, direct your attention to your playing gear. Even "sensing" your own perspiration (as a vital, joyous sign of health) can keep you from letting (left-brain) self-doubts get the best of your natural ability.

Yoga Tennis, Inner Tennis—and "Sensing"

Anybody can play a perfect game of tennis; the best strokes are still inside you. Don't try—let it happen. These are the suggestions of Tim Gallwey, whose concept of *inner tennis* has captivated thousands of fans for his North American television program. Similar to those turbaned gurus who teach the new breed of "yoga tennis," Gallwey is (unawares) talking SA and the concept of left-brain/right-brain integrations. All roads lead to the perceptive mind; as Gallwey suggests those who learn tennis should learn it as a totality—rather than piece by piece, rule by rule. (Danish tennis star Torben Ulrich agrees. Look at the court as a mandala for meditation, he recommends. There is no opponent—only the tennis ball.) Learn total tennis by suspending your ego, Gallwey adds. Don't make judgments on how you are playing, just continue. "Ninety percent of the bad things students do are intentional corrections of something else they are doing." Let the body experiment and bypass your mind. Or get preoccupied with the ball: watch the seams on it as it turns. (Torben, who has played at Wimbledon, Forest Hills, and in Asia, says each locale has its special tennis sound. "Sense" the sounds and you'll play a better game.)

All agree that after rudimentary basics, your body will naturally seek the best form if you don't let your mind get in the way. Concentration, in the Gallwey definition, is not *trying*. Look for things that will quiet the mind, these sportsmen agree. Talk to your body gently, soundlessly. Ask your wrist to snap at the top of the arc. Don't force: it will happen of itself.

It is unlikely that Gallwey (former captain of the Harvard tennis team) ever studied SA-Selver. His path to the inner tennis he preaches came by following the Guru Maharaj Ji. But Gallwey talks about what is essentially sensory awareness when he tells tennis servers not to "think" about their ability to serve. Rather, as you bring back your arm, count your breaths (one, two; one, two) and serve. Focus body awareness on the ball or the court, not on any internal verbalizing about good shot, bad shot.

Should the learner's mind communicate to the body? If

need be, says Gallwey, but do this in the body's language, not the use of words, spoken or thought. The native language of the body is sight and feel. At the outset of learning, it is mostly sight that will help. So don't let your instructor just tell you what he means—ask him to show you. (And attend with your senses, and your eyes especially, rather than making critical observations.) Before verbal instructions can be understood by the body, they have to be translated.

I've discussed the Gallwey method with leading tennis players (some of international caliber). Many shrug it aside, claiming they do these things automatically.

The operative word, of course, is "automatically," and most top players appear in unwitting agreement with Gallwey and exponents of the new yoga tennis. The difference is that the players I spoke with already had acquired confidence, suspending their (left-brain) analytic mind for the joy of playing. It is the unsure player and the beginner who will benefit most from "sensing"—and concentrating on the here-and-now of game implements.

Archery, Zen—and a German Named Herrigel

When tennis gurus advise that the way to master the game is to remain mindless, attending to the ball (or the sound of your racquet), they follow in the footsteps of a *grandpère* of this nuptial joining of Western sports and Eastern spiritual disciplines. He was a philosophy professor, German-born Eugen Herrigel.

Decades ago, Herrigel studied archery in Japan under a Zen master who taught that the effortless way was the masterful way. It took Herrigel a year just to learn to "draw the bow spiritually." Another five years passed (so he says) before he could strike the bull's-eye "without aiming at it." As the alert reader has doubtless surmised, all this comes full circle to an underlying theme of SA-Selver: the goal is to have no goal.

Or that Zen maxim I mentioned earlier, "Let the mind abide nowhere."

How can you use SA to improve your proficiency at your own sport or game, whatever it is? Release your pent-up ability by readying your shot with a quiet mind, opening up your senses. Then (as you draw, aim, kick, or serve) focus your attention on your breathing.

CHAPTER
14

SA AND YOUR LOVER

Charlotte Selver was talking to me. "Our work helps you in dancing, in singing . . ."

"In sex?" I asked.

Her clear green eyes twinkled, then she looked down, nodded, then added quietly: "But we cannot say that. It would . . ." (She pushed downward with her palm.)

"Downgrade the 'work?' "

She nodded.

PERSONAL RECOLLECTIONS

Like a dancing, golden-rimmed song of your best self, love turns your day-to-day life into a ballad of sensory beauty. You feel tuned into the warmth of life, and your body (and your senses) becomes more vital and responsive.

When you're falling in love especially, life's sensations take on a heady impact, more fulfilling and important, as your sensory being comes more alive. Your skin tingles with happiness, the chirping of birds was never more cheering, the fragrance and colors of flowers were never sweeter nor more exciting. People and sounds that might have been annoying in the past now seem charming or quaint.

The blissful changes that falling in love can bring are more than emotional. Some scientists claim falling in love actually speeds up the metabolism. You've opened up more of your physical being, so sensory channels become alert. Often this sensory effect builds, orchestrates, and helps along the unlikely process of two persons glowing and growing together as one.

Another wise definition of romantic love is the "willing suspension of disbelief"; for love, at its romantic and most fulfilling, is a right-brain experience. You sit for hours, dreamily meditating about vague fantasies and present beauties. Mindless passion is right-brained; doubts about love are one's rational (left-brain) self. Physical affection is right-brained; skepticism is left-brained. Belief and trust are right-brained; so are satisfying moments of sexual encounter.

Lovers practice sensory awareness without knowing it, particularly in the early romantic stages. One of the first pleasures that lovers enjoy is finding excuses to touch each other— hands, hair, sitting closely. In itself this lowers the walls of rational (left-brain) resistance. Falling in love has been described as jumping off a precipice—if you stop to think about it, you don't do it.

Shared sensory experiences, such as sensory awareness or Psychosound (described later in this chapter) will make a relationship more meaningful. When love becomes habit, it is exciting to add a soupçon of sensory fun for spice and savor. This also can return romance to any longtime relationship and put sparkle into the routine of marriage. And last but never least, sexual intercourse is more satisfying when it is sensually imaginative.

Seventeen Ways to Use Sensory Methods for Sexual Enrichment

In addition to keeping love young and romantic, the following will help you deepen your relationship and enjoy life more. Shared sensory experiences speed up the growth of a love, as a couple becomes one being, with the dignity and beauty of (as one poet described) "a wonderful, two-headed horse."

Here's what you can enjoy:

1. *Dancing as sensory experience.* Suspend all thinking as you dance. Place full awareness on body parts, and let your limbs flow with the music.

2. *Cooking together.* Share scents, different feels of various foods. (This is a wonderful prelude to the methods that follow.)

3. *Feeding each other.* Oranges, raisins, grapes, tomatoes, cucumbers—the more succulent the foods you select, the more sensual can be this experience.

4. *Walking barefoot together.* In a garden, in sand or on poolside cement or just on a thickly tufted rug, this can restore a youthful exuberance to any relationship.

5. *Please touch.* Letting your bodies mingle as one can do wonders at restoring equanimity after a disagreement: knees touching, hand holding, even casual contact when the public eye looks—but only lovers see and know.

6. *Musical back rub.* This is fun for both of you, particularly after a stressful workday. Choose a rousing march song or upbeat show tune as musical background.

7. *Slapping as stimulant.* This is one of Selver's favorites: on head, neck, shoulders. Slap briskly to stimulate circulation, warmth, and a feeling of life.

8. *Foot massage.* Because adults keep feet shod and protected, a mutual foot massage becomes a giving and sensual

experience. Further, there are beliefs in acupuncture-related foot-zone therapy—stimulating foot parts will revitalize aging body organs.

9. *The eucalyptus bath.* A scented, shared bath is a beautiful experience. Garnish it with bubbles, if you like; or try some of the bath products that change the color of the water to azure or turquoise.

10. *Body massage.* A shared massage becomes even more sensory with some of the agreeably scented skin creams that are available. It also leads naturally to the following:

11. *Discovering new erogenous zones.* Body sensual spots vary, as do inhibitions (or lack of them). Most important is working out an intimate relationship that respects each other's feelings—and lets you discover new excitements in an ever-changing, vital love partnership.

12. *The bower bed.* It is a lyrical gesture to make love on a bed scented with natural petals or greenery. In addition to eucalyptus, try the green shrubbery called Japanese Pittis-sporum. When in season, magnolia blossoms add a heady touch.

13. *Hair care.* It can be glorious to share hair care, him shampooing her hair, her brushing his and massaging his scalp.

14. *Meditating together.* Meditation is more fun in a group, even a twosome. Set an alarm clock, sit tailor-fashion on the floor, if you like, and enjoy this soothing path to enlightenment—together.

15. *"Sensing" together.* Hands joined, you'll deepen your relationship in a park or the countryside by silently and physically reveling in body awareness. Do this: take two minutes each to sense the feeling in your knees, calves, ankles, feet, arches, then (if possible) each toe separately.

16. Hara-*warming.* This is guaranteed to smooth over quarrels: wearing a bikini and low trunks, the two of you will reach new heights by "sensing" in the sunshine, warmth touching below the navel area directly. When holding hands,

this brings a new oneness to the relationship. (*Note:* It is important here for the sun to be in *direct* contact with the *hara*, or lower abdomen.) After ten or fifteen minutes, "sensing" each other's *haras* is a serenely wonderful invitation to lovemaking.

17. *Your own sensory gamesmanship.* Shared preferences can dictate new sensory directions: silently sharing concerts (live or recorded); playing musical instruments together; even wearing similar colors or unisex fashions brings its own sensory camaraderie. For extra fun: get his-and-her Japanese wraps for lounging—an easy reminder that the two of you are growing as one (even in your spare moments).

The foregoing sensory enrichments, at their best, can serve as sexual foreplay (or a sexual denouement). Whatever the recipe for sensual lovemaking that you and your sexual partner concoct together, don't be shy about touching each other's body. Direct his or her hands and lips to those spots on your physical self that long to be caressed: lower back, buttocks, earlobes, the nape of the neck, anus, the tips of the breasts. Like enjoined love offerings, your two bodies are more fulfilled when intermingling comes naturally, without forethought or predictability. What I am saying is, don't continue your rational sensory planning in bed—just let it all happen.

For there is nothing shameful between two adults who love each other. As the Bible suggests:

My spikenard sendeth forth the smell thereof. A bundle of myrrh is my well-beloved unto me; he shall lie all night betwixt my breasts . . . My beloved put in his hand by the hole of the door, and my bowels were moved for him. I rose up to open to my beloved; and my hands dropped with myrrh, and my fingers with sweet-smelling myrrh, upon the handles of the lock . . . I am my beloved's,

*and my beloved is mine: he feedeth among the lilies
. . . Behold thou art fair, my beloved, yea, pleasant: also our bed is green. The beams of our house
are cedar, and our rafters of fir. Set me as a seal
upon thine heart, as a seal upon thine arm; for love
is strong as death.*

Psychosound—A Sensory Romp for Lovers

When love is going well, you and your lover can increase
your delight in each other with sensory games.

Psychosound is a sensory method that is related to Bioenergetics, where breathing exercises restore natural energy
flows. In Psychosound, primal play (as animal frolics) adds an
element of fun. After such sensory games, a marvelous feeling
of well-being seems to flow throughout the body; in itself this
can be a prelude to shared intimacies and the most joyous lovemaking.

Psychosound was developed by a former Viennese singing
coach, Susanna Jutasi, who founded the Center for Natural
Voice Development in New York City. She claims anybody
can use his voice to restore confidence and calm. Every normal
baby breathes beautifully. We lose this harmonious breathing
flow as we grow older, because stress and polluted air force us
to become shallow breathers. (Shallow breathing patterns
bring on anxiety and neurosis, according to Reichean psychotherapists.)

The following Psychosound exercise game has just two
requirements: you must be shoeless on a comfortable rug.
And, finally, don't think of what you want to do, just relax
and be. Let your body take the lead and let your mind follow.

HERE'S WHAT YOU DO: (The first two movements are
keyed as warm-up exercises.)

1. Stand relaxed, hanging your head. Then turn it around in a slow circle to loosen the neck muscles (two turns in each direction).

2. Twist the torso from side to side while swinging your arms. (This relaxes chest tensions.)

3. Now say ha-ha-ha on a single note. (Continue for one minute.)

4. Say ha-ha-ha on a slightly raised note. (One minute.)

5. Say ha-ha-ha on a still higher note. (One minute.)

6. Swing your head and body, saying ha-ha-ha on any note.

7. Make facial grimaces, now, and let any sound flow from you. (Really contort facial muscles as in facial isometrics exercises.)

8. Down on the floor, pretend you're any animal and emit any sounds that flow naturally.

9. Romp and roll around, animal-like, as you let primal sounds flow.

10. Now hold each other's hands, as you form a tiny, intimate circle. Then, eyes closed, emit whatever primal sounds come forth. Then continue romping on the floor if you like. The antic fun of this final exercise is a natural inducement to sexual by-play and lovemaking.

Even an early relationship that has not evolved into physical intimacy will benefit from this kind of primal play. As a sensory memory, it can fan the spark of romantic attraction into the glorious fires of love and passion. (Says Jutasi: "Sound waves bring into motion the inner life.") The mutual sense of well-being you both will enjoy also seems to induce an element of tenderness into the relationship, even in the early stages.

Celebrate Yourself Exercise No. 10: An Imagery Game for You and Your Lover

This sensory imagery experiment is an adaptation of "The Wise Thing in the Cave," a technique used in psychosynthesis. It is fun for two to play together, and it will tell you much about your lover's inner self—and new insights about yourself.

HERE'S WHAT YOU DO: When you are both relaxed and in a good mood (over cocktails, perhaps), ask your lover to play this little fantasy game. Tell him or her to imagine there is a wise thing waiting in a cave. This is the wisest creature in the world, and your lover has the privilege of visiting it to ask a single question.

Without further preparation, ask your lover to describe his journey aloud. There are only three rules: (1) There should be obstacles (rocks, trees, turbulent seas, etc.) he must overcome en route; (2) He must use many colors and sensory sensations in his description; (3) The cave can be at the bottom of the sea or high in the mountains. But once your lover is "inside" it, he must let whatever wants to appear or happen, happen. (Notes one expert, we have all sorts of material within us that we usually ignore.)

Whether the "wise thing" is a man, woman, or neuter is up to your lover. What counts is to take several minutes to describe the journey, using as many colors, sounds, feelings, and mood adjectives as possible. Then when your lover reaches the wise thing, have him or her ask a question. Then you say quickly, "What does the wise thing answer you?"

Take turns commenting on the first fantasy. Then repeat the experiment, giving your own description of a journey to the thing, and what happens. Remember, this experiment is most revealing when sensory impressions are included in the narration: cool winds, sun hues, wetness, the touch of twigs, leaves.

One further note: don't be reluctant to disclose your innermost thoughts to your loved one. Candor and trust help two persons construct a shared understanding of other things and situations. Between lovers, this game will not likely be a critical, abrasive encounter: when love is true, it is also kind. And the more giving of yourself you are in the game of love, the more you deepen your own ability to enjoy love's delicious fruits.

When Love Goes Wrong—Sensory Awareness Helps

Shakespeare said that "love is a spirit all compact of fire." Love can bring jealousy, and the purple demon usually turns your emotions into a churning bundle of self-destructive confusion.

The following sensory exercise can ease the pangs of love, including the fevers of jealousy or anger. (It helps, jealousy experts suggest, to recognize your turmoil as resulting from plain, old-fashioned jealousy. Strangely, this lessens the confusion, perhaps due to what California psychologists term the "Rumpelstiltskin effect"—or, give it a name and it may disappear.)

This exercise requires just a few minutes, and the presence of a friendly dog or cat. The pet used can be yours or a friend's, but it should be trim and docile enough so you can feel its heartbeat. (Do this exercise at home, alone.)

HERE'S WHAT YOU DO: When you are emotionally disturbed, get your pet to lounge alongside you, the two of you sitting relaxed and comfortable. (Sit in sunshine, if possible; this adds to the physicality of the experience and quiets the troubled mind.)

Place your hand on the pet's back or underbelly; start to gently rub, smoothly, rhythmically. As you move your hand back and forth, empty your mind of all thoughts, including observations about this experience. Let the stroking establish its own energy. Feel this pulsating through your fingers. Feel it in your palm. Feel it flowing up through your hands, up your arms.

Close your eyes. Now imagine your center palm can "see" your pet's fur. Stop stroking, resting your hand lightly on the fur. Try to sense the fibers without moving your hand. (How does your palm feel? Does the fur feel warm? Let this warmth move through your hand and up through your arm.)

Now seek out the pet's heartbeat through the fur. Let its vibration enter your body. Breathe low in your abdomen, steadying yourself as life flows into life. If you like, count to yourself as you breathe: one, two, one, two. Spend at least four minutes sensing your little friend's being and its heartbeat. Feel yourself warmed and emotionally revitalized by this loving, giving vitality.

How Sensory Exercise Can Help You Over the Loss of a Love

Loss of a love strikes a mortal blow. At such times, you can't think clearly and the hours drag by; more than sensory distraction is needed to quiet the agonized mind. When this searing emotional turmoil occurs, you can use left-brain/right-brain interplay for *thought-stopping*. The more often the following power chant is practiced, the faster it works. Soon the thought of the words alone will silence disagreeable mental images and accusations. (*Note:* The chant contains power words that must not be substituted; it is patterned after a Carlos Castaneda concept.)

HERE'S WHAT YOU DO: Imagine a tabletop, covered with a dark blue tablecloth. Everything specific in your life can be spread on this tabletop: your lover or spouse, your children, other relatives, your job, boss, friends, parents, co-workers. Everything that can be given a name or common noun will fit on this tabletop. We shall call the tabletop the *tonal*. For purposes of this exercise, identify your unfaithful love as the mainstay of your problem. (The exercise can also be used for other problems; a disobedient child, a jealous co-worker, an unjust boss, etc.)

Outside the rim of the tabletop are those mysterious powers and forces you now have access to use; all you need is to try. Call this outer, formless area the *nagual* (pronounced "na-wohl").

In proposing the concept of the *tonal* and the *nagual*, Carlos Castaneda does not use the term "left brain" and "right brain." An alert reader will grasp the similarity. You can put this to work for you, using it to quiet your internal agonizing. (One rule: if you use this exercise to ease you past the loss of a love, it works best if you say to yourself that the loved one is dead and shall never return. This must be final, and a foregone conclusion; repeat it often and whenever his or her name comes to your mind. Then continue the exercise.)

Envision the tabletop, or *tonal*, as your brain's left hemisphere. Whatever person, place, or thing is bothering you is atop this, sprawled, growing, and ready to topple over the *tonal*. If your love is "dead," imagine the dead form of your loved one, lifeless and out of your life forever.

For support in this, in your mind's eye, reach for the

power of the right-brain *nagual*—formless, unstructured, but strong and ready to be summoned. Think of
it in this case as a friendly genie, powerful and ready to
do your bidding. The *nagual* is a mysterious force and
can be put to work for you.

When hurtful thoughts begin, imagine that your *tonal*
(tabletop) begins to wobble; imagine yourself "reaching" for your *nagual*. Firmly press this gigantic shape
under the imaginary tabletop, steadying and firming it.
As you envision this action, say to yourself, purposefully:
"Use the *nagual* to prop up the *tonal*."

Repeat this several times, with military insistence, until it becomes an imperative command. Say it now: *Use
the nagual to prop up the tonal.*

This is a power phrase. When you get accustomed to
using it, the mind expansion exercise works even better with
this: envision your *nagual* as a red-brown mass, perhaps semi-
transparent. Soon, just replaying the power phrase serves as a
thought-stopping technique. This is a powerful exercise. Practiced correctly, it can get the most emotional person past the
first few days after loss of a love; it lets you function nor-
mally, with a minimal amount of emotional stress. As a
thought-stopping salve, it lets your raw emotions have valuable time to heal naturally. As you use this, whenever the
name of your loved one appears in your mind, say to yourself
"He (or she) is now dead." Then force your thoughts to your
environment, or the here-and-now task at hand.

I used this exercise with astounding success to heal emotional hurts over the Christmas holidays, during the preparation of this book. Under ego-deflating circumstances, my
fiancé and I decided to stop seeing each other. It was Christmas, not a time for me to remain alone with just my thoughts.
This occurred during my first Christmas in Bermuda; I was
in a foreign land, for me, without family or friends. To make

matters worse, I had sent my daughter to New York for a holiday visit with her father and stepmother.

This *nagual-tonal* power phrase got me through the bleakest of holidays, with a minimum of anger and internal dialogue. Best of all, when the man in my life and I were reunited (at New Year's), he said it was all the sweeter because I had no recriminations and showed no anger or hurt feelings. This sensory *thought-stopping* technique had so succeeded in silencing all the questions and self-doubts ("How could he do this?" or "Why did this happen to me?"). I had remained emotionally open, warm, and ready for love—instead of becoming emotionally bruised and coldly alienated from it.

Love (and its cousin, hate) can be the most powerful of emotional destroyers. For emotionally charged persons, it can be self-consuming and prematurely aging. When this sensory exercise works for you—and it will if you need it—you will feel a sense of awe, perhaps be even a bit fearful, at your own untapped mind power. Castaneda tells us that when a warrior (one who bids for mind power) accepts the frightening nature of knowledge, he cancels out its awesomeness.

In itself, knowing you can call upon your *nagual*, as a *thought-stopping* technique to help when you need it most, brings serenity. Once you know beyond a doubt that you can use sensory power to go inside yourself for sustenance, it becomes an uplifting feeling. As Albert Einstein said, "The most beautiful experience we can have is the mysterious."

And now that you soon will finish the main part of this book, I'd like to remind you of a promise I made earlier. In the Foreword, I promised that "sensing" would change your life, as it has mine. The big difference comes when you begin practicing what you have acquired in these pages. Sensory awareness information isn't knowledge until it is used.

Already, in quiet ways, you have started growing into a more assured, more interesting person. (As George Bernard

Shaw once told a friend, "There are no endings in life, only unrecognized beginnings.") For now, I envy you a bit for the new joy that tomorrow has in store. And the wondrous thing you will discover is that (like a serenely hidden but radiant beam of light) it was waiting inside you, all the time.

CHAPTER
15

SA AND SPECIAL PROBLEMS

[If there are problems in life, it helps if we remember that] we are constantly in connection with something, and therefore are never alone, never isolated.

CHARLOTTE SELVER

It has been said that space age problems require space age solutions. Because sensory awareness works in deep and persistent ways to open up hidden needs (and it shores up human individuality against civilization's tendency to coerce people into fixed behaviors), SA has a unique application for some of today's problems. I'll mention a few of these in this chapter and describe how "sensing" can bring salutary benefits. Again let me mention that like the Zen Buddhism with which it fits so congenially, SA-Selver works its most sweeping changes when it is pursued for its *own* sake. (As Charlotte Selver says in SA workshops: "Don't expect anything: just see what happens.")

Scientists have shown TM and other right-brain activities can be therapeutic: they offset the effects of stress and calm troubled minds. It is my belief that, because it works on the brain in similar ways, sensory awareness practice can prove a good backup to clinical therapy. Indeed, medical experts have found "sensing" can aid patients in turning around *emotionally related* bad habits.

SA—for Dieters

That's right, SA practice can help with our culture's most health-disturbing illness: overweight. For dieters, SA builds much-needed self-esteem. And by shoring up body awareness and a sense of self, it gives persons with chronic compulsions—like the compulsion to overeat—a clearer idea about who they really are (and what it is that makes them want to overeat). Often, ovcreating relates to body-image problems, and the new self-honesty that SA practice brings will pay dieting dividends.

It remained for two women psychologists studying an overweight disorder called "anorexia nervosa" to see this hitherto unrecognized use of SA training. Anorexia nervosa is one of the most challenging overweight problems, because it combines a physical disorder with deep-seated behavior problems. Victims fall into two groups: those who literally starve themselves, and those who get in the habit of going on eating binges, regularly followed by self-induced vomiting or other purging—all to maintain a trim figure at any cost.

Psychologists Marlene Boskind-Lodahl and Joyce Sirlin of Ithaca, New York, noted: "The emaciated anorexic, denying both her hunger and her real physical proportions, has such a distorted self-image that she tries to shed plumpness that isn't there . . . she may even **die of** starvation." Their anorexic patients, they found, were generally women—and they were women with a low opinion of themselves as persons. This worked against building up the willpower needed for normal dieting. Yet, despite protestations of fatness, many of the patients were neither unattractive nor grossly fat: their frequent purgings had disturbed their digestive patterns, as well as contributing to real confusion about their appearance. As one of the psychotherapists observed, "It was as if they saw themselves in some internal fun-house mirror."

Such topsy-turvy emotional distortions obviously made therapy difficult. Some of these binge eaters had already been under psychiatric treatment for other problems, but they never revealed their wild eating/purging episodes to other clinicians. Lying and deception was a habit pattern, for the more a person binges on the sly, the more defensive he or she becomes, evading even those who would help them.

Patients that Boskind-Lodahl and Sirlin concerned themselves with had a specific form of anorexia nervosa, called bulimiarexia by the psychologists (from "bulimia" meaning "insatiable appetite"). In this disorder, a patient can eat enormous amounts of food, then attempt weight control with vomiting or laxatives. One patient was taking sixty laxatives daily. Another victim said she would sneak into her refrigerator after midnight, jam a whole pound of butter into a loaf of bread and eat the mass standing up so her sleeping husband wouldn't find out.

The psychologists concluded that much of this gorging-purging was brought on by a compelling urge to keep fashion-thin; where women patients were concerned, it coincided with a social compulsion to be pleasing to men. The female anorexics all came from affluent homes, and most had parents who set great store by beauty and success—and success, they were taught, depended largely on a girl's appearance.

In addition to sensory awareness training, group therapy and discussions were used to help the binge eater. She learned that others had this affliction, and that gorging-purging was an emotional ill that warranted professional care.

But it was sensory awareness that was responsible for

giving the more than 100 patients in the Ithaca study a re-
newed and stronger sense of identity; it helped clarify their
thinking, by improving their body images. This self-esteem
building was buttressed with assertiveness classes, and the
women patients were encouraged to find interests and activities independent of the men in their lives. (So deeply imbedded
was this core feeling of success-in-life equals success-with-men
that one patient said: "If a woman doesn't like me, we're in-
compatible. If a man doesn't—I'm worthless!")

Sensory awareness practice also helped the patients become more attuned to what incidents would trigger their
compulsive behavior. By the end of the therapy, Boskind-
Lodahl reports, all had come to view their overeating-purging
neurosis as resulting from causes and specific situations. "They
learned to stop and sift through their feelings when they felt
the urge to gorge."

Can sensory awareness help anyone with an overeating
problem? Yes; it can help you, too. Try this the next time
you've an urge to eat unnecessarily between meals: distract
yourself briefly, perhaps with whichever is your favorite Celebrate Yourself sensory exercise in this book. Then take another
look at your food craving. If your urge to eat is in response to
an emotional situation, consider an alternative way of easing
your hurt feelings over this temporary hurdle. And if you
have serious dieting problems, consider formal training in SA-
Selver. It will put you in steadier and more serene contact with
yourself than coconut creams or other palliatives. Then, once
you are in touch with your emotions, you'll better understand
why you have cravings to nibble and overeat.

SA—and Chronic Drinking

Some people begin to imbibe frequently because they're
lonely. Or they start out taking a drink to celebrate, whatever

the occasion. Or they console themselves with a drink, whatever the problem.

This leads to emotionally dependent drinking, and the person involved is routing himself into a serious drinking problem. For anyone whose chronic drinking has not yet reached the stage where one-to-one professional counseling or therapy is needed, consider the use of sensory awareness to derail a drinking compulsion.

Here's how SA can interrupt a downward emotional spiral, rational or irrational. The right-brain "sensing" activity turns off left-brain "chatter" and internal dialogues. The calm that results eases inner turbulence; whether the emotional upheaval was due to a lost love or a lost job, it's all the same in terms of impact. If you "need" a drink to quiet your thoughts (or until "your mind goes 'click'" as an alcoholic in a Tennessee Williams play described it), sensory awareness practice promotes a quiet mind.

Try the following sensory experiment next time you want a drink on impulse.

DO THIS: Focus in on any nearby humming noise (an auto or airplane engine, an air conditioner, your kitchen refrigerator, etc.). Then close your eyes and try to envision the sound waves entering your body. Let them flow as the color spectrum, perhaps, or as tones of a single color. (If the particular sound reminds you of a design or pattern, envision this.) Let this vibrating energy settle at your body center. Begin breathing deeply at this center. Feel this vibrant energy warming you, strengthening. As your inner power builds, continue breathing deeply: flatten your diaphragm as you exhale, expand it as you inhale. Continue for several minutes this way, using your lower abdomen as a bellows.

Complete this sensory experiment by standing and briefly shaking each arm and leg separately. Then busy yourself with an immediate task—your mind (and body) are no longer obsessed with hungers beyond your control.

SA—for Breaking the Smoking Habit

Body awareness, and SA especially, proves to be a super antidote for cigarette smoking. Once you discover the miracle of your sensory self, you lose interest in things that would mar or mutilate this new body song. That's why you'll seldom see cigarette smokers around advanced sensory awareness workshops. There's no deliberate anti-smoking campaign; smoking just loses its hold on the serious "senser."

If you've tried to quit smoking, and found it a problem, I suggest you consider formal sensory awareness training with a qualified instructor (see Appendix listing). In the meantime, the following sensory exercise can help.

Celebrate Yourself Exercise No. 11: A Sensory Walking Meditation for Overcoming Bad Habits

SA offers a special avenue of support if you've embarked on the road to self-improvement. It lets the person with bad habits find renewal and meaning in the exultation: It's great to be alive. Enjoy the following anytime you're trying to rid yourself of a compulsive urge—for a cigarette, to master drinking problems, or to change your overeating behavior. In short, whenever you're attempting to rid yourself of a bad habit, this sensory awareness "walk" makes a game out of self-discipline. (For bonus benefit for dieters, especially, practice this at the exact same hour daily, perhaps between 3 and 4 P.M., when midafternoon hunger pangs have been found to be most troublesome.)

HERE'S WHAT TO DO: Preparation for this chanting meditation is easy. Just select a familiar poem or a rousing song (such as "America, the Beautiful," or "God Save the Queen.") I like to use a marching tune, like "She Wore a Yellow Ribbon"; if you like, try "Onward Christian Soldiers" or "This Land Is My Land." Or perhaps you'd prefer an inspiring poem you memorized in childhood. (During an emotional crisis, I got great results with "If" by Rudyard Kipling.) If none of these appeal to you, you might like to use the lyrics to the melody you picked for our first *thought-stopping exercise*, mentioned in Part I of this book.

Whichever tune or verse you select, it should have a lilting cadence. It also should boast an upbeat message, and the words must be as familiar to you as your own name. This way you'll open up healing reinforcement that can be almost mystical in its impact. What will happen is that you'll begin to synchronize your internal body processes, coordinating breathing with heartbeat. This soothes from the inside out, for the monotonous, effortless tattoo of the chanted lyrics can restore (right-hemisphere) composure. With regular practice, just beginning your meditative "song" will hasten well-being and a smiling state.

HERE'S WHAT TO DO NEXT: Plan a walk that begins with a long, uninterrupted stretch of easy walking terrain. If you're a city resident, select a park or area that bypasses traffic lights, intersections, or other interruptions—at least for several minutes.

After a few minutes of walking, begin your sensory meditation with either your right or left foot, it doesn't matter. What counts most is that, soon after, you begin to pace your steps as you silently "repeat" the chosen tune's lyrics, using an orderly, almost drumlike regularity. Walk briskly in march step to this song or poem: without your doing anything, your breathing will adapt itself.

Repeat your meditative rhythm as often and as many times as you like. For the more often you practice this, the quicker it can restore mind/body harmony and serene control.

SA—to Ease Insomnia

The sleepless person is usually beset with turbulent thoughts. As we've seen, sensory awareness brings a quiet mind, soothing restlessness and bringing restorative sleep without the unpleasant side effects or morning-after sluggishness of sleeping pills.

Consider the following example of the way "sensing" hastens drowsiness. (It can work for you, also.) A Broadway actress of my acquaintance found the months she spent on hectic road tours with national theater companies left restlessness on her spirit, burdening her with tension-filled nights. And the more sleep she lost, the more she worried about sleep; of course, this made ready sleep even more elusive.

Then, on one tour, she was assigned a hotel room that had gently flashing lights on the ceiling, during post-midnight hours; this was curiously calming, making a silent, changing, but regular pattern in her bedroom. Within a few minutes it lulled her to deep sleep. (A left-brain/right-brain expert would explain the silent shadow effect brought a physical meditation, quieting her left-brain "static.") Today, when and if she encounters sleeping difficulty, she recalls in her mind's eye that curious, silent pattern of shade and shadow on her walls and ceiling. Then she breathes regularly and from the diaphragm. Relaxed, she drifts off to deep sleep.

I've learned to put this *remembered patterns meditation* to work as a sleep-inducer. One can deliberately insert into one's memory banks sense memories such as the reflexion of a goldfish bowl on a sunny wall, or sparkling water effects in a brook or inlet. Even filmy curtains billowing in the breeze can be used, but this is more effective when it is a combination of light and shadow, perhaps including a touch of color.

HERE'S WHAT TO DO: Select a pattern such as is mentioned above, or perhaps use a mechanical lighted sculpture with moving water beads. Do this: focus your rapt attention on the pattern as you breathe quietly. Continue for several moments; then focus attention on your abdominal breathing, and breathe in long, rolling exhalations. Return attention to the pattern or figure, now, remaining mindless; let your senses take over.

Continue meditating easily but without distraction upon the moving pattern for several minutes. Then close your eyes, and try to transfer this remembered visual impression to the dark velvet walls of your closed eyelids. Then open your eyes and again gaze at the visual meditation for several minutes more. (This entire experience should take at least four or five minutes.)

Next time sleep won't come, close your eyes and open your memory to this moving, delicate interplay of light and pattern. Eyes closed, let the remembered patterns move silently across your recollection—lulling, calming. Accompany this with body awareness attention to the lower abdominal area. (Touch your "center," if this is easier: let your gently curved palm rise and fall with your respiration.) Mental and emotional turbulence will cease. What follows will be a deep, more restorative sleep than usual.

Other sensory appeals play a role in the sleep seeker's drama: the low hum of an air conditioner; billowing curtains at an open window; satiny coverlets, scented pillows and sheets; water beds; filmy lingerie. Does your spouse or lover snore? Think about the incessant z-z-z-z as a resonant, specially designed sleep inducer. Listening to it with slowly breathing, mindless attention lets the sound vibrations seem to enter your being. This rapport increases when you quietly snuggle closer, making body contact. Relaxing body tensions and thus clearing your mind, the *sounding* will serve as an aural meditation—it can ease you to sleep like the z-z-z-z of a manmade electronic sleeping aid.

SA—to Overcome a Special Fear

Scientists have shown that daydreaming becomes a right-brain activity when you are relaxed and just let your imagination unwind itself lazily. You can learn to do this deliberately, building inner strength by making it a guided fantasy. This becomes spell-binding and even self-healing when you come to include sensory imagery in your daydream. For some, it can prove as educational as a sleep-learning recording or taped message.

The idea of using guided fantasy to help persons rid themselves of emotional hangups was the idea of a French psychiatrist, Dr. Robert Desoille. (This concept also parallels Zen Buddhist theory and is used today among leading Japanese psychiatrists as self-help therapy.) For best results, guided fantasy themes should be loosely structured, such as "A Visit to the Cave of the Wizard," or "A Visit to the Bottom of the Ocean." When a troubled person describes such an imaginary journey, just letting thoughts flow, it unblocks impeded but deeply rewarding material within the human mind. And when *sensory* phrases and words are used for the teller's description of his "journey," it becomes a more powerful assurance builder (such as "the turquoise blue ocean," "the cool winds chilled my legs," etc.).

Fantasies and daydreams can become the foundation of

serenity and bring more purposeful lives, according to an expert specializing in the use of fantasy as an emotional health tool. Dr. Jerome L. Singer claims that imaginative people find it easier to relax; a rich inner life makes one less dependent on outside events. By contrast, people with an inability to fantasize are more likely to use everyday life as outlet for bottled-up aggressions. Further risks of an undeveloped fantasy life include susceptibility to alcoholism, use of drugs, overeating, and delinquency. Use daydreaming as an instant vacation when you feel stressed or depressed.

Can you also use fantasy to rid yourself of anxiety or fear? Yes, according to German psychiatrist Dr. Albert Frankel; he calls this technique the system of *paradox intention*. The idea is that it helps to stay with an emotional pain, working your way through it and thus ridding yourself of it. This is similar to certain zazen theories: the differences is that you're overcoming an emotional ache rather than a physical one. And there's an extra ingredient—with *paradox intention* you try to "sense" your lower adbomen as you breathe during your therapeutic daydreaming.

In the following sensory experiment, what you can do is to deal with your fear or anxiety by facing up to it and weaving a meditative daydream around such an action or event. This sensory daydream can prove useful for anyone with a fear of flying, fear of heights, fear of elevators, fear of burning buildings, and so on. (Remember: whether you fantasize aloud or silently, use imaginary phrases that relate to sensory things—and then focus awareness attention on your lower abdomen as you breathe.)

HERE'S WHAT TO DO: Sit down and recognize and pinpoint exactly what makes you uneasy. Then sit quietly, breathing in long, rolling motions; remember to focus attention on your lower abdomen as it moves with respiration. Now imagine you are in a situation where you must encounter your frightening circumstance, event, or person. If you are fearful of speaking in public, imagine you must return, time and again, to a speaking platform where you must speak before hundreds in an assembled audience. No matter how uncomfortable the thought makes you, stick with it. Act out (in your mind) all possible exigencies. Eventually you'll find new strength surging through your fantasy; the endings will become more satisfying.

If you're afraid of flying, think of several good reasons why it would be to your advantage to make quick air trips (a prize trip, a professional award ceremony, visiting a new in-law). Continue to force yourself onto the plane (or platform/into stalled elevator, etc.); continue to cope with imaginary versions of your problem situation, as you breathe deeply and slowly. Practice this for at least four or five minutes, two or three times a week. Continue until the real-life prospect of your fear situation no longer makes you ill-at-ease.

Note: This sensory meditation offers extra benefits when it is practiced at the *same time daily* for several days. Deliberately concentrating one's creative mind on an unpleasant possibility—and practicing this over and over—will develop an unexpected mental power and strength, advises a world-famous Oriental psychiatrist.

SA Can Help with Headache

Headaches come more often these days, perhaps as a result of stress and urban din. One out of five persons has regularly occurring headaches. Ninety percent of these are tension or migraine headaches, according to records of a New York headache clinic. Despite myth and legend, experts find that headache pain is caused mostly by blood flow: the brain itself has no nerve endings and cannot suffer pain.

Migraines and unexplained head pain should be diagnosed by a physician. (The headache might be organic in origin.) In cases of simple tension headache, sensory awareness can help. Often tension headaches result from taut muscles: wherever muscular tension exists becomes a site for pain. Jaw clenchers get aches in their temples, habitual frowners get pains in the center forehead or hairline. For tension headaches, the following sensory experiment can relax and ease away pain. As before, don't try to figure out what is happening. Just let your (right-brain) creative forces lead the way. The experiment begins with a relaxation dynamic.

HERE'S WHAT TO DO: Eyes closed, drop open your jaws. Let cheeks and jowls relax and hang. Then tense and relax your forehead several times. Try to wiggle your ears, then relax them. Roll your head around loosely, to ease your neck. Then, with your eyes closed, have a friend ask you the following (or put this into a tape recorder for convenient playback). Think of your headache in terms of color. Does it have one or several colors? Is it a light or a dark shade, or a pattern? Where is the color deepest? Is the color moving or stationary? Now breathe evenly for several moments. How big is your headache? Consider colors, size, and tones. Is your headache pain the same now as at the start of this experiment? Now focus awareness attention on the palms of your hands. Try to "warm" them by thinking of them in bright sunlight. Envision your headache color. Is it still the same, or changing? Has it lessened?

Nine times out of ten, your headache pain will fade away. Pain is a signal, and you have said to your headache, Okay—pain signal received. Now, over and out.

SA—and Too Much Tranquility

In certain instances, perhaps you don't need calm or serenity; what's required is more get-up-and-go. As I indicated in the Foreword, in this book we are not using "serenity" in the sense of tranquility alone, but in the Oriental sense— that is, as the composure and inner pride needed as a first step to self-realization.

For some, there is no denying the fact that too much tranquility can make one lackadaisical. It can work against taking those positive actions sometimes needed to turn your life around. As one of my favorite sayings puts it: Rome was not built by a tranquilized Italian.

So when you want to work up mental push to get things moving, try the following two steps: (1) Practice any of the special Celebrate Yourself exercises (especially 1, 2, or 3) to "psych yourself up" when spirits are sluggish. (2) Then let the following left-brain/right-brain interplay spur your rational mind to activity.

HERE'S WHAT YOU DO: Lying down easily, center your breathing in your middle and upper (not lower) chest. Take firm, medium-sized breaths, not long and rolling but breaths of energetic interest. Continue this for a few moments. *Then,* using your right hand, pretend to adroitly throw an imaginary baseball against the opposite wall. Don't worry about "catching" it—concentrate on throwing. Continue this for several minutes. Then return your awareness to your upper chest and what is (by now) your speeded-up breathing. Shake your right hand briskly, as if loosening the joints. Then see if you don't feel like busying yourself with an immediate task.

(*Note:* This right-brain/left-brain exercise was designed for right-handed persons. If you are left-handed, experiment with either hand to see which seems to activate your practical mind.)

SA—and Filth, Litter, Unpleasantness

One of the two most curious side effects I found in practicing SA-Selver was this: when I first became more present for outside environmental sensations, I came to note filth and litter more than previously. In the antiquated hotel on Monhegan Island, the first thing to catch my eye when I entered my room was any area of cracked, fraying plaster or a torn or rough spot in the rug or draperies.

Could SA thus become a problem, particularly for city dwellers and those in polluted areas? Once one came to be more attuned to what is beautiful in the environment, would he become uneasy around what is not? (Since then, I've found that even a tiny hair of beauty, sensorially appreciated, will displace all less pleasing aspects of one's surroundings).

At the time, it worried me: Can "sensing" open us up to ugliness also? I asked Charlotte Selver whether one must also learn to "turn off" sensory awareness. She paused, going deep inside herself for the answer. When it came, the words were profound:

"There is too much today of this [*gesturing to the push-button on her hearing amplifier*] 'turning off' and 'turning on.' There *is* ugliness in this world—and old age. We have got to learn to embrace everything!"

I persisted. "Should I have tried to 'work through' the experience, and the ugliness [of my rundown hotel], instead of trying to distract from it, or ignore it?"

Selver nodded. "You know Buddha—and Jesus—did not shun the ugliness of this world. They overcame it."

The next time you're faced with a disagreeable sight, sound, or circumstance, don't turn away or distract yourself. As advised in Zen doctrine, stay with the "pain" and work through it. You'll uncover new depths in yourself (and perhaps an uncommon beauty elsewhere)—and this will become all the more meaningful because it is unplanned and unexpected.

SA—and Decision-Making

The most far-reaching way that sensory awareness practice will serve you is in the decision-making process. Like an overworked computer, your logical mind can become steamy with emotional problems and thoughtful confusions. "Sensing" lets your hidden desires and true feelings rise to the surface. This provides perceptivity and builds wisdom, as well as generally organizing your overview of the situation. SA practice helps you to avoid impulsive decisions and bypass changes that are not right for the person you really are.

With practice, you'll hit upon your own favorite "sensing" method to shut down turbulent (left-brain) rationality and open up perceptions and inner truths. As you'll see in the examples that follow, the main idea is to use sensory awareness either as a focus for rapt attention on your inner processes or to make you more open to environmental events. Try any of the following the next time you need to unsnarl an emotional problem or keep cool decision-making on your agenda. To clear your mind, practice at least four or five minutes or longer, relaxed, breathing naturally.

DO THIS

Walking barefoot around the garden or a rocky area, focus awareness attention on the varying textures beneath your arches, between your toes, foot to foot, and so forth.

OR

Lying in the sunshine, practice ways to relate to the surface beneath (giving up weight/holding back/

limply relaxed/in partnership and tonicity). Then just enjoy *being* (choose the day and hour when the sun mellows rather than burns).

OR

Playing a stimulating record, choose music without lyrics or any emotional association with the past. Then turn up the volume and lie comfortably, eyes closed. Open your body as well as your ears to the musical tones; this shuts down (left-brain) dialogues or the clickety-clack of your mental computers. When thought won't cease, focus attention on your breathing: one, two, one, two. Let your breathing rhythm synchronize itself to the musical flow. (Do not force this; when your body relaxes, your respiration will follow.)

OR

Gazing at goldfish, you'll find their shimmering, darting unpredictability makes for visual meditation at its most relaxed.

OR

Walking in the rain, let raindrops touch your skin, "sensing" the unique sensation of water (itself a minor sensory miracle) and warm flesh. Also take time for the childlike distraction of walking through a few puddles.

OR

Wrapping your palm around your left ear, cup it for inner sounding. Quietly hum a single note for several moments. As the sound dies away, inside your listening station, see if you sense vibrations lingering within. Repeat this inner sounding several times. Or, if you prefer, use the "om" sound to provide more sweeping body resonance. Either activity does much to revitalize right-brain/left-brain interplay.

OR

Practicing lying as relating (as Selver terms it), you can enjoy this indoors, any time of year. Put the following questions into a tape recorder for playback (or ask a neighbor to read them aloud to you). Then relax, head cushioned if you like, on floor or rug. Let your body rather than your mind take the lead, as you consider: Are you pressing your arms to your sides? Are you pressing your legs together? Is your back (or your head) pressed against the floor? Try to carefully feel out the difference between pressing and not pressing—arms, legs, head.

Spread your legs gracefully. Do your legs feel lonely or awkward when they come apart? Do they just lop sideways? (Remember, in SA-Selver there is no correct or incorrect way of doing things: it is finding *your* way that is important.) Now raise one leg, letting it gently return to the floor. How does the surface of the rug or floor feel now? How long does it take until you have fully "arrived"? Repeat with your other leg, then each arm. Then return to your legs, and practice raising the weight of each leg without leaving the floor.

Consider your neck. Raise it, then let it return to the floor. Is there stiffness of which you were unaware? Use your hands now to raise and lower your head. Now raise both arms and lower them gently. Repeat, sensing the feel of raising and lowering each separately—then compare the experience. Then use lying to become more awake in your pelvis and groin. Raise your pelvis slightly; holding it in the air, notice how this affects breathing. Lower it gingerly. Does your pelvis now relate differently to the rug or floor?

Now relax your entire body, tensing and then un-tensing each finger, arm, foot. Try to open yourself up more within for circulation and energy flow. Stretch your legs again. Do you have enough space or would you like more? (For just your arms and legs, or for your life also?)

PART

IV

ADVANCED
SA INFORMATION

CHAPTER 16

IF YOU ARE A MAN READING THIS BOOK

More than women, men need the subtleties of sensory awareness practice to restore the sensory gifts and perceptions of which civilization has robbed them. There is a desensitizing nature in our Western culture, and its macho influences still makes men embarrassed to betray sorrow, deep love, or other "unmanly" emotions. In itself, this can signal disunity between mind and body, leading to a psychopathic neurosis, or "split." This brings on further ailments, many of which can chronically endanger health: recurrent colds, ulcers, psychosomatic disorders, asthma, and even cancer.

Consider your own attitudes toward your body. While many easy exercises to test masculinity are suspect (and even use of the word "masculine" might be outdated), the following was designed by psychologists; as a key it helps you open the door to more understanding of your body awareness—or lack of it.

If somebody asked you to point to that part of your body that represents "self," where would you point?

In other words, where, in an imaginative sense, does "self" reside in you?

(Point to this area.) Psychologist Phillip Himmelstein found most men point to their heads as "self." In comparison, women point to their chests, or the heart area. Notes another psychologist, "This difference in where self is assigned is vividly congruent with the diminished importance that the body, as such, has for men in our society."

For the average woman, the body is the matrix for most major events in her life: she is encouraged from girlhood to make her appearance a central focus, and whether she pursues a career or not, the average woman feels more secure about her body boundaries than does the average man.

However, in our culture, boys are encouraged to attribute more status to mental pursuits. Only on the playing fields are they permitted to reintegrate body and mind, and even such sports activities can be curtailed first in schools when budgets are cut. There are always superstitious warnings and threats against the "evils" that result from a boy's having too much contact with his physical self. This anti-body intimidation takes its toll in faltering self-confidence. A girl can sit for hours before a mirror, studying face and form—the boy who does so is regarded as peculiar or deviant. The distortions in body awareness that result should not be surprising: Dutch psychologist Van Lennep found boys are not only less aware of their bodies than girls but this difference widens as the two sexes pass into adulthood.

What body awareness a male child receives comes under the form that psychologists term *phallic body orientation*, in itself another distortion, and one that sets up the adult man for hypertension and that scourge of big-city living: "hurry sickness." Dr. Seymour Fisher, leading researcher in body awareness attitudes, sums up these misleading male indoctrinations: legend emphasizes the notion the male body must move swiftly and easily. The male comic book hero, among other stereotypic influences, is portrayed as traversing great distances, or he gets from place to place in record time to accomplish his daredevil missions. The concept of speed in childhood toys is also part of a boy's upbringing (trains, scooters, model cars, and airplanes), more so than in those toys mostly marketed for girls (dolls, toy dishes, cutouts).

Early on, the boy child learns that anything that is not speeded-up or forceful is unmanly, or, that worst thing in some circles, a "time-waster." He is encouraged to lead a life that emphasizes goals and action. ("He's going to be a real doer!") Several authorities and pundits on the nature of sexuality (from Margaret Mead to Norman Mailer) have noted that men generally acquire their feelings of sex identification by *doing*; women identify by *being*.

Such frenzied activity works against those quiet moments that every thoughtful person needs for introspection and a sense of self. (Compare the Austrian folk saying: "Out of silence comes knowledge.")

Sensory awareness or other sensory practice permits a quietude that can serenely punctuate the hectic day, building willpower and ego strength in other avenues of life as well. When a man leaves himself open to sensory messages, it spills over into courageous inner soundings on other matters: Do I really like my life? My job? How would I change it? What's the preliminary for this? The next step?

For men, especially, the Western culture's speeded-up emphasis on action might account for the reason retirement after middle life becomes an overwhelming stresser for some. Such a priority placed on constant activity is diametrically opposite the Oriental concept of the Tao "no place"—this is an alert time of quiet "listening" to one's inner stirrings, a time when self-actualization begins. And there's another ominous result of our action-oriented emphasis, influencing the manchild's psyche: it incites an inner unrest that might explain why men's life spans remain shorter than those of women.

Despite improved health care, mortality rates for men are still sixty percent higher than they are for women in the United States. Medical surveys indicate that, if auto accidents don't get you, heart attack will. Forty percent more men than women die of heart disease, a direct result of the competitive, aggressive (masculine)behavior termed the Coronary-Prone Behavior Pattern. Other causes of death are also linked to attempts at macho behaviour, says psychologist Ingrid Waldron. One-third of the premature deaths in men are due to habits encouraged more in males than in females: recklessness with guns and cars, habitual drinking, smoking, working at hazardous jobs, and seeming to be socially fearless. (While women now smoke and drink in greater numbers, it is not encouraged as a statement of sexual worthiness. And despite increased smoking among women, notes Dr. Waldron, "As much as half of the sex differential in life expectancy from the ages of thirty-seven to eighty-seven may be due to the effects of higher rates of cigarette smoking in men.")

Recklessness and rebellious behavior are also tolerated more in boys than in girls; parents and teachers allow boys more independence and expect girls to be more obedient. Such macho conditioning comes to the forefront in death statistics from motor accidents due to driver recklessness. And while genetic influences have a hand in shorter life spans in men, scientists now suspect this is not the all-pervasive influence it was once thought. Among species that are our close relatives, the birds and mammals, female death rates are even with male death rates. Adds Dr. Waldron, it is mostly our industrialized, macho-oriented society that kills off males at younger ages. In many countries, female death rates have exceeded male death rates between ages one and forty, and in some cases at older ages as well.

Sensory awareness brings a new oneness of mind and

body that can offset all this. It also relieves another painful side effect of our cultural conditioning, and a contributor to sensory desensitization in itself: many boys learn early to equate heavy drinking with masculinity. In a so-called masculinity survey by a psychology journal, one male respondent explains: "I feel that because I don't drink as much as the other guys, that there might be some doubt if I am a 'real' man."

Out of touch with his body and urged to prove his sexuality on every front, it is a bitter irony that macho attitudes (helped by the reinforcement of chronic drinking and tissue-saturation) can lead to out-and-out alcoholism. Says the U.S. National Council on Alcohol Abuse, one recurring trait of the latent alcoholic is an insistence that he is able to drink well and to "hold" his liquor. This is the drinker who imbibes more frequently, and who orders drinks of higher proof as an act of boastfulness to his comrades.

Sensory practice can also condition a man to a change like growing older. Dr. Seymour Fisher has conducted numerous experiments proving that women are conditioned to be more adaptable to changes or modifications in their physical selves. This makes women more open and aware of their bodies and more likely to attune themselves comfortably to their body sensations. (It may be that men are as intuitive as women are credited with being, it's just that boy children are discouraged from listening to such inner messages.) This is shown by the way women change fashions and even hair color to express mood or whim. Dr. Fisher says women who alter their appearances frequently may be attempting mastery of those body events that are disturbing to them (menstruation, etc.). Such women are asserting, in essence, "I am not afraid of body change. In fact, I instigate such change in myself." For if she can bring about the changes deliberately, she feels in charge of them.

Lack of confident body awareness gives men, on the

other hand, a shyness about abrupt transformation of their appearance. This shows itself in the conservative attitude toward men's fashions, although this is easing somewhat. The fact that such body uncertainties go deep was shown in an experiment psychologists performed with young men and women of college age. Each was asked separately to stand in front of a mirror, eyes closed, in a darkened room. A lifelike mask was then slipped over the subject's head, a woman's face on the men, and a man's face placed on the women. A spotlight was briefly flashed on their heads, after they opened their eyes, and each subject was asked to tell what he saw. Psychologists found the men showed more confusion and were more upset by seeing distortions in their appearance than were the females. Concluded one researcher, weighing all the evidence: "Women are better able to cope with changes or distortions in their usual physical appearance." This carries unfortunate overtones in daily living for the man who is not in easy contact with his physical self. Men might not adapt easily to growing older, or to sickness. When entering a hospital for treatment, males have greater body anxiety than females. When a parent is chronically ill, the male children are more disturbed by persistent contact with such illness.

When body awareness conditioning overcomes the macho influences, life becomes easier for the male. Even among younger men today, with macho indoctrinations fading, there is an easier assurance about self. However, there is still much uncertainty among men about what is expected of them in today's society. In a survey of 28,000 respondents, the same psychology journal mentioned previously found most young men today want to be warm, open, and loving— but still not as much as the women wish them to be. Several respondents noted a new and confusing ambiguity. Wrote one Georgia minister: "I feel I *must* say very loudly, I'm tired of American male stereotypes. I have a beard, two biceps, a penis, *and* I'm capable of showing warmth, sharing housework, and shedding a tear. Why are so many men threatened by that combination of characteristics?"

One thing was obvious about the men in attendance at all sensory awareness workshops I've participated in: they were manly, quite physical, and apparently confident of their sexuality and of themselves. Indeed, it was my impression that these enlightened young men were attending this workshop as they partook of other humanistic studies, finding the human potential movement is more intellectually provocative as a self-improvement road than yesteryear's Dale Carnegie speech courses. I dwell on all this merely to exorcise any doubts in men readers as to whether sensory awareness is too "feminine" or "sensitive" a preoccupation. There are many styles of masculinity today, and, as Kinsey learned, heterosexuality and homosexuality are not either-or categories. No longer, if ever, can our world be divided into "sheep and goats." And as women are more liberated, they want their men to be warm, more emotionally open and more loving. And as I shall discuss shortly, sensory awareness will make a man a better lover, for reasons that are both physical and emotional.

Women's interest in the warmer, more romantic man is shown by the statistical responses to the masculinity survey I mentioned previously. More women than men said they placed priority on romantic personality traits in a man (66 percent of women compared with 48 percent of men); more women wanted their men gentle, compared with men who welcomed this attribute (86 percent compared with 64 percent); able to cry (51 percent to 40 percent); and even soft (48 percent compared with a scant 28 percent of men.)

While many men still feel it is "unmanly" to betray fears and uncertainties, particularly in front of women, today's woman would encourage this openness. It deepens mutual understanding and enhances and broadens their loving relationship. In short, women want a man who is able to express his emotions but is not a slave to them. Such easy grace in communicating how you truly feel is facilitated and enriched by sensory practice, as I shall discuss later. And in lovemaking, sensory awareness directly benefits the man-woman relationship.

Sensory Awareness Will Make You a Better Lover

What are the biggest complaints about men as lovers? He's not considerate, says one. He has orgasm too early, says another. Most agree there is not enough sexual foreplay. Yet body awareness—and sensory awareness in particular—will open up a more satisfying sexuality, for both partners (see Chapter 14: "Sensory Awareness and Your Lover"). For the man, it makes him a more considerate, more enlightened, and more sophisticated lover; in itself, this increases the responsiveness of his sexual partner. Direct physical benefits (resulting from opening up neural-sensory sensitivities) include the bringing of orgasm under more voluntary control, thus avoiding premature ejaculation. Lovemaking and coitus also are extended, when the sexual partners so desire, and there is more frequent orgasm during each sexual encounter.

And perhaps of greater significance, sensory practice will increase your pride in your body and deepen your own capacity for love. Marital counselors and sex therapists agree, the heartfelt emotional warmth and mutual consideration that emerge with true love will enrich the sexual experience. And this love-sex relationship comes full circle: when you are a more open, more warm and more human person—and adventurous in the way you go out to meet life—exuberant, rich lovemaking will be a manifestation of this new magnetism. For the man who is confident and aware of his body as self is more appealing to others—and especially desirable as a sexual partner.

Sensory Awareness Helps You Communicate How You Feel

More than in previous eras, there's much talk about getting in touch with one's true feelings. This can be difficult for some men, perhaps because men are less emotionally responsive than women (as noted by Dr. Alexander Lowen, of Bioenergetics fame). Yet self-help psychology experts claim wide benefits for such honest expression. You'll accomplish more in business when you can articulate how you feel about a project or situation; you'll improve social transactions and establish more meaningful friendships; you'll enjoy a more fulfilling emotional life. Yet, as one Manhattan executive complains: experts talk lots about getting in touch with feelings—but nobody tells how to do this.

I'll tell you how: let sensory practice accustom you to heeding your inner stirrings and respecting yourself as a unique person. Self-assertiveness comes as sure as dawn follows fading nighttime—and the ability to nimbly convey your likes and dislikes, and what you expect of others.

Scientists have found that, in the vast majority, the right brains of men are less developed than those of women. This is one explanation for generalizations about men as more fact-loving and pragmatic. I think this left-brain dominance in men (which sensory awareness can balance and integrate) is due to educational conditioning and use. From knee-high up, boys are encouraged to ignore or dismiss any perceptive talents they have as trivial hogwash and part of the collective illiteracy known as female intuition. Our culture trains the male, above all, to be rational. Logic and cause-and-effect are emphasized and body feelings and perceptive lore shunted aside.

Yet, as one psychologist points out: "Body feelings may not infrequently be a better guide to action than carefully teased-out chains of logic." Unfocused and undefined feelings of body pleasantness or unpleasantness (or mental discomfort) can stem from very real causes; they can result from fundamental matters of fit or appropriateness between an individual and a situation. In a business sense, his reason might tell a man it's to his advantage to pursue some task until it is completed; yet perceptions could interpose intuitive feelings that such a project is unsound. (It is probably true, in a left-brain/right-brain sense, that certain Nazi guards in concentration camps had to overcome feelings of perceptive horror and repugnance about their work in favor of [left-brain] reasonableness. Nothing, when you think about it, is more "logical" than unquestioningly following a military order because a respected superior passes it down to you. Hannah Arendt, political scientist, argues that Adolf Eichmann was a detail-minded, unimaginative bureaucrat, more interested in obeying orders than able to consider the holistic [right-brain] cataclysm that resulted.)

When you learn to place a high value on your intuitive, perceptive feelings, it helps you sift and sort other factors and improves decision-making. As enlightened self-interest, sensory practice helps a fellow strike a mutually profitable bargain with life. And when you, as a confidently integrated person, can verbalize what you feel, the man that emerges out of what Gindler called this "opening up at a later stage" will more courageously resemble the man you always wanted, deep down, to become.

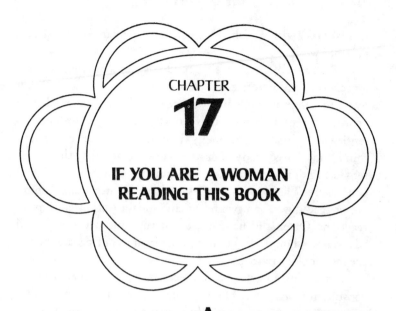

CHAPTER

17

IF YOU ARE A WOMAN READING THIS BOOK

As a woman, how often do you enjoy tuning in to just enjoying life and being radiantly physical—feeling the warmth of being utterly human and all woman? I don't just mean relaxing, if your mind continues to tap out nervous thoughts, reviewing the day's disjointed menu of problems. I mean those times when you give up all thinking and enjoy mainly physical sensations, such as one feels in a warm tub when tired and cold.

Do you experience love, sex, and orgasm as much as you've heard women are capable? Sensory awareness practice helps with these things, letting you focus in (with dignity and taste) on our culture's new physicality. And it does this with a minimum of nonsense and mumbo-jumbo.

For centuries women have been encouraged to be socially retiring and dependent on others, so it builds a special pride in self when you find that, with SA reinforcement, you can depend on yourself rather than outside persons. For the woman homemaker, SA practice offers a special dividend, as we discuss in the section on "Sensory Awareness at Home" (Chapter 9). That is, it can add sparkle to those tedious menial tasks with which the traditional homemaker must still pace her week.

Best of all, for big-city residents (and mature women especially), SA practice lets you control nervousness. You'll learn to summon up what one poet said was richer than a crown—the quiet mind. This sidesteps a fatigue peculiar to sensitive, high-strung women, those who have an overactive mind and a tired body. For the working woman, this over-tensed mind/body syndrome can muddle thinking and affect composure. The woman professional can let her trained mind get bogged down in a swamp of emotional reactions and over-reactions. Often this happens just at the time when, as Virgil advised, we should "yield not to misfortunes but press forward the more boldly in their faces."

In their report, *The Managerial Woman*, management consultants Margaret Hennig and Anne Jardim note that many women executives err by insisting on either/or, like-or-dislike relationships with fellow workers. When they see the way men of diverse interests maintain a working rapport, they say: "How can they pretend to like each other? How can they be such hypocrites?" Needless to add, the executive who manages to steer clear of interoffice hostilities is the one to get promoted, for he appreciates the value of teamwork. Especially for the working woman, sensory practice works in nonverbal ways to lift the barriers that separate mind from mind. It builds tolerance and what is known in Zen as the one-mind, and the gift of being able to see things as they are.

There is a related reward that sensing brings, one I spoke of in the Foreword, and one that has greatly changed my own life. Sensory awareness practice opens up the ability to love in the fullest, most romantic sense of the word. In her memoirs, actress Liv Ullman said: "I believe that the overpowering happiness—when the whole world is fragrant and the sun shines and one is almost unconscious for emotion—I believe it comes less frequently." I respectfully disagree: this need not be the case. For once sensory awareness is practiced regularly, a woman comes to reverse the desensitizing and alienating crippling of age and survivalistic, stress-ridden experiences. No matter how closed up life has made you, your heart can open to love in all its passionate intensity.

This might be due to the fact that sensing brings emotional renewal and an almost childlike zeal for finding beauty and goodness in others. It might also be rooted in the self-pride and inner glow that sensory practice brings. Like other forms of beauty, the magic of romance is also in the eyes of the beholder. And this relates directly to one's body image. Says Dr. Seymour Fisher, "A woman who has been told (or thinks she's been told) in various ways that her body is ugly may not be able to grasp the existence of beauty elsewhere." You feel beautiful inside, so you're opened up and less critical of the warmth and kindness that comes from others. You even have more courage to seek it out. At any age and under any of life's circumstances, sensory awareness will lift the binding shutters from your emotions, freeing you for the more fulfilling peaks of happiness.

Many women don't have sufficient confidence in their physical resources, due to cultural traditions. When a woman senses her body rhythms with clarity, she grows in self-esteem. This builds body awareness and that enhances emotional health, according to body-consciousness research.

Sensory Awareness and a Woman's Self-Image

With stress or neurosis, women begin to acquire a distorted self-image, and this increases the more they are out of touch with their physical selves. Dr. Alexander Lowen says this disharmony can even dictate the direction of mental illness: a neurotic tries to dominate the body; a schizoid denies the body; a schizophrenic dissociates from the body. He warns that the unresponsive body can lead to emotional impassivity and the inability to love.

Even that woman who only has a rare and infrequent hangup can find that her identity (or lack of it) relates to her body's physical responsiveness. "The feeling of identity," says Lowen, "stems from a feeling of contact with the body. To know who one is, an individual must be aware of what he (or she) feels . . . without this awareness of bodily feeling and attitude, a person becomes split into a disembodied spirit and a disenchanted body."

When this "split" between mind and body continues, the intelligent woman, especially, becomes inwardly perverse. Soft and compliant on the outside, she comes to find secret satisfactions in doing unexpected and perverse things: flirting with a girlfriend's beau, pushing a project she knows the boss disapproves of, sleeping with peculiar sexual partners, stealing things from luxury stores or supermarkets. It is all a matter of degree, with perversity a measurement of a woman's deadness of body/mind and her own inability to love warmly and trustingly. Said one Bioenergetics patient, a woman whose coldness and alienation showed itself in sexual high-jinks: "I felt most alive when I felt most perverse."

Still other women, without the emotional stabilizer of body awareness, become outer-directed; they invert, living their lives by the standards of others: community, husband, family, friends. Rather than expressing what they want, they do what is expected of them, awaiting approval as if they were obedient children.

These women cling to roles, acting out a part rather than custom-tailoring life to their own wants and needs. Some go to stereotypes: the cool secretary, the dutiful mother. The role-playing can become so necessary to mobilize her body and get her moving mornings that what is unreal approaches what is real, or seems to. However, it is a facade that comes to hide an emotionally dead, alienated person. Again, this is a matter of degree, according to Lowen. "When the role dominates the personality, when the whole is lost in the part (the part acted out), when . . . the person cannot be seen or reached behind the mask and the costume, one is justified in describing such a personality as schizoid." Role-playing, he adds, is a substitute for an emotional commitment to a situation.

And, to a lesser degree, many of us because of our conditioning play roles that limit our brain growth and personal development.

How Limiting Life-Styles Stunt Brain Development (and How Sensory Practice Helps)

In Chapter 1, I discussed how the adult brain can perfect itself, whatever your age, and how brain studies on left brain and right brain relate to this. Before we see the way this can be worked into your own life, try a little test. Get a friend to give it to you, and test each other. You'll both enjoy learning whether you are right-brain dominant, or, like most people in our Westernized educational culture, left-brain dominant.

> **HERE'S WHAT YOU DO:** Casually, during talk about other matters, have your friend ask you a question that requires quick figuring, as "Count the number of letters in the name of Minnesota," or "For a monogram, how many letters are there in both your names?" Have your friend track the direction your eyes turn when you start to count.

If you're like most persons, turn they will—this indicates which side of the brain is more easily activated. It also might indicate which hemisphere *dominates*. However, you should bear in mind that this test is not scientifically conclusive, for each person's brain is individual. Also, it may be that future research on this new frontier will show that many brains alternate in dominance, depending on the task at hand. (Trick is, of course, to be able to call on this brain power at will.) All the same, this test (proposed by Dr. Merle Day, neurologist at the Veterans' Administration Hospital in Downey, Illinois) has a surprisingly high degree of accuracy. It is recommended by Dr. Ernest Hilgard of Stanford University, another specialist in brain function.

> WHAT EYE MOVEMENT REVEALS: When your eyes shift to the right, it suggests your left brain dominates (as with most people). If eyes shift to the left, it probably indicates you are one of the special people with a keen right brain, the seat of intuition and perception. (Each one of our cerebral brain "twins" controls the eye muscles on the opposite body side, remember?)

If you are a mother with children over the age of ten, try the test on them—it might give you a few surprises. (I was delighted to learn that my younger daughter, age fifteen at this writing, had untapped right-brain [artistic] talents.)

How does an adult brain develop? According to the way it is used (or misused). Consider your own day-to-day life. Have you built a life with variety in it? If you work, does your job call for verbal abilities? Have you balanced this off with a right-brain activity like meditation? The sensory exercises and experiments in this book will add spice to your life.

If your eye movements show you have right-brain dominance (with strong perceptions and artistic talent), you'll want to balance this off with such things as vocabulary learning, studying a foreign language, more detail work like setting up recipe or telephone files, and so on.

Most important, of course, is the kind of activity that fills your normal day. And if you are a full-time homemaker, there is a special problem for you to consider: the hazard of routine. ("Conform and be dull," said J. Frank Dobie.) It might be that parental urging, or life's entrapments, pushed you into a situation that is not as mentally stimulating as you'd like it to be. There are ways that sensory practice can put more sparkle in your days (and lift the dust covers from little-used portions of your brain).

First, let's consider ways that, unaware, you might be limiting your brain growth—and your own growth as an interesting person.

1. *Routine scheduling of tasks brings monotony.* Whatever their jobs, today's women share a common pitfall, encouraged by many women's service magazines. Do everything on a daily schedule, they urge. The efficient woman is the organized woman. Eat at a certain hour; do laundry at a special time on specific days; stack and wash dishes right after mealtime—each and every day. All this urging of humdrum routine is backed by incessant TV commercials, urging women even to stay indefinitely with the same beauty soap (or switch to the advertiser's brand and then make it another dull routine in your life). Worse, when babies arrive, this emphasis on routine scheduling becomes almost mandatory: baby must be fed at precise times; outings must be regularly scheduled like clockwork. Even those moments the busy mother can set aside for personal care should be dropped into an organized agenda, where presumably they will not disturb her demanding schedule of errands or chores. A working woman is even more overscheduled. (What happens, of course, is that when, finally, a woman gets some time to herself, she is too depleted to make the most of it.)

What's wrong with this picture of the sweetly smiling, self-sacrificing woman? When it is a role the woman plays that does not reflect her true self it carrys its own seed of destruction. Boredom is a stressor, and this is why there are so many cases of chronic depression, particularly among well-educated women. In a report on body breakdowns and stress, Walter McQuade and Ann Aikman address a warning to that person who gradually sacrifices bits and pieces of her true self in efforts to get along with everybody: "You learn to smile when you are really angry . . . You give up an eccentric hobby; you read the right books and say the right things about them. Pretty soon not much can be seen of you anymore but a bundle of correct reactions." While your inner self might not be destroyed, it's been robbed of its chance to expand and grow. So, like a primitive monster, it goes underground; frustrated in natural development, it becomes your enemy. Body breakdowns may come gradually, perhaps all at once: heavy smoking, chronic drinking, migraines, frequent backache. Perhaps the chief symptom is a chronic feeling of being tired. In itself, this combination of symptoms leads to serious emotional problems: one psychiatrist calls it "the trauma of eventlessness."

2. *Rigid following of life-style routines brings depression.* Boredom and eventlessness lead to depression. This might be due to lack of real feelings of accomplishment, a problem for many homemakers, especially. As Germaine Greer noted, one of the peculiar curses of housework (as opposed to most office routine) is that each and every chore must be repeated precisely the same way the next day.

Yet, consider the possibility, as the boss of your home "office," of putting your own wishes foremost. Let what you genuinely want to do with yourself go at the head of your agenda (if you're a scheduler). Organize your work routine around self-growth; fun activity with your family; beauty care. You'll be amazed, and pleased, at how much better you'll be treated by your children and husband when you come to emerge more as a person in your own right. This is what psychologist David Reisman termed the *inner-directed* person. Lowen of Bioenergetics fame says such people have internal sureness and self-pride. "His (or her) primary identification is with himself as a person, and his activities are an expression of who he is. He finds his fulfillment in his response to the world, rather than in the world's response to him."

(Elsewhere in this book, I suggest ways that sensory practice can bring more satisfaction from homemaking routines, such as making cooking a sensory feast. Right now, let's consider the most serious result of unrelenting household routine.)

3. *Day-by-day routine leads to mental impoverishment.* This is a common worry of many stay-at-home women, who fear they could get mentally rusty from lack of stimulation. For the homemaker can find herself getting rusty. This, in and of itself, affects coping ability and brain growth. No matter how bright you were in school, lack of regular stimulation can dull the edge of your intelligence and talents. Unrelieved, it also can keep you tensed-up and your senses depleted. This is due to what is called *habituation*. Without distractions, you can lose your flair for handling emergencies. One stress expert explains, "Habit seldom solves problems, and almost never seizes opportunities."

There's another mentally impoverishing aspect to this for the woman at home: working during the daytime in the same environment where one sleeps at night limits variety and enriched experience; this might be a traditional factor to explain women's smaller brain size. In medical textbooks, including those used by physicians today, women are said to have smaller brains by weight and volume than men. This, it is suggested, indicates lower intelligence for the female than the male. (Medical male chauvinism aside, neuroscientists still measure head size and estimate brain weight to assess human intelligence.)

How can you overcome the effects of mental impoverishment in your own life? Remember the medical research mentioned early in this book, where scientists measured results of *enriched experience?* (See Chapter 1, "Sensory Practice Can Boost Your Mental Ability.")

The scientific research was conducted by neuroscientists in France and at the University of California, among other institutions. Results agreed worldwide: problem-solving ability and brain capacity are increased when there is challenge and enrichment in one's day. Testing involved laboratory animals raised in what is termed an impoverished environment. Those laboratory animals kept in what is termed the enriched condition (EC) thrived as many as twelve at a time in a larger cage. Food and water were freely available. But when stimulation is included in the living environment (ladders, wood blocks, brushes, etc.), brain size and mental abilities were increased. This was true regardless of whether several subjects lived together, or whether they were alone.

Even animals whose brains had been deliberately damaged, with lesions, showed brain improvement when enrichment training was made part of their life-style. And in one experiment, the enriched experience was found equally beneficial when it was only given for a sixty-day period (for two hours daily). Neuroscientists say this research shows the living brain is capable of growth and perfectibility. The findings, says one scientist, relate also to improving learning ability and memory.

Can you boost your own mental abilities (as well as problem-solving) by putting variety into your daily life-style? Yes, indeed; elsewhere in this book I suggest sensory activities that will do this at work and play, and by incorporating sensory touches into the interior decor of your home.

Save Time for Daydreaming

So brainwashed have many of us been by Western education's left-brain one-sidedness that we feel a bit guilty when we take time to ourselves for "idle" daydreaming. If an activity involves other than physical movement, and does not produce a practical or tangible result, we feel it has no merit. Not so, claim psychologists. Aggression studies have pointed up emotional health gains from daydreaming. Psychologist Jerome L. Singer of Yale University insists that fantasy is good for everyone: persons who fail to enrich their lives with fantasy or daydreams have been found to become bored easily, and they are less relaxed. More serious signs of an underdeveloped fantasy life are angers, overeating, violence, delinquency, and use of dangerous drugs, including chronic drinking.

Celebrate Yourself Exercise No. 12: A Guided Daydream Experiment

Sometimes a woman can be reluctant to face a difficult situation, such as a first-time experience under unusual conditions. Others are reluctant to assert themselves: asking the boss for a raise, making a speech before club or civic group, entertaining a boyfriend's parents. The following fantasy technique can build assurance and proves of special benefit to shy women especially. Imagery exercises are an accepted part of psychophysical therapy, and even work in the sports world. (Olympics champion Bill Toomy claims he improves his pole-vaulting ability by sitting still, imagining the "feel" of each body muscle as he approaches the vault, lifts, and arches himself over. He says it has boosted his timing as much as hard practice.) For yourself, also, acting out an upcoming event in your mind, bit by bit, will be as good as a "dress rehearsal" of the real thing.

HERE'S WHAT YOU DO: Remember these four procedures: (1) Sit comfortably, eyes closed. (2) Concentrate on the details of your imaginary situation: what you will wear, how the office or room will look, how others appear, talk, sit. (3) Rack your mind to anticipate all reactions, for everybody involved in this psychodrama, particularly the objections and difficulties they might raise. Script others as well as yourself. Be prepared to cope with these responses on a replay of your guided daydream. (4) Set up an imaginary obstacle that must be overcome or climbed in your fantasy (stairs, a locked door, a huge rock, etc.). In fantasy therapy, this is a technique for building inner strength and self-esteem.

How Sensory Practice Can Make Difficult Times Endurable

Because it is a cousin to the here-and-now of Zen, sensory practice lets you endure difficult times, maintaining composure with grace and style. A Zen story communicates this:

> A man traveling across a field encountered a tiger. He fled, the tiger after him. Coming to a precipice, he caught hold of the root of a wild vine and swung himself over the edge. The tiger snorted at him, sniffing from above. The man, trembling, looked down to where, below, another tiger waited to eat him. Only the vine he held sustained him. Then two mice, one white and one black, started to gnaw away the vine, little by little. Looking about, the man saw a luscious strawberry growing near him. Grasping the vine with one hand, he plucked the strawberry with the other hand. How sweet it tasted!

Celebrate Yourself Exercise No. 13: A for-Women-Only Meditation

On busy days, a woman sometimes only has a moment here and there to snatch for herself. Until such time as you can ease up on your schedule, put these random minutes to work for you; relax mind and body with this little meditation. It is based on both Zen and yoga practice, particularly the Zen concept that one learns to control the mind by regulating body actions. The following lets you put your eye muscles to work to ease and relax (left-brain) mental turbulence.

HERE'S WHAT YOU DO: Sit quietly, feet comfortable, back erect but relaxed, hands lightly cupped. Close your eyes. Breathing quietly, try to center breath in the lower abdomen. Now focus your (closed) eyes on the center of your forehead. Keep your gaze controlled but easy; do not strain. Breathe gently, then relax your eye muscles, as you maintain body awareness at the forehead area. Say silently to yourself: "At the center of all peace I serenely remain: naught can harm me here." Repeat this several times, until the words seem to flow down from your forehead, through your arms, down to your toes and beyond. (Experiment with this briefly.)

In addition to soothing emotional tensions and so-called brain noise, the above experiment might let you awaken hidden mind power, if one heeds a yoga legend. The forehead center is said to cover an intuitive "third eye," and this exercise is known in yoga as the *tratakam*. Whether it makes you more perceptive or not, this sensory meditation provides a little island of calm in the midst of the hectic day. And when a woman sits calmly, sufficient unto herself, it works in gentle but steady ways to bring contentment.

There is an English country saying that describes this: happiness is a butterfly that, if you pursue it, will elude you. But if you sit down quietly, it can alight on you.

**SA-SELVER
ON YOUR OWN**

SA Source Information

For further information about the location of the closest instructor in Charlotte Selver's sensory awareness system, contact: The Charlotte Selver Foundation, 32 Cedars Road, Caldwell, New Jersey, 07006.

RESEARCH
NOTES

*Chapter 1: What Sensory Awareness Is—and
What It Can Do for You*

Charlotte Selver's statement comes from an article she
and Charles Brooks prepared for a humanist psychology textbook, *Explorations in Human Potentialities* (Springfield, Ill.:
Charles C Thomas, 1966). The Selver chapter is entitled, "Report on Work in Sensory Awareness and Total Functioning."

Dr. Frederick "Fritz" Perls's comments, quoted here, are
taken from his taped talks at Esalen Institute. Interested readers can locate them in the book *Gestalt Therapy Verbatim*,
edited by John O. Stevens (Moab, Utah: Real People Press,
1969).

Dr. Alexander Lowen's link between apathy and pathological depression is a core concept of Bioenergetics psychotherapy. Details can be found in any of the Lowen books,
particularly *Depression and the Body* (New York: Coward,
McCann & Geoghegan, Inc., 1972), and *The Betrayal of the
Body* (New York: The Macmillan Company, Inc., 1967).

*Background on the way sensory talents deteriorate with
disuse* and misuse can be found in my first book, *Revitalize
Yourself: The Techniques of Staying Youthful* (New York:
Hawthorn Books, 1972); paperback edition from New York:

Barnes & Noble, 1974). I refer specifically to Chapter X: "Revitalize Your Senses."

Dr. *Rene Dubos* long has emphasized that man should lean more on his human physiology for environmental appreciation and adaptation. Observations about man's sensory input appear in several of his books, including *So Human an Animal* and *A God Within,* both published by Charles Scribner's Sons (New York, 1973). Further observations of mathematician/philosopher Alfred North Whitehead will also be found in *A God Within.*

Uniqueness of the individual human brain is increasingly a phenomenon to brain probers. Indeed, experts predict that in the data-conscious future world we shall use brain-prints as well as fingerprints as official identification. Such brain-wave readings could serve as a barometer of emotional predictions, revealing almost any kind of eccentricity—emotional as well as intellectual. British neurologist W. Grey Walter claims we have barely touched this rich resource: only one hundredth of one percent of brain data has yet been decoded and put to use.

George Kelly's illuminating theory about consciousness as a personal construct appears in his book, *The Psychology of Personal Constructs* (New York: W. W. Norton & Co., 1955).

Sensory deprivation studies are reported in books by the best-known pioneer in this field, Dr. John C. Lilly. His works include *The Center of the Cyclone* (New York: Julian Press, 1972), from which this chapter draws. A popularized account of such work appears in the provocative *An Index of Energy and Power,* was compiled by The Catalogue (an organization) and published by Clanose Publishers, Ltd., London, distributed in America by Pantheon Books, New York (1974). This ambitious and well-illustrated book covers many of the New Enlightenment subjects, such as the martial arts, Gurdjieff, the Lorenz theory, Sufism and Zen sects. It is entertaining as well as engrossing, and I recommend it highly for the tyro reader.

Robert E. Ornstein, PhD, has been termed the "guru" of the left-brain/right-brain field. His illustration of habituation comes from his early work, *The Psychology of Consciousness* (San Francisco: W. H. Freeman and Company, 1972). While he and I have had passing differences (he chauvinistically resists being interviewed by female journalists, such as this author), his research work is beyond reproach. Indeed, it was Ornstein's recognition that Sufi stories offered right-brain stimulation that opened the door to our premise that sensory awareness practice fulfills a similar role. And, with Ornstein, I am concerned that left-brain/right-brain know-how (as you will read of it in the next chapter) will be oversimplified and bastardized by commercial reductionism. So for an enlightened look at the technocracy of this "new" psychology, I direct any serious reader to Ornstein's books, mentioned in more detail in my Notes for chapter 2.

Karl Pribram's description of the "Bowery El" effect comes from his article, "The Neurophysiology of Remembering," *Scientific American,* January, 1969.

More on enriched experience research (a term scientists use) will be found in our chapter for women (chapter 17); I believe the self-help concept of brain-building through this approach offers special promise for the stay-at-home wife and mother, as you will read in that section.

Comment from the multi-talented Dr. Charles Shaw comes from conversations and interviews with him at the hospital of which he is medical director, King Edward VII Hospital, Hamilton, Bermuda.

Charles Brooks is the husband of Charlotte Selver; he is a Harvard graduate, linguist, ex-furniture designer, and a highly cultured gentleman in his own right. He is also the co-leader of the sensory awareness movement. The statement quoted is from the first textbook written on SA-Selver (and required reading for those who would pursue this subject further): *Sensory Awareness: A Re-Discovery of Experiencing* (New York: Viking Books, 1974).

Shamanism has become a challenging subject for research and is now discussed openly at leading medical schools and reviewed in seminars such as those during the spring of 1977, at Esalen Institute, Big Sur, California.

Dr. Hans Selye, one of the world's most respected stress authorities, discussed this with me during interviews at his Montreal Institute for Experimental Medicine (affiliated with the University of Montreal) during February, 1970.

Body/mind tensions (and their diagnosis) are described in Will Schutz's book, *Here Comes Everybody: Bodymind and Encounter Culture* (New York: Harper & Row, 1971).

Psychosomatic body/mind breakdowns are reported at greater length in the lucid book by Howard R. and Martha E. Lewis, *Psychosomatics* (New York: The Viking Press, 1972).

Charlotte Selver's statement comes from her essay, "Begining of Beginnings," appearing in a bulletin of the Charlotte Selver Foundation.

More on Richard Suinn's noteworthy work in sports psychology will be found in Chapter 3. Our data and background come from his article "Body Thinking: Psychology for Olympic Champs," appearing in *Psychology Today*, July, 1976.

Chapter 2: Left Brain/Right Brain—How "Sensing" Builds Mind Power

The Selver quote comes from her article, "Beginning of Beginnings," appearing in a bulletin of the Charlotte Selver Foundation.

Technical data in this chapter is based on the following articles (which are recommended reading for readers interested in pursuing this subject further): Maya Pines's pioneering report, "We are Left-Brained or Right-Brained," in the *New York Times Magazine*, October 9, 1973; and the Left Brain/Right Brain special issue of *Human Behavior*, June, 1976. The latter publication features three articles of reliable clarity: Craig Buck's "Knowing the Left from the Right"; a profile of Robert Ornstein, "A Mind for Metaphor," by Edwin Kiester, Jr.; and Wayne Sage's "The Split Brain Lab."

Serious students of lateral specialization will enjoy Robert Ornstein's laudable book, *The Psychology of Consciousness* (San Francisco: W. H. Freeman and Company, 1972). A Penguin Books edition is also available (1975). Chapter 3 of this basic reference will be particularly helpful ("The Two Sides of the Brain"). While I politely disagree with Ornstein's (early) tendency to lump human emotions into a right-brain catch-all (anger can be interpreted as irrational left-brain mental dialogue), one must give unrelenting credit to Ornstein's pioneering research in this field, together with his associate, David Galin. Ornstein's more recent books should also be included in any formal bibliography: *The Mind Field* (New York: Grossman Publishers, 1976), and *The Nature of Human Consciousness* (San Francisco: W. H. Freeman and Co., 1973).

In this book, the chapter test involving "goatee" and "zig-zag" is my own. Distinguished Rene Dubos discusses *"entheos"* as a core theme of his book, *A God Within* (New York: Charles Scribner's Sons, 1973). The anecdotes about Descartes and Poincaré evolve from this source.

For deeper study, there is a growing and rich literature about this exciting new field. Professionals are referred to the following for initial but specific data. All articles are written by eminent contributors, and our space here permits only a partial listing of available sources: Joseph E. Bogen's "The Other Side of the Brain," *Bulletin of the Los Angeles Neurological Societies*, Vol. 34, No. 3; Michael S. Gazzaniga, "The

Split Brain in Man," *Scientific American*, August, 1967; Brenda Milner's "Interhemispheric Differences in the Localization of Psychological Processes in Man," *British Medical Bulletin* Vol. 27 (1971); Roger W. Sperry, "The Great Cerebral Commissure," in *Scientific American*, January, 1964; and a collaboration, "Right Hemisphere Specialization for Depth Perception," by Margaret Durnford and Doreen Kimura, appearing in *Nature*, June 11, 1971.

Chapter 3: The Peak Experience—"Joy and Flow" from SA Practice

The Selver comment came from her observations at a SA workshop I attended at New York University, New York City, October, 1975.

SA workshop sessions are generally held with participants barefoot, on Japanese mats.

Our civilization's attitude toward time modes (favoring linear, as opposed to simultaneous or cyclic) is a favorite topic of Robert Ornstein's. He feels that the clock as we honor it is the embodiment of sequential, left-brain thinking. As Ornstein notes in *The Psychology of Consciousness*, if we assume that the contents of a normal person's consciousness are a personal construct (i.e., self-selected), then we should begin to consider the possibility that our "normal" mode of experiencing time is really just one construction of reality. As research advances in the new Enlightenment, other modes of time will become increasingly accepted. It is here worth mentioning that Dr. Joseph Bogen, leading medical researcher in left-brain/right-brain specialization, said one of the distinguishing differences between the twin sides of the brain is the extent to which a linear concept of time participates in the ordering of thought. The left brain processes sequentially and the right brain simultaneously, creating a "patterned whole."

Dr. Suzuki was the pioneer in teaching Zen Buddhism in

Western civilization, starting in England and Europe, during the thirties.

Dr. C's landmark research into the phenomenon of the "flow" experience can be found in William Barry Furlong's super report, "The Fun in Flow," appearing in *Psychology Today,* June, 1976.

John Brodie's experiences are included in a report on "Sports as Yoga," written for the Esalen Institute *Bulletin* by founder Michael Murphy, and publisher in December, 1974. Further details will be found in a report Brodie himself prepared for the *Intellectual Digest,* December, 1972.

The golf anecdotes are from Michael Murphy's book, *Golf in the Kingdom,* an Esalen Institute book, from Dell, 1973.

Stories about Billie Jean King and Jean Claude Killy appeared in Richard M. Suinn's article "Body Thinking: Psychology for Olympic Champs," appearing in *Psychology Today,* July, 1976. The Bill Toomy story came from Will Schutz of Esalen Institute.

The concept of the "play-professions" was designated by Dr. Hans Selye and appears in several of his books, including *Stress Without Distress* (New York: J. B. Lippincott Co., 1975). I have also discussed this with the distinguished stress expert during several interviews for my newspaper column, 1969–1975.

Counting your breaths is central to the "Relaxation Response" of Harvard's Dr. Herbert Benson, discussed with this author during a New York University seminar, November, 1975.

Chapter 4: Charlotte Selver and the Sensory Awareness Movement

Charlotte Selver's anecdote is taken from conversations I had with her on Monhegan Island, Maine, in 1976.

The Bess Mensendieck exercise system is reportedly still taught in Dutch medical schools. Readers can investigate it further by reading Jennifer Yoel's *Re-Shape Your Body, Re-Vitalize Your Life* (Englewood Cliffs, N.J.: Prentice-Hall, Inc., 1972). Descriptions of the work of *F. Matthias Alexander* will be found in *The Resurrection of the Body*, edited by Edward Maisel (New York: University Books, 1969).

The Alan Watts comments are from a radio address he delivered on a San Francisco station in the fifties, and are reprinted in bulletins of the Charlotte Selver Foundation.

All other material in this chapter is based on personal conversations with Charlotte Selver, teachers in SA-Selver workshops, and various bulletins of the Charlotte Selver Foundation.

Chapter 5: SA and Breathing as Sensing

Charlotte Selver's comment comes from a pamphlet, "On Breathing," published by the Charlotte Selver Foundation.

The breathing awareness teacher mentioned is San Francisco's noted Magda Proskauer.

Zen expert Chogyam Trungpa is the author of "The Myth of Freedom & The Way of Meditation," (Boulder, Colo.: Shambhala Publications, 1976).

Chapter 6: Your Hara, Centering and Body Awareness

The Charles Brooks quote is from his book, *Sensory Awareness: The Re-Discovery of Experiencing* (New York: Viking Press, 1974).

The hara and its physiological background are discussed at greater length in Dr. Tomio Hirai's book, *Zen Meditation Therapy* (Tokyo: Japan Publications, 1974).

Tai-chi ch'uan and related exercise systems from the Orient are best learned from an instructor, present to call and supervise exercise sessions. I am therefore not listing supplementary books on these systems, as I feel the interested reader would benefit more from consulting his phone directory and personally sampling the complimentary demonstration that most martial arts and *tai-chi* instructors offer.

Centering background, and extra centering exercises for women especially, can be found in the comprehensive *Getting Clear: Body Work for Women,* compiled by Anne Kent Rush, and distributed by Random House, New York, 1973, and The Bookworks, Berkeley, Ca.

Moshe Feldenkrais, PhD, is among the most creative of the new breed of psychophysical scientists. Formerly a successful Israeli industrialist, Feldenkrais was the enthusiast who taught the late prime minister Ben-Gurion yoga and revitalized the Israeli political leader after he was in his seventies by teaching him head stands. Readers interested in learning more about the exercise approach of this respectable "body engineer" are refered to his book, *Awareness Through Movement* (New York: Harper & Row, 1972).

Dr. Seymour Fisher's research into body image and awareness will be of interest to readers. I heartily recommend his book, *Body Consciousness: You Are What You Feel* (Englewood Cliffs, N.J.: Prentice-Hall, Inc., 1973).

Chapter 7: Zazen—The Sensory Awareness Meditation

The Charles Brooks description of zazen comes from his book, *Sensory Awareness: The Re-Discovery of Experiencing* (New York: Viking Press, 1974).

Data regarding medical research on zazen meditators comes from the writings of Dr. Tomio Hirai, particularly *Zen Meditation Therapy* (Tokyo: Japan Publications, 1975). Notes on rhythmic breathing and the note from an ancient Buddhist text are also taken from this source.

The Sufi story is used by Robert Ornstein; this, and other Sufi folk tales, can be found in books by debonair

Indries Shah, leading exponent of Sufism in America and the United Kingdom. This particular story is taken from Shah's *Tales of the Dervishes* (London: Jonathan Cape, 1967; New York: E. P. Dutton, 1970). *The Zen story*, and others, can be found in Paul Reps book, *Zen Flesh, Zen Bones* (New York: Doubleday, 1961).

All other details about zazen are from my personal experience as a regular zazen meditator, and from SA workshop instructions and fellow meditators' experiences.

Chapter 8: Sensory Awareness at Your Work

The Charles Brooks comment comes from *Sensory Awareness: The Study of Living as Experience* (New York: Viking Press, 1974).

Roger W. Sperry's landmark research is reported in Wayne Sage's article, "The Split Brain Lab," appearing in *Human Behavior*, June, 1976. Sperry, a PhD, has contributed his own noteworthy articles to professional publications. The reader is referred to his "Neurology and the Mind-Brain Problem," in *American Scientist*, 1951, Vol. 40.

Japanese industrialists' case histories and their use of Zen exercises to broaden the attention span come from Tomio Hirai's *Zen Meditation Therapy* (Tokyo: Japan Publications, 1975). This highly readable book offers added background about the Zen concepts of *samadhi* and *mokusho*.

The mind power sensory meditation from Adam Smith comes from his book, *Powers of Mind* (New York: Random House, 1975). This meditation, of course, can rely on other poems or lyrics, the more familiar to the user the more effective.

Dr. Leopold Szondi's pioneering work is little known to Americans, and a promising subject for fellow science writers. My description of his "A" and "B" mind-concept comes from private conversations with his staff, 1957–1958.

Charles Brooks's erudite comment on chairs comes from my conversations with him, and an essay, "On Sitting," published as a bulletin of the Charlotte Selver Foundation.

F. Matthias Alexander was one of the truly original forerunners of today's body/mind cult. An ex-actor in Australia who spent years studying the relationship between body tensions and emotions, his work is described in *The Resurrection of the Body*, edited by Edward Maisel (New York: University Books, 1969).

Dorothy Sarnoff's "teapot exercise" was given to this author in personal interviews in New York City, 1969–1972. More details on her work can be found in her book, *Speech Can Change Your Life* (New York: Doubleday and Company, 1972).

Chapter 9: Sensory Awareness at Home and for the Homemaker

The Charles Brooks comment comes from his book, *Sensory Awareness: The Study of Living as Experience* (New York: Viking Press, 1974). The Brooks book is must reading for anyone who wishes to pursue sensory awareness as a serious study.

Juvenile neurosis that results from a lack of tactile contact during the early years of life has been reported widely in the medical literature. The lay reader is referred to the *Psychology Today* report by Karen Turok, "Babies" (April, 1977) and research on the insecure aftermath of parental coldness, an ongoing interest of Dr. Gordon Clanton, San Diego (Ca.) State University.

Chewing as a sensory awareness experience is recommended to any reader wishing to brighten gloomy hours (or interrupt a downward spiral of emotional thoughts). Charlotte Selver suggests fruit or nuts. Next time you're alone (and lonely) try this experiment to get the sensory most out of an apple or pear. Suspend all thinking and give yourself over to tactile and mouth awareness. Notice the abundant juices, the rich, lush sounds, the way the taste you savor changes as you chew. Give three or four long minutes to this SA experience and I'll wager your gloom has lifted by the time you've finished.

The Christmas Humphreys comment is from his book, *A Western Approach to Zen* (London: London Buddhist Society, 1971).

Johnny Cash's home living style comes from recollections by a Cash family visitor, *TV Guide* N. Y. Bureau Chief, Neil Hickey. Other celebrity life-style glimpses are from popular sources and interviews for my syndicated newspaper column. *Mitzi Gaynor* and *Ann Miller* descriptions came from our personal conversations, 1968–1975. *Lyndon Johnson's* habits come from my own and friends' recollections, gleaned during my political work during his 1960 and 1964 presidential campaigns.

Rene Dubos's observations are taken from his book, *A God Within* (New York: Charles Scribner's Sons, 1974). Dr. Dubos also includes a description of the Luria studies on memory in those pages.

Several books on the Senoi Indians of Malaysia are now available. Of these, I recommend *Creative Dreaming* by Patricia Garfield (New York: Simon and Schuster, 1975). Carlos Castaneda describes the teachings of the enigmatic Don Juan in several books; this dream-power concept was suggested by *Tales of Power* (New York: Simon and Schuster, 1975).

Chapter 10: Sensory Awareness in Your Travels

Charles Brooks's cultural observation appears in his essay "Sitting," published as Bulletin No. 5 (Fall, 1963) of the Charlotte Selver Foundation.

The human seat muscles described in the exercise under "SA—for Revitalizing" are the gluteus maximus muscles. As a further sign of the great unsuitability of much of our "civilized" education in terms of the person and our innate gifts, consider the structural stiffness of waiting room and institutional seating. (As Charles Brooks notes, even high-energy school students are obliged to spend a large part of their time in seats whose designs "have no relation to the person's organismic functioning." This deleteriously affects vision, circulation, and mental acuity.)

That chronic sore throats are an urban problem (and one found even in cities without air pollution) has been observed by Will Schutz, Feldenkrais teacher and member of the faculty of Esalen Institute, Big Sur, California.

Chapter 11: Sensory Awareness in Health and Beauty

Charlotte Selver's comment appears in an article she wrote for the Charlotte Selver Foundation, appearing in *Bulletin* No. 1, Winter, 1971.

Dr. Popov's work with aromatics has been reported by various beauty magazines, as well as in his own books. For background on the use of sensory aromatics for rejuvenation purposes, see the pioneering book by Patrick M. McGrady Jr., *The Youth Doctors* (New York: Coward-McCann, Inc., 1968).

The late Dr. Erno Lazlo (beauty advisor to some of the world's most perpetually ageless women such as the Duchess of Windsor, Greta Garbo, and others) recommended this cool water splash.

Our sensory beauty meditation is also known as "color breathing," and was reported at length in *Harper's* and *Queen* magazines, October, 1976.

The Rockefeller University experiment with mice, teaching them to "blush" in one ear at a time, was supervised by

far-sighted Dr. Neal Miller; much of Dr. Miller's work led to
today's Biofeedback technology, and he is hailed worldwide
as being one of the early psycho-physiologists (or scientists
concerned with the medical and anatomic background of
behavior and psychology)

Chapter 12: Sensory Awareness and Your Child

Charlotte Selver has for decades been concerned about
the way children's sensory selves can be stunted. This comment is taken from an article she prepared in collaboration
with Charles Brooks, "Report on Work in Sensory Awareness
and Total Functioning"; it appears in *Explorations in Human
Potentialities* (Springfield, Illinois: Charles C Thomas, 1966).

The incident about the little girl is a favorite of Charlotte's, and is told at SA-Selver workshops by various teachers.

Dr. Emmy Pickler has been quoted by Selver on several
occasions, including the report mentioned above. Other Selver
quotes in this chapter are taken from verious bulletins of the
Charlotte Selver Foundation.

The term "the Take Society" was (to my recollection)
first used by *Fortune* magazine editor Walter McQuade.

The concept of time sense, or *"zeitgedächtnis,"* was
originated by German scientist Von Buttel-Reepen. It refers
to that inner awareness that prompts instinct-oriented beings
to "know" when it is a specific hour (or to awaken precisely
at the hour they choose, without benefit of alarm clocks).
This concept, which predated today's knowledge of bio-
rhythms, is explored in Ritchie Ward's excellent book, *Living
Clocks* (New York: Alfred A. Knopf, 1971).

Falling and emotional health (as related by Dr. Alexander Lowen) was discussed by him in conversations with me
in 1975 in New York City. The concept also appears in this
esteemed psychiatrist's books, including *Depression and the*

Body (New York: Coward, McCann & Geoghegan, Inc., 1972).

Sensitivity training and sensory awareness training can overlap; while several private preparatory schools give sensitivity training to a limited extent, the only nontuition school teaching it, to my knowledge at this writing, is Julia Richman High School, New York City as part of their fine psychology class.

The Ramstein class experiment in teaching sensory awareness was reported in *Human Behavior*, July, 1976.

The belief that sensory experiences open up memory banks is shared with this author by Will Schutz of Esalen Institute, who has discussed it during workshops.

The "primal play" game is based on Psychosound by Susanna Jutasi, founder of the Center for Natural Voice Development in New York City.

Our quote about the "noisy impertinence" of children comes from James Russell Lowell, who ever had an eye for the "suchness" (in Zen terminology) of healthy youngsters. His full description (from an essay called "A Good Word for Winter,") tells of the "noisy impertinence of childhood, the elbowing self-conceit of youth." Again, the alert reader will note that this kind of ready, youthful confidence is at polar opposites from the (sensorily deprived?) adult who needs to seek out so-called assertiveness training.

Chapter 13: Sensory Awareness in Recreation and Sports

Charles Brooks's comment comes from SA-Selver classwork and observations in his book, *Sensory Awareness: The Study of Living as Experience* (New York: Viking Press, 1974).

For further information on individual sports, tennis

players are advised to seek out Tim Gallwey's *Inner Tennis* (New York: Random House, 1973); golfers will enjoy Michael Murphy's *Golf in the Kingdom*, distributed by Esalen Institute, Big Sur, California; I have heard rumors of a book on *Zen of Running*, but at this writing am unable to locate any publisher for it. Meanwhile, all athletes (present and would-be) will benefit from a reading of Eugen Herrigel's *Zen in the Art of Archery*, recently reissued by Random House (1971). And an overview of his mind/body approach to sports will be found in the Adam Smith book, *Powers of Mind* (New York: Random House, 1975).

Chapter 14: Sensory Awareness and Your Lover

Charlotte Selver's statement was made during a personal conversation we had in August, 1976, at Monhegan Island, Maine.

Physicality (particularly the sensory awareness of sexual body contact) is a right-hemisphere activity to a large extent. I think there is a related truth here that is worth noting, also: for years, those married couples whose marriages were in difficulty and who sought out sexual counseling (even from top experts like Masters and Johnson) inevitably got divorced anyway. Sexual proficiency alone did not bolster their foundering relationship. Here's my theory, admittedly a debatable one: during intercourse, too many rational (left-brain) directives about sexual technique can work against the bliss of lovemaking in the fullest sense of the term. For most persons, love (in the romantic sense) remains a glorious, unfathomable, right-brain experience—with holistic delicacies that can be destroyed by inordinate emphasis on the how-to of sexual activity.

The biblical passage was taken from that most sensual of books, the Song of Solomon, excerpted from Chapters 5, 6, and 8.

Identifying jealousy as such is a step toward conquering it, according to jealousy therapists Gordon Clanton and Lynn G. Smith. For details, readers are directed to their book, *Jealousy* (Englewood Cliffs, N.J.: Prentice-Hall, 1977).

The "Rumpelstiltskin effect" is a familiar reference in writings on current psychology, and was mentioned by Adam Smith in *Powers of Mind.*

The Castaneda concept of the *nagual* and the *tonal* can be found in his book, *Tales of Power* (New York: Simon and Schuster, 1975). Use of this concept as a mind-power exercise, with sensory awareness overtones, is my suggestion.

Declaring your lost lover as dead is key to my SA exercise. Here's why: hope springs eternal, particularly for those who would unconsciously hold onto love (and most of us would). So to speed adaptation to loss, it is emotionally healthier to stamp out any latent hope for reconciliation. Then, if all works out well anyway, your spirit is whole and unscarred—instead of a bundle of overstressed contradictions.

Einstein's quote was used by Lyall Watson in his highly original work, *Supernature* (London: Hodder and Stoughton, Ltd., 1973).

The G. B. Shaw statement was made to Valerie Pascal, the beautiful European actress who was married to Gabriel Pascal (the only film producer whom Shaw really trusted with his works). Valerie is now married to debonaire philanthropist George Delacourt, and lives in New York City.

Chapter 15: Sensory Awareness and Special Problems

Charlotte Selver's quote is taken from a pamphlet (based on her various talks) entitled "On Breathing," published by the Charlotte Selver Foundation.

The right-brain nature of meditation (and even listening to Sufi tales) has been scientifically established by America's leading expert, Robert Ornstein. For data and details, see his books, including *The Mind Field* (New York: Grossman Publishers, 1976).

Anorexia nervosa, and SA training as therapy, is reported in the literature by Dr. Marlene Boskind-Lodahl. Here I quote from an article prepared by Boskind-Lodahl and Joyce Sirlin, "The Gorging-Purging Syndrome," from *Psychology Today,* March, 1977.

The gorging story about the stand-up midnight eater is an incident related me by Jean Nidetch, founder of Weight Watchers International, when we talked during the spring of 1970.

The drinker's (left-brain) rationale came from the Tennessee Williams play, "Cat on a Hot Tin Roof"; the character was Big Daddy's favorite son, who imbibed to turn down the mental dialogue in his rational mind.

The dieter's hazard hour (between 3 and 4 P.M.) was a fact I gleaned from an extensive survey of American dieters that I conducted in association with the Diet Workshops, as research for my book, *BodyPower.*

Repetition and cadence as meditative tattoo can eventually bring self-healing, according to various early Christian legends, including sources described in Ornstein's *The Psychology of Consciousness* (San Francisco: W. H. Freeman and Company, 1972). For a curious parallel in a noted literary work, I call the reader's attention to the J. D. Salinger short story, "Franny and Zooey." In this story (believed to be autobiographical), Franny and her boyfriend are at dinner. He notes she is carrying a book, *The Way of a Pilgrim,* telling of a Czarist Russian peasant who seeks out a *starets,* or holy man. The *starets* advises him that if he can keep saying "Lord Jesus Christ, have mercy on me" over and over, it will have healing and salutary effects. "You only have to do it with your *lips* at first," Franny describes. "Then eventually what happens, the prayer becomes self-active . . . [that is] the words get synchronized with the person's heartbeats, and then you're actually praying without ceasing . . . Which has a really tremendous, mystical effect on your whole outlook . . . The marvelous thing is, when you first start doing it, you don't even have to have *faith* in what you're doing . . . All you have to have in the beginning is quantity. Then, later on, it becomes quality by itself . . . [like in] the Nembutsu sects of Buddhism, people say 'Praise to the Buddha' over and over . . ." In similar ways, I believe, there could be self-healing benefits to the Zikr of the Moslem who repeats *"La ilaha illa'llah."*

Restless sleep and insomnia might relate to intensive left-brain stress. Consider the research on patients with right-hemisphere brain damage, cited by Dr. Paul Bakan of Simon Fraser University in British Columbia, who has written extensively on this subject. He says such patients lose the ability to dream. At Cambridge University, three such brain-damaged patients also were unable to visualize an image with eyes closed! For pertinent details, see Dr. Bakan's "The Right Brain Is the Dreamer," in *Psychology Today,* November, 1976.

Fantasy as a science is a subject eminently explored by Dr. Jerome L. Singer, who has become a distinguished authority on this provocative field. Among his books, readers will enjoy *The Inner World of Daydreaming* (New York: Harper & Row, 1975).

Overcoming fears with sensory meditation is advocated by Dr. Tomio Hirai. For information about this, and the concept of *paradox intention* of Dr. Frankel, see the Hirai book, *Zen Meditation Therapy* (Tokyo: Japan Publications, Inc., 1975).

That unexpected mental powers can result from concentrating the meditative mind is a belief of Tokyo's Dr. Tomio Hirai, among others.

Headache survey figures and therapies are taken from the Daniel Goleman article, "Why Your Temples Pound," appearing in *Psychology Today*, August, 1976. A related sensory headache treatment to the one I suggest is called "The Great Central Philippine Headache Cure," and was included in Adam Smith's fine book, *Powers of Mind* (New York: Random House, 1975).

The other side effect of SA-Selver training is one that might concern only advanced (or otherwise predisposed) persons. Because of its natural link to Zen, SA-Selver builds awareness of, and respect for, all "sentient beings," as the Zen prayer terms it. So I found a repugnance developing in me for carnivorous gorging. At this writing I have become more vegetarian, even excluding certain forms of seafood. This (not unhappy) side effect was brought home to me when I stopped overnight at a Port Clyde, Maine, inn, en route home from my last visit to Monhegan. At my request I was served a beautiful Maine lobster, glowing red-orange in the vitality and health it had so recently enjoyed. Although hungry (and paying for the repast), I was unable to eat that lobster and found myself filling up on salad and vegetables. I offer no further explanation for this, other than to reiterate that "sensing" can change a person's outlook in unexpected ways.

Lying as relating is enjoyed to a deeper extent in SA-Selver workshops. It is described in Charles Brooks's excellent book (required reading for anyone who wishes to seriously pursue sensory awareness), *Sensory Awareness: The Study of Living as Experience* (New York: Viking Press, 1974).

Chapter 16: If You Are a Man Reading This Book

Psychosomatic illnesses that can result from a prolonged mind/body "split" have been described at length in medical journals. Readers interested in data or bibliography are referred to Howard R. Lewis and Martha E. Lewis, *Psycho-*

somatics: How Your Emotions Can Damage Your Health
(New York: Viking Press, 1972).

The Himmelstein test (to establish where "self" resides)
is from his report "Sex Differences in Spatial Localization of
the Self," appearing in *Perceptual and Motor Skills* 19:317,
1964.

The Psychologist quoted is distinguished Dr. Seymour
Fisher. Dr. Fisher's body-image research is reported extensively
in the medical literature. Lay readers are referred to the landmark book by Dr. Fisher (on which this chapter leans
greatly), entitled *Body Consciousness: You Are What You
Feel* (Englewood Cliffs, N.J.: Prentice-Hall, 1973).

Disregard for physical training as part of education was
shown by budget cutbacks during the 1975–1976 recession
in the United States, especially in the Philadelphia school
budgets.

The Van Lennep report is found in "Projection and
Personality," an article appearing in *Perspectives in Person-
ality Theory,* edited by H. P. David and E. Von Bracken
(New York: Basic Books, 1957).

Sex identification differences are noted in the Carol
Tavris report on the masculinity survey, reported as "Men
and Women Report Their Views on Masculinity," *Psychology
Today,* January, 1977.

Retirement inactivity as a stressor has been variously
reported, including a 1974 U.S. Conference on aging, reviewed by the *New York Times.* Advocates of meditation
(and other right-brain esoteric disciplines) suggested then
that enrichment training could help the retired elderly find
meaning in lives of lessened physical activity.

Life span statistics come from the publication, *Vital
Statistics of the United States, 1970,* United States Depart-
ment of Health, Education and Welfare, Public Health
Service, Vol. II—Mortality (Washington, D.C.: Government
Printing Office, 1974).

The Waldron report, "Why Do Women Live Longer Than Men?" appeared in two parts in the *Journal of Human Stress,* beginning in March, 1976, Vol. 2, No. 1. This section of our chapter is largely taken from Dr. Ingrid Waldron's comprehensive report.

Educational world attitudes to boys vs. girls are discussed in a report "Responses of Female Primary School Teachers to Sex-Typed Behaviors in Male and Female Children," by T. E. Levitin and J. D. Chananie, appearing in *Child Development,* Vol. 43, 1972.

Insistent alcoholic attitudes are described in my book, *BodyPower* (New York: Simon and Schuster, 1976).

Male attitudes toward family illness (reflecting body-image distortions) are discussed in Dr. S. H. Arnaud's article, "Some Psychological Characteristics of Children of Multiple Sclerotics," appearing in *Psychosomatic Medicine,* 1959.

The emotional responsiveness of men in general was discussed by Dr. Lowen in private conversations with this author, during the winter of 1975.

Right-brain development in American males is discussed in an article in *Human Behavior,* June, 1976. The article, "The Split Brain Lab," was extensively researched and written by Wayne Sage. Also as relates to the male drinker, another report in that same issue, called "Narrow-Minded Alcoholism," suggests that chronic alcoholism specifically depletes right-hemisphere-related skills. This includes a loss of left-ear performance for right-handed alcoholics, and lower left-hand coordination among chronic drinkers as compared with occasional or non-imbibers.

Body feelings as a superior guide for decision-making was suggested by Dr. Seymour Fisher, noted body-consciousness researcher.

Regarding Eichmann's left-brain/right-brain lateral specializations, the speculations are, of course, my own. No brain probe was taken of the Nazi war criminal during his days of captivity. However, Hannah Arendt describes his personality and traits in her book, *Eichmann in Jerusalem,* and this subject was carefully explored in a book review by Richard L. Rubenstein, "The Nuremberg Mind: The Psychology of the Nazi Leaders," that appeared in *Psychology Today,* July, 1976.

Chapter 17: *If You Are a Woman Reading This Book*

"The Quiet Mind" was lauded as long ago as the sixteenth century by poet Robert Greene, in his work, *Farewell to Folly.*

The tense body/overwrought mind is a link generally recognized by the majority of today's psychophysical experts, such as Dr. Alexander Lowen, Moshe Feldenkrais, Ida Rolf (of Structural Integration), and others.

The Hennig, Jardim book, *The Managerial Woman,* was published by Doubleday & Company (New York: 1976).

This gift of Zen (and forthcoming with long-term SA practice) is described in most books on Zen Buddhism, such as those by Christmas Humphreys and Dr. Suzuki.

The Liv Ullman quote comes from her memoirs, *Changing,* published by Alfred A. Knopf Publishers (New York: 1977).

Dr. Seymour Fisher's astute observation comes from his book, *Body Consciousness: You Are What You Feel* (Englewood Cliffs, N.J.: Prentice-Hall, Inc., 1973).

Dr. McClelland's comment comes from an article he co-authored with N. F. Watt, "Sex Role Alienation in Schizophrenia," *Journal of Abnormal Psychology,* 1968, Vol. 73.

Dr. Hilgard's little test for left-brain/right-brain dominance is quoted in the Maya Pines article, "We Are Left-Brained or Right-Brained," *New York Times Magazine,* September 9, 1973.

The story about my daughter's right-hemisphere activity is true. I attribute it to her devoted love of a toy called the

Spirograph during her dominance-determining growth years, ages three to nine. (Yes, she also receives top honors in left-brain subjects like mathematics and vocabulary testing, proving that hemisphere integration exercises indeed pay off in mental acuity during childhood.)

The Frank Dobie comment appeared in the introduction to his book, *The Voice of the Coyote* (London: Hammond, Hammond Publishing, Ltd., 1949).

The way that feigning complicity (and burying your own yearnings) can bring illness and stress is discussed in the book by Walter McQuade and Ann Aikman, *Stress: What It Is, What It Can Do to Your Health, How to Fight Back* (New York: E. P. Dutton & Co., 1974).

The David Reisman concept of the inner-directed person appeared in his book, *Lonely Crowd: A Study of the Changing American Character* (New Haven: Yale University Press, 1969). It is also discussed by Alexander Lowen of Bioenergetics fame, in his book, *The Betrayal of the Body* (New York: The Macmillan Company, 1967).

Head circumference to measure brain development was used as a medical criterion as recently as 1975, at the Society for Neurosciences meeting in New York City. The research paper to which I refer is "Nutrition, Poverty and Brain Development in San Diego," submitted by Dr. R. B. Livingston of the University of California Medical School, at San Diego. The reference to woman's brain being smaller and of lighter weight than the male's appears in the current edition of *Blackwell's Medicine*, in most medical libraries, and on the shelves of many medical practitioners.

The promise of enriched experience training is signaled by the report, "Effects of Enriched Experience on Recovery of Rats from Cortical Lesions: Problem-Solving Scores and Brain Reserves." This was submitted to the Society for Neurosciences 1975 session, by Dr. Mark R. Rosenzweig, University of California, Berkeley.

Salutary functions of fantasy and daydreaming are espoused by leading researcher Dr. Jerome L. Singer. Interested readers are referred to his book, *The Inner World of Daydreaming* (New York: Harper & Row, 1975). He also authored "Fantasy: The Foundation of Serenity," appearing in *Psychology Today*, July, 1976.

The Olympics champion story (about Will Toomy) is told by Will Schutz at Esalen. It is also Schutz's note that the technique of fantasy therapy is bolstered by an imaginary obstacle to be overcome. For further information, see his book, *Here Comes Everybody: Bodymind and Encounter Culture* (New York: Harper & Row, 1971).

The Zen story is taken from Paul Reps collection, *Zen Flesh, Zen Bones* (New York: Doubleday and Company, Inc., 1961). The *tratakam* exercise is from yoga, and the reader is referred to *Fundamentals of Yoga* by Mishra Rammurti (London: Julian Press, 1959).

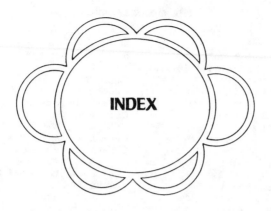

INDEX

Papyrus of Thebes, 152
Paradox intention technique, 212–213
Parasympathetic nervous system, 74
"Patterns game," 167–168
Peak experience, 35, 36–40, 45, 132
Perceptivity, 43, 145–146, 166, 174
  benefits in business world, 98, 102–104
  disparagement and neglect of, 31, 162
  power heightened by SA, 14–15, 34, 70, 102–104
  a right-brain function, xiii, 29, 98
  sharpened by meditation, 89
Perls, Frederick "Fritz," 4, 9, 16, 20, 23, 32, 57–58, 70, 82, 249
Permissiveness, parental, 161
"Personal constructs," 11–12, 250
Personality:
  split, 235–237
  Type A, xi–xii
Pets, 130–131
Phallic body orientation, 224
Phobias, coping with, 212–213
Physical activity, right-brain involvement in, 183–185
Physical affection, right-brain involvement in, 189
Physical education, 32, 269
Physical illness, 15–16, 223. *See also* Health benefits of SA
Physicality, 32, 43, 85, 264. *See also* Body awareness
Piaget, Jean, 167
Pickler, Emmy, 161
Pines, Maya, 27
Placebo effect, 19
"Play professions," 48, 255
Poincaré, Jean Henri, 33
Polarity squat, exercise, 76–77
Polarity therapy, 76
Popov, Ivan, 152
Posture, 109–110
Pribram, Karl, 13, 251
"Primal play" games, 167, 193, 263
Problem-solving ability, 13–14, 27, 31, 241–242
Psychic Research Society, London, 14
Psychophysical therapy, 16, 59, 163. *See also* Bioenergetics
Psychorhythm experiment, 122–124

Psychosomatic illness, 16–17, 87, 119, 223, 252, 269–270
Psychosound, 189, 193, 263
  exercises, 193–194
Psychosynthesis, 195

Racial prejudice, 81
"Rain game," 173
Raja Yoga, 9
Ramstein social behavior experiment, 163–164, 263
Reasoning, 30–31, 162
Recreation, 47, 181–187
Reich, Wilhelm, 16, 17
Reilly, Eileen M., 164
Reisman, David, 240
Relaxation, 47, 62
  of conscious thinking, 43
Religion, Western, and Oriental meditation, 85
Religious holidays, 133–134, 137
Remembered-patterns meditation, 209–210
Respiration. *See* Breathing
Retirement inactivity, 225, 269
"Return to Center" exercise, 74–75, 79
Reynolds, Burt, 133
Rhythmic breathing, 92–93
Right brain:
  damage, consequences of, 267
  neglect of, in Western education, 30–32, 35
  neglect in men, 231, 270
  non-verbal center, 27–29, 97
  seat of subconscious, 34
  testing strength of, 238
Right-brain functions, 27, 29, 30, 33–35, 106, 183, 189
  artistic creativity, 29, 30, 33
  holistic thinking, 29, 31, 32
  intuition, xiii, 29, 43
  meditation, 29, 86, 202, 266
  perceptivity, xiii, 29, 43, 70, 98
  physical activities, 183–185, 264
  recall of tunes, 25, 29, 167
  spatial relationships, 27–29, 31, 32, 180
  stimulated by SA, 14, 26, 34–35, 70
  synthesis function, 29, 32–33
Right-handedness, 27